Giant Creatures in Our World

Giant Creatures in Our World

Essays on Kaiju and American Popular Culture

Edited by
CAMILLE D.G. MUSTACHIO
and JASON BARR

McFarland & Company, Inc., Publishers
Jefferson, North Carolina

LIBRARY OF CONGRESS CATALOGUING-IN-PUBLICATION DATA

Names: Mustachio, Camille D. G., 1975– editor. | Barr, Jason, 1976– editor.
Title: Giant creatures in our world : essays on kaiju and American popular culture / edited by Camille D.G. Mustachio and Jason Barr.
Description: Jefferson, North Carolina : McFarland & Company, Inc., Publishers, 2017 | Includes bibliographical references and index.
Identifiers: LCCN 2017028007 | ISBN 9781476668369 (softcover : acid free paper) ∞
Subjects: LCSH: Monsters in motion pictures. | Monster films—Japan—History and criticism. | Popular culture—United States—Japanese influences. | Monsters—Symbolic aspects.
Classification: LCC PN1995.9.M6 G53 2017 | DDC 791.43/67—dc23
LC record available at https://lccn.loc.gov/2017028007

ISBN (print) 978-1-4766-6836-9
ISBN (ebook) 978-1-4766-2997-1

BRITISH LIBRARY CATALOGUING DATA ARE AVAILABLE

© 2017 Camille D.G. Mustachio and Jason Barr. All rights reserved

No part of this book may be reproduced or transmitted in any form or by any means, electronic or mechanical, including photocopying or recording, or by any information storage and retrieval system, without permission in writing from the publisher.

Front cover image © 2017 fotokostic/Grandfailure/iStock

Manufactured in the United States of America

*McFarland & Company, Inc., Publishers
Box 611, Jefferson, North Carolina 28640
www.mcfarlandpub.com*

Table of Contents

Introduction	1
Kamen Rider vs. Spider-Man and Batman: American Superheroes as Kaiju Villains SE YOUNG KIM	17
Notes from the Land of Light: Observations on Religious Elements Seen in *Ultraman* JUSTIN MULLIS	35
Monsters of the Rift: Kaiju as Ciphers of Unbalance JASE SHORT	59
Archetypes at War: Kaiju as Cult Icons in *Pacific Rim* NICHOLAS BOLLINGER	77
"Was it me? Did I kill them?": The Monsters and the Women in *King Kong* (1933), *Gojira* (1954), *Monster Zero* (1965), *Destroy All Monsters* (1968) and *Gamera III: Revenge of Iris* (1999) SIGMUND C. SHEN	92
Soft Power: Narrative of Neutrality in *King Kong Escapes* and *Frankenstein Conquers the World* FERNANDO GABRIEL PAGNONI BERNS and EMILIANO AGUILAR	109
The Confused Nation: Hitoshi Matsumoto's *Big Man Japan* KENTA MCGRATH	123
Japan's Anti-Kaiju Fighting Force: Normalizing Japan's Self-Defense Forces Through Postwar Monster Films JEFFREY J. HALL	138

The Ideology of Disaster: Godzilla, Gorillas and Geopolitics in the Global 21st Century
 JAMIE MACDONALD   161

"We are eating Gamera": *Mystery Science Theater 3000* Consumes the Kaiju
 KAREN JOAN KOHOUTEK   178

Collecting Kaiju: How Nostalgia Influences Adult Toy Collecting
 JASON BARR   193

About the Contributors   203
Index   205

Introduction

The animated show *Uncle Grandpa* has an episode, "Big in Japan," in which the character Gus, a lizard-man sort of creature, lands a job as a kaiju. His measured responses to the endless demands to destroy the cardboard and wooden city around him contain many layers, but his question, "what's my motivation?" is an important one. For many kaiju films, the writers and the directors often struggle to give the creature anything more interesting beyond a distinct creature-ness. Within many kaiju, we may find size, grotesqueness, and sometimes even some sort of biological origin, but, in the end, the kaiju is often thought to represent only one thing: destruction. Such an overemphasis on destruction, either on the part of the filmmakers or emanating from fans or critics, leads to a consistent underestimation of the kaiju genre and the themes it routinely explores.

This has led, in many ways, to the outright castigation or marginalization of the kaiju film in academic and critical circles. A kaiju film, by its very nature, has to have some form of destruction, but not necessarily at the expense of thematic content or characterization. In other words, the kaiju genre has been damned by, at best, faint and misplaced praise. Yet, new releases of franchise icons such as Godzilla or King Kong are often met with sneers or indifference by many critics. Fans have also been at times guilty of treating the kaiju genre as necessitating parody as well: beyond several well-written texts by William Tsutsui and Peter Brothers, among others, the focus has often been on history and the learning of what could be considered arcane or technical (even trivial) knowledge: who put together what suit, who was assistant director on a film, and so on. Even fan-driven works have often succumbed to the temptation—often spurred by shame or by simple fear at losing credibility—to poke fun at the films as well as their own observations. A simple search on any book-selling website, for example, will uncover dozens of (mostly self-published) works whose focus on mocking or belittling kaiju franchises is its primary selling point.

Such a process has led to a lack of understanding regarding what the

2　Introduction

kaiju genre actually *is*. If one accepts that *King Kong* (1933) was the first kaiju film, then the cinematic genre has been in existence for around eight decades now, almost as long as horror and science-fiction genres. Although there has been some critical prestige associated with science fiction, and horror, as well, has recently begun to receive more serious academic consideration, kaiju films have continued to be ignored, save for a few instances of discussions of *Godzilla* (1954) or *King Kong* (1933). In those films, at least, the respectability of history provides a safeguard for critics to explore these films without fear of outright academic shunning.

There are numerous reasons why the kaiju genre has been neglected, and to enumerate them all would fill an ample portion of this volume. Some of the most prevalent reasons have been a sense of critical discomfort with the concepts therein, often driven by the "campy" or "cheesy" nature of the films themselves. Additionally, the kaiju genre has often been lumped into the science fiction genre, forcing it into a subset, a critical backwater where only the boldest critics dare to tread. More controversially, it is also important to remember that cultural values may also play a role in how kaiju films are treated in the West, particularly in the United States. Western critics have often been quick to deride kaiju films, and a small portion of this may be due to the cultural expectations and differences at play between Western audiences and critics and Asian filmmakers.

Even though the kaiju film has yet to gain much critical acceptance in the world, the very concept of a kaiju has become an intrinsic part of both American and Japanese pop culture. Like students who know the basic plot of *Moby Dick* without reading it, and can spot references to Ahab or the White Whale in pop culture from afar, kaiju have also become a sort of cultural touchstone, a shorthand for communication and representation. Americans who have never seen a Godzilla film recognize Godzilla on sight, and they can understand references such as those in *Uncle Grandpa* as a clear homage or parody to, if not Godzilla specifically, then to kaiju in general.

This volume, therefore, intends to examine the manifestation in, and intersection of, kaiju and American pop culture. Kaiju such as Godzilla and, to a lesser extent, Ultraman and Gamera, have become knowledge-based byproducts of our very existence. Beyond advertising and beyond cheap parody, however, representations of kaiju in pop culture abound with nuance and subtlety, no small feat for the usage of overly large creatures. In fact, everything Godzilla is fiercely protected by Toho because the kaiju and every aspect of it—from the name to the basic silhouette—has been co-opted for everything from the name of restaurants to bootleg t-shirts. It is no surprise that Godzilla, in particular, is so ubiquitous, precisely because the great beast is a sort of shorthand for largeness, destruction, and, sometimes decidedly Asian perspectives. In other words, Godzilla has become a pop culture touchstone that embodies not only everything that people associate with Godzilla, but also represents the totality of kaiju themselves.

Before we try to understand the relationship between kaiju and pop culture, however, we have to understand exactly what *kaiju* means. This sounds, on the surface, to be a simple idea, but, when we pull back the layers of semantics and meanings of the term, there is much, much more nuance. As a result, we asked several of the authors that appear later in the text to provide their own short summary of what a kaiju is to them. The answers (which appear in no particular order) are as varied as they are interesting, and although there isn't a clear consensus across all perspectives, it does appear that some progress has been made in determining some of the foundational aspects of kaiju.

The first essay of the volume, by Se Young Kim, examines the Japanese television show *Kamen Rider* and its depictions of the decidedly American superheroes Batman and Spider-Man. Justin Mullis explores another Japanese television show and its titular superhero, Ultraman, and the series' use of religious iconography. Jase Short discusses how kaiju films such as *Godzilla* and *Pacific Rim*, among others, use kaiju as a dislocator, a way of unbalancing the world for audiences. Nicholas Bollinger also focuses on *Pacific Rim* as he attempts to determine if the film has a place among the kaiju genre. Sigmund C. Shen analyzes the portrayal of women in a variety of kaiju films, including *King Kong* and *Gamera II*. The authorial team of Fernando Gabriel Pagnoni Berns and Emiliano Aguilar addresses the political implications found in *King Kong Escapes* and *Frankenstein Conquers the World*. Kenta McGrath examines how *Big Man Japan* and *Shin Godzilla*, in particular, depict the Japanese social and political world. Jeffrey J. Hall uses the depictions of the Japanese Self-Defense Forces to exhibit how the country's relationship with its military has changed over the past half-century. Jamie Macdonald uses kaiju film to decipher the geopolitical landscape of the 21st century. Karen Joan Kohoutek questions the sometimes problematic jokes directed at the original *Gamera* series by the crew of *Mystery Science Theatre 3000*. And finally, Jason Barr deconstructs the potential origins of kaiju toy collecting, which isn't just for children anymore.

One final note: because of its origins as a Japanese word, and its later co-option into the English language, there are variations on the way kaiju should be spelled. For the sake of clarity and ease of use, we have decided to simply use kaiju as our term for this volume, with the first usage of kaiju in each essay italicized.

What Is Kaiju?

Before we go further, we need to consider a simple question that can have a complex response: what is kaiju? Literally, *kaiju* is roughly translated to mean "strange creature" or "strange beast." Yet, that label or idea seems to be extraordinarily inclusive of any number of cinematic creations, from Nosferatu to Leatherface. More appropriately, the term should be *daikaiju,* a term which also incorporates the idea of strangeness, but also largeness. So, how do we define the edges of the term kaiju? Is it a rigid definition? Or is it something that we only know when we see it? In order to understand the varying interpretations of what makes a "kaiju," we asked several authors in this volume to share their thoughts.

Jason Barr: I've come to the understanding that kaiju has become a popularized term, and I point primarily to *Pacific Rim*, which uses the term kaiju to refer to their creatures. Over time, the idea of a daikaiju being different from kaiju has lessened, so much that the term kaiju now represents large beasts such as, say, Gamera or Godzilla, although it would be more literally used to describe the human/mushroom hybrids in *Matango*. It no longer seems to me that the popular usage of kaiju has any requirements save for an overly large beast. It is the same situation, to me, as asking for a Kleenex and receiving a tissue. When someone asks for a Kleenex, the understanding is that a tissue would suffice. I think the same has come true for kaiju; when it reached a more popular usage, the general public, from the layperson to the scholar, has come to the tacit understanding that kaiju represents overly large creatures, even though the literal translation belies that assumption.

As far as applying the term to cinema, the kaiju eiga (kaiju film) seems to focus on a deeper set of problems. In spite of the literally dozens of movies that feature kaiju, the films almost always seem to center on the same issues that confront humanity on a global scale. Indeed, the incredibly large creatures often represent or attack overly large, but real, human issues: colonization, pollution, scientific ethics, and so on.

One can find a clearer delineation in a film like *Jurassic World*. Creatures such as the Tyrannosaurus rex or the Velociraptor do hold fascination for many Americans; however, they don't quite fit the "strange" part of the definition of kaiju themselves: these dinosaurs actually existed and are not unnatural. The Indominus rex, however, which is the product of genetic manipulation and has what can only be described as superpowers for a dinosaur, could conceivably be a kaiju.

Pursuing this line of thought, it would be somewhat easy to exclude some films which feature kaiju, such as *Sharknado*, because they descend into farce or camp and never quite achieve some sort of commentary. As the kaiju genre seems so prone to critical accusations of camp or cheese, it seems paramount for critics to divorce films such as *Sharknado* from the rest of the genre. This means, however, that some films such as *Son of Godzilla* or *Gamera: Super Monster*, even though they feature some of the most recognizable kaiju in cinema history, may not fit this definition.

Karen Joan Kohoutek: Growing up as a monster fan in the American Midwest, in a time before the Internet gave us access to more accurate information about Japanese culture, I generally heard "Godzilla movies" as a generic way to refer to what would now likely be called kaiju films. The phrase could be used unscientifically to mean movies about Godzilla, the most representative of the class, but also any of the related monsters. "I like the Godzilla movies where Godzilla is a bad guy" would mean one thing, but "I love Godzilla movies; especially *Gamera*" would not, colloquially, have been an incorrect statement. Even though the borders are always disputable—just like deciding what's really "punk"—it's still a relief to have the term kaiju instead.

It may be because I first heard the term used specifically to refer to Godzilla and his cohorts, but to me, the term kaiju has always included a connotation of largeness. The smaller the monster, the less kaiju seems like an appropriate term. Largeness alone isn't enough; however, the strangeness in "strange beast" is also important. The giant ants of *Them* are strange, but in the end, they're just big ants.

Opinions will certainly vary on this, because yes, magnifying the size of a creature will render it strange, certainly stranger than a normal-sized creature. But a thing simply made big, even as big as King Kong, lacks the uncanny peculiarity I associate with the term kaiju. Godzilla is more than a large lizard, Gamera is more than a large turtle, and Mothra is more than a large moth. While size is a part of the equation, they are strange beasts in more than size, with additional, often peculiar characteristics, rendering them in some way unreal. They're not beasts that can be found in nature, even in a smaller form.

Similarly, I rarely think of large humanoid beings as kaiju, although I give a pass for the creatures of *Frankenstein Conquers the World* and *War of the Gargantuas*, which I doubt I could defend intellectually.

In defining the common features of kaiju films, not just kaiju monsters, I'd agree with Jason Barr's assessment that they tend to feature "issues that confront humanity on a global scale." On the other end of the spectrum, I also have a strong prejudice that a kaiju film needs to show its kaiju wreaking some destruction. If there isn't a monster smashing cities and power plants, or at least brawling violently with another weird, giant creature, then it's not, to me, going to seem like it's truly part of the genre. Whether that reaction is simply the result of childhood imprinting on the Godzilla template, or if it speaks to the anxieties of the post-nuclear world, wanton destruction still seems like an essential element.

Sigmund C. Shen: "Largeness," yes. A story that takes on global issues like pollution, etc., yes. But the genre is also partly defined by its associations with Asian culture. The term "strange creature," all by itself could describe *The Creature from the Black Lagoon* or the great white from *Jaws*. But the genre is not "strange creature"—it's kaiju. So to decide whether the story "qualifies," I think it helps a lot if your monster is either Asian or significantly Asian-influenced. We wouldn't have a problem identifying the "boys adventure" genre made famous by Jules Verne, Rider Haggard, and Edgar Rice Burroughs as historically European; or the boarding school genre, from Sarah Fielding and Charles Dickens to J.K. Rowling, as uniquely British.

An important qualifier here is "or significantly Asian-influenced." The British *Gorgo*, the Danish *Reptilicus*, del Toro's interdimensional invaders of *Pacific Rim*: all kaiju. The flip side of this coin is that kaiju eiga is implicitly a culturally hybrid genre, much like South Asia's Bollywood musicals or Italy's spaghetti westerns and *giallo* films. Ishiro Honda was directly inspired by *King Kong* and the Rhedosaurus from *The Beast from 20,000 Fathoms*, and look at the *Aliens* homage in *Godzilla vs. Destroyah*.

Thanks to the Meiji Restoration, which ultimately led to Hiroshima and the birth of Godzilla, it also helps if the story is infused with a modernist anxiety about science-driven, post-industrial social upheaval, hurtling cultural change, and the feared karmic consequences thereof. So Vermithrax Pejorativ of Disney's *Dragonslayer*, despite being a terrific giant monster, doesn't really fit. But the Sin of Sloth from the medieval text *Piers Plowman*, being a tremendous being that roams the countryside emitting metaphysical waves of debilitating despair, might be, depending on how one defines modernism. And so might the eponymous Allosaurus from *The Valley of Gwangi*, who allegorically dies trapped in a burning church on the Western frontier. Even Gabara from *Godzilla's Revenge* dies because he's all the bullying that arises from deteriorating social structures and latchkey kids.

Another part of what makes a kaiju "strange" is context—it is a kind of fish out of water, bumbling around causing destruction almost by accident because it doesn't belong in a human city. So King Kong, yes, especially after he was made Asian by association, both in the coining of the portmanteau of Gojira's name in 1954 and in the international box office success of *King Kong vs. Godzilla* in 1962. (It's not clear to me how the natives of Skull Island perceive Kong, and maybe the upcoming Legendary film will shed light on the question, but in the racist logic of the boys adventure story, all that matters in the original story is that he is strange to the American expedition.) But the Toruk dragon native to planet Pandora in Cameron's *Avatar*, or the Sando Aqua Monster in *The Phantom Menace* (or, for that matter, the Exogorth Space Slug in *The Empire Strikes Back*) don't count because they were in their natural habitat. In those alien places, it's the humans who are the "strange creatures."

The feel of the kaiju genre also, in my opinion, is disrupted by a focus on gore or other bodily fluids because they make the threat feel very personal as opposed to societal. This goes back to Honda's decision to nix the original shot of Godzilla's head appearing over that hillside with a cow in his mouth, because the image was too disturbing. Likewise, something like *Q: The Winged*

Serpent is just too bloody, even though Quetzalcoatl is much bigger than the comparatively modest-sized kaiju Gwaemul from Bong Joon-Ho's *The Host*. Of course, the green blood in *Godzilla vs. Gigan* and the various Gamera movies gets a pass. I don't know if the giants from *Attack on Titan* get the same pass just because they're Japanese though—their appearance is so horrific they almost evoke zombies. And the hentai beast Overfiend from *Urotsukidoji* fails the same test for all sorts of reasons.

So, to sum up: (1) Asian-ness, (2) gigantic size, (3) intrusion upon a human society, (4) modernist anxiety over social upheaval. And (5), an avoidance of human gore and body horror, so as to keep our focus on cultural problems rather than physical human mortality and disease (such as symbolized in zombies, vampires, werewolves, etc.). The satisfaction of no single one of these rules would be sufficient all by itself, but the more of them I can check off, the easier the call for me.

In my own writing, I am most interested in the fourth rule, as I think it is what drives the apocalyptic anxiety of the genre. Because the terror of post-industrial change, partly wrought by scientific advancement, implicates the rise of machines and cities, one could argue that every Godzilla film is a "vs." film, because cities are the biggest monsters of all. (In her indispensable study *Tracking King Kong*, Cynthia Erb says that this is precisely why Kong scales, and falls, at the art deco colossus of the Empire State Building, which was considered a pinnacle of modernism in 1933.) Michael Bay's CGI Transformers are a little bit too anthropomorphic to score very high on the "strange" metric, but have you ever seen pictures of the German TAKRAF Corporation's Bagger Bucket Excavator? It's a truly terrifying colossus that evokes the end of the world—any person in her right mind would prefer Godzilla.

All of the above having been said, looking back over the history, including the weird elements of the 70s *showa* installments and this year's *Shin Godzilla*, we must acknowledge a sixth rule. The kaiju genre would not exist without the Japanese Godzilla series itself. So it should be allowed, all attempts to find a totalizing theory be damned, that any Godzilla film is automatically kaiju, and therefore, any element introduced in that way, no matter how unexpected, could potentially "qualify" other films as part of this evolving genre.

Justin Mullis: When attempting to define kaiju in an academic context I would begin by stressing that we need to be conscious of the fact that kaiju is a Japanese word first and foremost, a fact which necessitates, in keeping with George Orwell's "Politics and the English Language," us asking the question of why we are using a foreign word to begin with when perfectly good English ones—like "(giant) monster"—are available and since doing so without just cause will only result in both obfuscating the subject of our inquiry and making us look somewhat pretentious.

To this end I believe it is important to bear in mind that in Japan kaiju is a generic term denoting any and all giant monsters. Evidence of this can be seen in acclaimed Japanese science-fiction writer Hiroshi Yamamoto's contemporary kaiju novel, *MM9* (2007), which features a dizzying array of allusions not only to familiar Japanese monsters like Godzilla, King Ghidorah and Biollante but also to *Reptilicus, Gorgo, The Beast from 20,000 Fathoms, The Amazing Colossal Man, Attack of the 50 Foot Woman, Tarantula, Them!, It Came from Beneath the Sea, The Deadly Mantis*, H.P. Lovecraft's Cthulhu as well as mythical and religious beasts such the Japanese Yamata-no-Orochi and the Great Red Dragon of the biblical Book of Revelation. Considering this fact we are then left with very little reason why we should opt for the use of the Japanese term kaiju over that of the English "monster" as they can be readily applied to the exact same set of creatures.

However, Tokyo-based art critic Ivan Vartanian persuasively argues against just such a conclusion in his overview of kaiju as a uniquely Japanese artistic mode of expression, writing that kaiju are best understood when considered along the same lines as other Japanese cultural exports such as *manga* and *anime*. In Japan, manga and anime are generic terms for comic books and cartoons, and yet both inside and outside Japan manga and anime are also recognized as clearly not being the same as American or European comic books and cartoons but rather a breed apart. (For more on this point see Scott McCloud's 1993 study *Understanding Comics: The Invisible Art*.) Likewise Vartanian maintains that while kaiju may share many attributes in common with non–Japanese giant monsters, kaiju should nevertheless be seen as being distinct from similar fictional creatures found elsewhere in the world—a point of view I also share.

But what is it about kaiju that makes them so distinct from non–Japanese giant movie monsters, aside from their country of origin? In a 1998 interview with the BBC, Showa-era Gamera director Noriaki Yuasa observed that "in a Japanese monster movie, the monsters have a different function. They can be heroes, friends, something like that" while in Hollywood films monster are usually restricted to the role of villains. For Yuasa this difference in the two culture's approach to the subject of monsters is a fundamentally religious one. Western religions, chiefly Christianity, "divide[s] man from the supernatural" notes Yuasa, "but Japan doesn't have that separation. We have many different kinds of gods. Even the water in this glass [*gestures to a glass of water sitting next to him*] contains some element of the divine."

As I come from the field of religious studies, Yuasa's explanation makes perfect sense to me. Christianity emphasizes the fallen status of nature through sin and the elevated role of man as having been made in God's image, placed at the head of all of creation and being the only aspect of creation worthy of redemption by God. Conversely the Japanese national religion of Shinto teaches that man is a part of nature and that all of nature is itself inherently divine. This underlying set of ideas creates, as Yuasa points out, two very different sets of monster movies. In Hollywood monster movies, monsters are an expression of nature's fallen, and in some cases overtly demonic, status. Hollywood monsters are only capable of expressing hostility towards humankind, desiring to chase us down, attack us, violate us, eat us, kill us, or make us into one of their own. The only recourse in such a scenario is for man to reassert his God-given dominance over nature by killing the monster.

In opposition, Japanese kaiju movies position their monsters into a variety of roles. Yes, some are villains, but they can also be heroes, victims, clowns, friends, role models and more. The kaiju which have appeared throughout the Ultraman series—the subject of my essay in this collection—have been all of the above and then some. Furthermore, even when serving as the heaviest of heavies, kaiju are still about more than just serving as opportunities for mankind to flex its muscles and demonstrate its alpha predator status. As my fellow contributors have all noted, kaiju are also almost always about warning humanity that we have somehow disrupted the delicate balance which exists between humankind and nature, a balance which must be corrected if we are to endure.

These factors, I feel, are more than sufficient justification for the use of the Japanese term kaiju, insofar as the creatures in question fit the above qualifications of being either Japanese or, to second the point previously advanced by Sigmund C. Shen, clearly influenced by the Japanese cinematic tradition, *kaiju eiga*. By adhering to such qualifications we can refine the focus of our inquiry thus avoiding the awkward situation alluded to above by Jason Barr concerning the question of whether or not such SyFy Channel *nanar* as *Sharknado* applies to our present examination without having to sacrifice genuine kaiju movies like *Son of Godzilla* or *Gamera: Super Monster* regardless of their perceived lack of subtext. This means that we would get to keep films like the UK's *Gorgo* and the American *Pacific Rim*, whose Japanese influence is well attested, but would also need to lose films such as South Korea's *The Host*, Norway's *Trollhunter* and Denmark's *Reptilicus*—unless Shen knows something about that last film that I do not—as there has been no acknowledgment of Japanese influence by any of the principal creatives involved in the production of these films.

Lastly to circle back to two points raised by both Karen Joan Kohoutek, who observed that gigantism alone seemed insufficient to qualify a creature for the status of kaiju, and Shen's quandary about whether or not the presence of excessive gore and body horror would detract from the essential qualities of what defines a kaiju, each writer may be interested to learn that both points were among the three self-imposed principals of seminal kaiju artist Tohl Narita (1929–2002) who designed numerous iconic kaiju for both Toho Studios and Tsuburaya Productions. The only problem here, however, is that it is clear that later generations of artists and filmmakers have not shared Narita's views…. Case in point, *Son of Godzilla*'s Kamacuras and Kumonga are truly nothing more than an enlarged praying-mantis and spider—indistinguishable from those found crawling across screens in numerous American 50s giant monster movies. Likewise on the subject of gore and body horror imagery we need to keep Ishiro Honda's *Matango*, with its fungus-infected humans, in mind. An example of both kaiju eiga and body horror, *Matango*, as noted by Anthony Camara in his insightful essay on the film, left an indelible imprint on Japanese cinema leading to such notorious cyberpunk flavored body horror movies as Sogo Ishii's *Electric Dragon 80,000V*, Shozin Fukui's *Pinocchio √ 964*, Yoshihiro Nishimura's *Tokyo Gore Police*, and most infamously Shinya Tsukamoto's *Tetsuo* trilogy. (Anticipating some objections here I will preemptively point out that both Nishimura's *Tokyo Gore Police* and Tsukamoto's first two *Tetsuo* films received the classification of kaiju eiga in the Japan Vol. 1 installment of Intellect Book's venerable Directory of World Cinema series, and that the studio started by Tsukamoto to produce his *Tetsuo* films was christened Kaijyu Theater by the director in an attempt to make clear what kind of movies he hoped to make.) Body horror and gore also play a role in Honda's *Frankenstein Conquers the World* and *War of the Gargantuas* as well as their contemporary thematic and visual descendent *Attack on Titan* whose creator, Hajime Isayama, cites not only Honda's Frankenstein films as a key influence but also the 1990s Gamera trilogy with its man-eating Gyaos birds. So yes I would say that the Titans in *Attack* would qualify as kaiju too.

Jase Short: Firstly, in defining kaiju I would like to make the distinction between kaiju as cultural objects and kaiju as theoretical constructs. We must not conceive of this as a hard and fast distinction, as the two inform one another considerably, but we can say that there is a cultural mythos and there are ways of understanding it. There exists a body of work and a web of references in the broader culture to this work, and that is the object of theoretical study. If the object is constituted by the things themselves (in this case films and other media, as well as popular references to these media), the theory is constituted by how we conceive of these objects both as immediate consumers of art and as critics of it.

Kaiju can be read as subsets of a broader genre of fantasy creatures that haunt capitalist modernity. If one were to make a kind of mythic taxonomy they would fall within the category of gargantuan beings that include everything from ancient alien gods like Cthulhu or massive robots like Voltron. Kaiju can be separated from other giant monsters first as a matter of scale, as they tend to be much larger than, say, a dinosaur or something like the Rancor from *Return of the Jedi*. They are meant to eclipse the size of buildings in large cities rather than merely tower above treetops.

Ultimately, though, their scale is less central to their nature than their status within a narrative as a quasi-mythical or divine being. They are instances of the grotesque, which in Istvan Csicsery-Ronay, Jr.'s formulation involves a "disorienting anomalousness" which destabilizes our sense of place in the world. We expect the world to conform to rules of scientific regulation, and kaiju are precisely those returns of the repressed which demonstrate that, at best, our sense of what orders the world is flawed—at worst, they represent the sensibility that the world is decidedly not ordered.

Whether in the form of terrifying space dragons or deities emerging from obscure islands and lakes, they carry with them something more than mere organic structure. This is to say that what sets kaiju apart from other giant monsters is that they are not merely animals—though they might be that as well—rather they are akin to the yokai of Japanese lore. A variety of giants populate ancient mythology from cyclopes to dragons, and yet these are not rehashed ancient mythologies, rather they are all too contemporary social constructs.

The proliferation of these beings in contemporary mythologies surpasses previous incarnations of the gigantic precisely because the modern world of roughly 1850 through today is defined by a sense of vertigo, dread, and awe in the face of the sheer massiveness of modern civilization. Contemporary civilization involves quantities of commodity production and human reproduction on a scale that bewilders the mind of a creature that evolved in small bands of dozens of individuals. A profound sense of destabilization and dislocation in the face of this vastness is the social precondition for the proliferation of gigantic beings.

In terms of kaiju specifically, the condition has been the vast expansion of humanity's destructive power over itself and the Earth. Kaiju were forged in the imaginations of those who survived the trauma of a world war that saw tens of millions killed and entire cities wiped out. They are the force awakened by humanity that remind us of our place in the world as subsets of nature. I would posit that what defines kaiju is precisely their status as grotesque beings conjured forth by nature—in the forms of Earth's dark spaces, or the Frankenstein-esque revolt of nature responding to human experimentation, or the otherness of outer space—to upset the balance of human civilization in order to restore a natural balance. They are mythopoetic creations that help us cope with the fact that we have overshot our place in the order of things. They reassure us of our insignificance in the face of a vast, inscrutable universe that will ultimately swallow us. They are acolytes of a death that we feel, on some level, our species deserves.

Kenta McGrath: Growing up in Japan, I didn't consider kaiju to be fearful or antagonistic as a matter of course. Sometimes they were, and sometimes they weren't. However, they were always gigantic without qualification. To this end I agree with Jase Short's observation that kaiju are "akin to the yokai of Japanese lore"; like yokai, kaiju can be frightening or innocuous, objects of dread and anxiety, or of goodwill and sympathy. As outlined by Justin Mullis in his wide-ranging response, this diversity can be attributed to cultural and religious factors, resulting in "two very different sets of monster movies" as represented by the near-uniform hostility of Hollywood's monsters, and the wide range of characteristics—often hostile, often not—embodied in the kaiju of the Japanese cinema.

For me, "monster" doesn't adequately acknowledge this multiplicity. Kaiju is most commonly translated as "creature" or "monster"—of the strange, giant variety, of course—but these two English words carry negative connotations that kaiju does not. By some definitions humans are considered "creatures," but we typically reserve the use of this word to describe species other than our own. King Ghidorah, my dogs, the fly that I'm swatting away as I type this under the hot Australian sun—are all creatures. However, we also use "creature" to distinguish between those species that we find safe, familiar, and lovable, and those we find alien, grotesque, and threatening. In an everyday context I'd never refer to my dogs as creatures, but a flying cockroach will remain a vile creature every hour of the day. Nigel Farage understood this convention when he referred to Obama as a "creature" after Trump's election victory—an insult designed to appeal to his base of followers who might chuckle at the racist undertone, and which simultaneously allows Farage to hide behind a word whose literal meaning, if one insists upon it, covers everything from American presidents to deep-sea fish.

"Monster" is a similarly flexible term. It can be used literally to describe fearsome (and sometimes, not-so-fearsome) imaginary creatures, but it's often used metaphorically—and often quite lazily—to ascribe moral value upon humans who have committed monstrous acts, or who have demonstrated cruel, antagonistic qualities that seem to transcend human-ness. Thus Mothra, King Kong, the Minotaur, the chupacabra, and the Grootslang are monsters in the literal sense, while Queen "Bloody" Mary, Josef Stalin, Jack Torrance, Nurse Ratched, and Trump may be considered monsters in a metaphorical sense. Kaiju, on the other hand, only describes; it doesn't connote anything other than a certain kind of (literal) monster, and it doesn't discriminate. This isn't to suggest that the differences in how Japanese and non–Japanese regard their monsters can be reduced to a simple matter of semantics, but there are clearly many connotations gained in translation when one describes a kaiju as a "creature," "beast," or "monster."

In any attempts to define kaiju it's crucial to consider cinema itself, as the medium—the *only* medium, really—responsible for the fame, interest, and study that this peculiarly Japanese breed of monster has attracted. In my view, kaiju and cinema (and to a lesser extent, television) are inseparable. Although the origins of kaiju can be traced back to long before *Godzilla* and indeed, cinema itself, the fact remains that the rise of kaiju in popular culture occurred in tandem with the rise of the kaiju eiga. But first we must be attuned to the fact that the kaiju eiga spans decades, covers many aesthetic trends, and varies widely in its use (and non-use) of allegory and socio-political commentary. It is not static but, like Godzilla, always evolving and adapting, according to when, how, and why it is produced, and who is behind the wheel. As with any genre, it has produced formidable works that will stand the test of time, and forgettable efforts designed to do little more than cash in on what came before it. Any attempt to impose a one-size-fits-all meaning for kaiju or kaiju films will inevitably result in a series of definitional dead-ends.

It's also worth reminding ourselves that the word kaiju didn't come into popular usage in Japan until it popped up in the title of a film, and it wasn't even Japanese. The Japanese title for the 1953 film *The Beast from 20,000 Fathoms* is *Genshi Kaiju ga Arawareru*, which translates as "An Atomic Kaiju Appears"—and "atomic kaiju" describes very well a famous Japanese monster that announced itself to the world just one year later. But it's *Godzilla* and not the earlier American film with which kaiju have come to be associated, and this isn't surprising. As clear "losers" in World War II, and in a nation still reeling from the trauma of the dual atomic bombings and the indiscriminate firebombing of its cities, the Japanese had more to invest in the allegorical potential of a powerful, destructive monster than anybody else. But it also has to do with the fact that *Godzilla* is a far more interesting, and far superior, film.

It still surprises me that *Godzilla* is more often discussed as a film that introduced a powerful, allegorical, and iconic monster, and less as a powerful, allegorical, and iconic work of filmmaking. The visceral impact of the film does not, and never did, rest on the shoulders of Godzilla alone. We mustn't underplay Ishiro Honda's inspired direction, he and Takeo Murata's superb (and in 1954, frighteningly relevant) screenplay, Akira Ifukube's modernist score, and Eiji Tsuburaya's special effects, which paved the way for an entire tradition of *tokusatsu* filmmaking, and which was worlds apart from how Western filmmakers were representing their monsters. It speaks volumes that Haruo Nakajima, the suit actor who played Godzilla in a dozen consecutive films between the 1950s and 1970s, was considered indispensable by both Toho and Tsuburaya, and is today regarded as a crucial factor in the films' success. Where many saw only the strange, giant monster, others recognized the art and craft behind the strange, giant monster. More than anything else, it is the art of cinema—the combination of image and sound, the collaboration of artists and craftspeople, and the considered use of the resources at their disposal—that allowed the meanings and allegorical potential of kaiju to be articulated in the first place. Beasts, creatures, monsters, and yokai—strange, giant, or otherwise—never needed cinema; it is just one medium in which they have appeared and flourished. Meanwhile, discussing kaiju as separate from cinema seems to me a fruitless exercise. Without cinema, kaiju are relatively unremarkable—just another variation of monsters of which there have been many throughout history.

In keeping with my view that kaiju and cinema are inexorably linked, my clearest understanding of kaiju is derived not from their physical appearance or their characteristics, but from something that could only be expressed in the audiovisual medium of cinema. It is not an image, but a sound. Regardless of the context in which it is heard, Godzilla's roar sounds to me in equal parts a warning of a horror about to be unleashed, like an air-raid siren, and the cry of anguish of a wounded and confused animal, which has found itself somewhere it doesn't belong. For me, it is this sound that is emblematic of kaiju, as both a genre and a cultural construct, in all their complexity and multiplicity.

Jamie Macdonald: I strongly agree with the sentiment that hard-and-fast definitions of kaiju are likely to prove reductive, and that it seems more productive to take a more inclusive stance. The definitions put forward so far are wide-ranging and personal, but are ultimately much more useful in my view. To build on Kenta McGrath's notion that kaiju are most at home on cinema screens, I'd like to put forward a few thoughts on how the special effects techniques used to bring them to life have influenced the development of kaiju as a cultural formation.

The "suitmation" techniques pioneered by Eiji Tsuburaya certainly did inspire an entire tradition of filmmaking, and for me one of the most distinctive markers of the kaiju is their quasi-humanoid appearance. Of course, this isn't always the case, as has been discussed earlier, but I'd argue that a kaiju's human-like aspects contribute to their uncanny quality. The actors playing kaiju imbue them with a live-ness that is magnified to a colossal scale: they are at once worldly and otherworldly. I concur with Jase Short's assertion that kaiju are frequently depicted as "quasi-mythical or divine"; deities are often portrayed as humanoid in form across art and literature, and as such the echoes of humanity which resonate through the onscreen appearances of suitmation-produced kaiju mark them out even more clearly as god-like entities.

Like gods, kaiju are beings with power that exceeds comprehension, and their potential for wielding this power is always latent in depictions of their colossal forms. It has been said that the particular appeal of the classic zombie lies in the inexorability of their march: one can run from their grasp but eventually, like death itself, the zombie will catch you. The archetypical advance of the kaiju through a city has a similar inevitability, but unlike the zombie the kaiju is not necessarily a harbinger of death and destruction. The kaiju's range of allegorical expression is broader, but in my view a unique part of this expression in many kaiju films is their reliance on human performers.

Again, this is just one aspect of a multifaceted concept, and I definitely would not insist that kaiju are by definition only portrayed by humans in suits. However, I do think it's important to consider how this aspect has shaped viewer expectations of the form. Plus, the human-like elements of kaiju are not necessarily confined to productions which use suitmation; while making *Pacific Rim* del Toro was inspired not only by Japanese kaiju movies, but by Francisco de Goya's painting *The Colossus* which depicts a human giant towering over a landscape. The film's computer-generated kaiju are designed to be vaguely humanoid, allowing them to maintain part of the suitmation "look." Similarly, *Godzilla* (2014) depicted the titular kaiju as a much more humanoid biped than in the 1998 iteration, and while it isn't exactly suitmation the performance capture techniques used on the film allowed human performers to shape the digital Godzilla's movements.

Kamen Rider vs. Spider-Man and Batman
American Superheroes as Kaiju Villains

Se Young Kim

On April 3, 1971, the first episode of *Kamen Rider* (*Kamen raida* or "Masked Rider") debuted on the Mainichi Broadcasting System (Jiminez-Varea and Perez-Gomez 92). The title sequence of the show frames an open field, filled by the sounds of a motorcycle. As the single figure closes in on the camera, the sequence cuts to a dolly-zoom on the helmeted face of the cyclist. A brazen musical cue alongside the stylized, hand-written words, 仮面ライダー, signal the advent of the titular hero. The sequence quickly establishes the series' protagonist: Kamen Rider is a masked superhero who rides a motorcycle, uses karate, and sports a grasshopper motif. The series was an enormous success, beginning a forty-five yearlong franchise that continues to this day,[1] initiating what has been referred to as the "Second Kaiju Boom" or the "Henshin Boom" (Ryfle, *Japan's Favorite*, 162; Bendazzi 360). *Kaiju* (怪獣) refers to the "strange beasts" of Japanese cinema while *henshin* (変身), or "transformation" points to the transforming superheroes such as Kamen Rider.

In its contributions to contemporary Japanese mass culture, the significance of *Kamen Rider* becomes evident. To be more specific, *Kamen Rider* was a crucial text to the *tokusatsu* mode of filmmaking, to which the Second Kaiju Boom or Henshin Boom, was a historical development. Translated into "special filming," *tokusatsu* refers to a practice of live-action science fiction filmmaking that heavily relies on special effects. The primary special effects of tokusatsu is the practice of actors wearing prosthetic suits. Suit acting, or "suitmation" (*sutsumeshon*) demonstrates the intimate relationship between tokusatsu and fantastical creatures, which extends to their respective origins. Tokusatsu and kaiju both arguably begin with *Godzilla* (*Gojira*) (1954) (Honda

Ishiro).² And yet, *sutsu akuta* "suit actors" are not limited to giant monsters. The kaiju of the Second Kaiju Boom required a nemesis, who would then in turn become the reason as to why the movement was alternately referred to as the Henshin Boom. That figure was the Japanese superhero. By Japanese superhero, I primarily refer to the heroes of tokusatsu television in the 1970s. That is not to suggest that Kamen Rider was the only iteration of a domestic superhero, nor was he the first.³ *Kamen Rider* serves as the object of study for this essay because it is the most vibrant example of phenomena that extends beyond the series' parameters and begins to gesture to the broader context of contemporary Japanese visual culture.

This essay will examine *Kamen Rider* as a prominent instance where kaiju are placed in opposition against a new superhero within a tokusatsu setting. The essay looks at *Kamen Rider* both because of its effect on Japanese media, but also because it allows us insight into the transnational movement of Japanese culture. Not only did *Godzilla* begin both the kaiju film and the tokusatsu modes, it was also able to establish Japanese genre cinema domestically and internationally. Relatedly, if *Kamen Rider* was responsible for the Second Kaiju Boom within Japan, then a possible third development could be said to have occurred in 1993—only this time it was in the U.S. It was then that the Japanese superhero (and by extension, his kaiju antagonist) was successfully exported via the *Super Sentai* "Super Task Force" series under the new moniker, *Mighty Morphin Power Rangers*. Super Sentai and Godzilla thus demonstrate the substantial international mobility of the kaiju and the Japanese superhero, somehow maintaining a specifically Japanese sensibility while simultaneously appealing to non–Japanese audiences. And yet, the cultural movement between Japan and U.S. flows in far more directions than might be immediately evident, especially in the latter half of the twentieth century. In this essay, we will investigate the way in which American superheroes were integral to the development of the tokusatsu hero. The essay will focus on the first two kaiju villains of *Kamen Rider*, who were perverse versions of the American superheroes, Spider-Man and Batman. Through a close reading of *Kamen Rider* approached within the historical context and legacy of tokusatsu, we will find further implications regarding the international movement of the kaiju. Ultimately, I will argue that the Japanese superhero and the kaiju of tokusatsu cannot be understood outside of the historical legacy of World War II and the atomic bombings of Hiroshima and Nagasaki.

A Taxonomy of Strange Beasts

The relationship that *Kamen Rider* has to the broader context of tokusatsu filmmaking is crucial to understanding the series. If *Kamen Rider* is the primary object of study, then this essay focuses on the dual figures of the superhero and the kaiju within the superhero genre of the tokusatsu mode. Superhero film and television is differentiated from the kaiju film, which constitutes a genre in and of itself. This essay proceeds with the idea that the superhero genre is a companion to the kaiju genre; while both fall under the category of tokusatsu, the two genres can be further divided into subgenres. In the case of kaiju, the term is often translated to "strange beast." More specific iterations include the *daikaiju* (大怪獣) (*dai* meaning "large") such as Godzilla and his offspring while *kaijin* (怪人) (*jin* meaning "human") describes the more humanlike creatures. The majority of kaiju in superhero tokusatsu fall under the kaijin category. As far as the superhero genre is concerned, the primary subgenres include the *kyodai* "giant" hero such as the *Ultraman* (1966–ongoing) franchise created by Tsuburaya Eiji, who was also responsible for the techniques used in *Godzilla*. The superhero genre also includes the henshin hero of which *Kamen Rider* is the most prominent in addition to the *sentai* heroes that consist of the *Super Sentai* series.

As Rick Altman notes, the practice of delineating genres is in some senses provisional, considering that the stability of a genre is always under question (Altman). In the case of tokusatsu superheroes, the difficulty lies in the fact that some texts are successful enough that they essentially create and constitute their own genre [take for example *Ultraman*, *Kamen Rider*, or the *Metal Hero* series (*Metaru hiro*) (1982–1998)]. Furthermore, as is often the case, the superhero films and television series rarely if ever strictly abide by the conventions of their specific subgenre. This is to say that the generic parameters are permeable membranes that the texts constantly manipulate. Broadly, we have the large categories of kaiju and superhero cinema. Within that rubric, the individual texts and subgenres are simultaneously specific while also interrelated. Ultimately, we are interested in this sense of play.

Much of the literature regarding kaiju cinema has made similar claims. And that is partially due to the fact that the question of categorization has been central to the ongoing conversations regarding the kaiju film. Many writers have approached the kaiju as simultaneously a national and international category. For Jason Barr and Ivan Vartanian, kaiju belongs in a genealogy that moves beyond Japan and begins rather with *King Kong* (1933) (Merian C. Cooper and Ernest B. Schoedsack) (3; 14). Along these lines, Vartanian explains how kaiju can be translated into "monster" and asserts that the term maintains close proximity to the original Latin of *monstrum* (10). Both Barr and Vartanian thus challenge the East-West distinction that positions the kaiju as entirely Japanese. At the same time, the writers also mirror other efforts to historicize kaiju cinema by locating it within premodern narrative traditions in Japan. Barr and Vartanian do this by moving outside of film and asserting that kaiju share a connection to the *yokai* (妖怪) "ghosts" of Japanese folk literature (5; 10). Similarly, writers analyze the kaiju as manifestations of nature itself, an idea that reads the strange beasts in relation to the *Shinto* tradition (Vartanian 14; Papp 120–123; Masco 22). Vartanian for example refers to the "animism" of kaiju and how early tokusatsu articulates a "lament for loss of connection to nature" (14). Such approaches to Japanese cinema has a precedent in Japanese film studies, as writers such as Noel Burch have drawn connections from pre-modern cultural traditions to contemporary media (Burch).

The writers mentioned above demonstrate the complexity of kaiju and tokusatsu cinema and the way in which they cannot be discussed as wholly Japanese, or entirely international. Indeed, one of the major tasks of this essay is to propose a way to navigate what is specifically Japanese in tokusatsu and kaiju cinema and how it simultaneously engages the global. Along these lines, I am less interested in establishing a connection with historical Japanese traditions by asserting that for example, *Kamen Rider* maintains an earlier Shinto tradition (although in some senses it certainly does). Instead, Shintoism is far more interesting because its connection to kaiju cinema is in the fact that it loses favor as a cultural practice beginning in the middle of the twentieth century, and that in turn can be attributed to the mandate decreed by the U.S. Occupation Forces following the end of World War II (Shibata 80). In that sense, instead of focusing on connecting *Godzilla* and kaiju to a Shinto tradition, I am interested in investigating how *Godzilla* appears at exactly the moment that Shintoism recedes. In other words, the relationship between kaiju and Shintoism is valuable inasmuch as the way it demonstrates that U.S.–Japanese relations cannot be understated in considering the kaiju.

By broadening the methodological framework of approaching tokusatsu and kaiju cinema as part of a larger movement of postwar Japanese science fiction,[4] then the historical significance of tokusatsu begins to emanate. We can begin with the idea of a specifically postwar tradition.

Books such as *The Best Japanese Science Fiction Stories* and *Japanese Science Fiction: A View of a Changing Society* have attempted to establish a history of Japanese science fiction in English-language scholarship, although already the problem of designating an entirely local tradition is evident in how the writers of the former must discuss that early twentieth century authors had access to and were influenced by literature from the U.S. and the UK (Apostolou 14–15). Even more interesting is the way in which *The Best Japanese Science Fiction Stories* opens by addressing the supposedly erroneous impression of Japanese science fiction, the "limited image" (Davis 9) of "a gigantic monster destroying parts of downtown Tokyo," which is "a gross misconception" (Apostolou 13). Two points can be made regarding *The Best Japanese Science Fiction Stories*. For one, this is another instance where Japanese science fiction studies overlaps with Japanese film studies, where writers based in the U.S. attempt to introduce English-language audiences to what they see as the authentic tradition, as with Joseph L. Anderson and Donald Richie's *The Japanese Film: Art and Industry*. Furthermore, in addressing what they see as a "gross misconception," Apostolou and Greenberg also demonstrate how kaiju is central to the dominant understanding of contemporary Japanese science fiction.

As the editors suggest, discussions of postwar Japanese science fiction inexorably refer to kaiju and almost always include *Godzilla*. Indeed, the very fact that writers refer to a designation of *postwar* Japanese science fiction suggests that there is some sort of internal coherence. Vartanian for example, separates yokai from kaiju by asserting that the latter is a postwar genre (13). Steven Ryfle on the other hand, refers to the "postwar monster movie" ("Godzilla's Footprint," 54) while Motoko Tanaka discusses contemporary science fiction in the context of "Japanese postwar culture" (2). If we maintain the link between kaiju, tokusatsu, and postwar Japanese science fiction then, the commonality would be the formal and aesthetic practices and more importantly, the relationship to history. Nowhere is this more evident than in the case of the pioneering *Godzilla*. Produced and released in 1954, *Godzilla* opened nine years after the atomic bombings of Hiroshima and Nagasaki. Perhaps more importantly, *Godzilla* emerged after the censorship implemented by the occupation forces was lifted. While the nation had in different ways attempted to negotiate and work through the trauma of the atomic bombs, *Godzilla* was without a doubt one of the most impactful addresses of Hiroshima and Nagasaki. In addition, the film also came immediately after the hydrogen bomb test at Bikini Atoll that irradiated twenty-three fishermen in 1954. The film opens on this very event, with the hydrogen bomb being the catalyst to Godzilla's awakening. In a very literal sense, the H-bomb begins both kaiju cinema and the tokusatsu mode (Hendrix 55; Dower 137; Allison 44–45; Ryfle, "Godzilla's Footprint" 46–47; Tsutsui 16–18; Szasz and Takechi 744). As Susan Sontag writes in "The Imagination of Disaster," "One gets the feeling, particularly in the Japanese films, but not only there, that mass trauma exists over the use of nuclear weapons and the possibility of future nuclear wars. Most of the science fiction films bear witness to this trauma, and in a way, attempt to exorcise it" (46). In a very similar way, we will find that an American presence triggers *Kamen Rider*, which in turn exhibits how nuclear anxiety reverberates throughout tokusatsu superhero television and cinema.

Kamen Rider, Japanese Superhero

Celebrating its forty-fifth anniversary in 2016, *Kamen Rider* is one of the most successful and enduring tokusatsu franchises. The franchise is split into two parts, referred to as the Showa era and the Heisei era. The first *Kamen Rider* series were produced predominantly during the Showa era of Japanese history (with a few exceptions), and ran from 1971 to 1989 with a new series debuting roughly every year. *Super Sentai* would adopt the same model beginning in 1975.

Following a brief sabbatical during the 1990s with intermittent theatrical release films, the franchise returned to television in 1999 with *Kamen Rider Kuuga* (2000–2001), considered to be the first Heisei era Kamen Rider. While the franchise is primarily based in television, it is multimedia and spans across motion pictures, comic books, video games, live shows, and of course, toys.

Kamen Rider is one of the core franchises in the tokusatsu superhero genre. Arguably, the franchise's success rivals that of the *Ultraman* series (which ostensibly initiated the genre) and the *Super Sentai* series (which was the most successful internationally). *Ultraman* is in close proximity to the daikaiju film, with both its heroes and villains growing to gigantic proportions (hence the *kyodai* hero designation). The *Super Sentai* series on the other hand, revolves around a colorful team of cybernetic heroes. *Kamen Rider* is distinguished by its lone hero, although each series maintains a cast of supporting characters and nearly every series (especially in the Heisei era) features numerous Kamen Riders. As the name suggests, Kamen Rider is determined by his—and in a very few instances, her—relationship to his transportation. One of the primary fixtures of the franchise is the heroes' vehicles, which are usually motorcycles. The other part of *Kamen Rider*, the *kamen* ("mask") displays some sort of motif. The majority of both Showa and Heisei riders implement an insect theme, with the first three Kamen Riders modeled after grasshoppers.

The name Kamen Rider is curious in that it is half-Japanese and half-transliterated-English. It also makes clear that Kamen Rider, like Godzilla, bears the mark of America. The influence is not readily visible, as Kamen Rider does not immediately resemble American superheroes. I would argue that this relates to the success of *Power Rangers*, which was near enough to an American sensibility that it allowed for profitable importation. Following *Power Rangers*, American children's entertainment producers scrambled to reproduce the show's success by importing other Japanese tokusatsu series. The *Metal Hero* franchise was imported as *VR Troopers* (1994–1996), and *Ultraman* led to *Ultraman: The Ultimate Hero* (1996) as well as *Superhuman Samurai Syber-Squad* (1994–1995). Haim Saban, who had started the entire trend with *Power Rangers*, attempted to replicate his own success with *Kamen Rider* in transforming the Japanese *Kamen Rider Black RX* (1988–1989) into the American *Masked Rider* (1995–1996).[5]

If *Kamen Rider* (and *Ultraman* and the *Metal Heroes*) did not share enough affinity to American superheroes to ensure successful exportation, then what exactly is it that links the series to the U.S.? To begin, the affinities that *Kamen Rider* shares with American superheroes concern both its broad thematic approach as well as its narrative structure. Consider that the series revolves around a single protagonist who possesses superhuman powers in order to combat an organization bent on global hegemony. Furthermore, *Kamen Rider* also exhibits the same totemic nature as many of the most well known American superheroes (a totemism that connects to but also moves beyond a purely Shinto animism). Kamen Rider channels the "spirit" of the grasshopper in the way that Spider-Man embodies his namesake arachnid. What further reinforces this connection is also the primary way in which *Kamen Rider* bridges Japan and the U.S.: by featuring its own version of Spider-Man.

American Superheroes in Japan

Decades before the influx of tokusatsu heroes into the U.S. in the mid–1990s, *Kamen Rider* was also crucial to what has been referred to as the "Japanization" of the American superhero (Goulding 945, qtd. in Jiminez-Varea and Perez-Gomez 84). And that Japanization was occurring both before and alongside *Kamen Rider*. In the latter half of the twentieth century, two American superheroes made a significant appearance in Japanese culture: Batman and Spider-Man. In the case of Batman, the success of the American television series produced between 1966 and 1968 led to its importation in Japan in 1966. A homegrown adaptation of *Batman* in the form of a serialized comic by Kuwata Jiro was developed following the substantial success of the show in Japan. Titled *Batman*, the comic ran from April of 1966 to May of 1967 (Kidd and Burnham). A similar trajectory occurs for Spider-Man. As with Batman, a comic adaptation by Ikegami Ryoichi was produced between 1970 and 1971 (Jiminez-Varea and Perez-Gomez 84). Interestingly enough, unlike the Batman comic, the *Spider-Man* series took substantial liberties with the property. In addition to being written and drawn by a Japanese comic artist, the *Spider-Man* comic moved the narrative to a Japanese context and featured a new ethnically and nationally Japanese protagonist. More relevant than the comic adaptations of *Batman* and *Spider-Man* is the tokusatsu *Spider-Man* television series produced by Toei Company, the same corporation behind *Kamen Rider* and *Super Sentai*. The result of a partnership between Toei and Marvel Comics, *Spider-Man* ran from 1978 to 1979 and featured a totally new Japanese Spider-Man (Jiminez-Varea and Perez-Gomez 86).

For Jesus Jiminez-Varea and Miguel Angel Perez-Gomez, the significance of the tokusatsu *Spider-Man*—and more precisely the Toei-Marvel partnership—was that the interchange was crucial to the tokusatsu superhero genre (87–88). The writers assert that the *Spider-Man* series was a form of localization, or even "Japanization" (84). The success of *Kamen Rider* six years prior to the *Spider-Man* series informed the latter production, and *Spider-Man* then played a key role in the 1979 *Super Sentai* series *Battle Fever J*, which was also a Toei-Marvel coproduction (85–88). To this, Jiminez-Varea and Perez-Gomez point out how *Spider-Man* was the first series to introduce a giant *mecha* (named Leopardon) for the hero to battle daikaiju villains. Giant mecha are one of the major elements in *Super Sentai*, and Leopardon directly led to the introduction of *mecha* in the franchise beginning with *Battle Fever J* (*Batoru fiba jei*)[6] (86). *Battle Fever J* was the second *Super Sentai* series following *Himitsu Sentai Gorenger* (*Himitsu sentai sorenja*) (1975–1977) and every single *Sentai* series since has featured a giant *mecha*. Considering that the franchise was still in its infancy, the claim that *Spider-Man* was essential to the success of *Super Sentai* and by extension, tokusatsu, seems undeniable. In the movement between *Kamen Rider*, *Spider-Man*, and *Battle Fever J*, we are thus able to observe a sort of feedback loop between American and Japanese heroes. It is the movement itself that is significant, and not the order or even the idea of coherent and stable categories of Japanese superheroes and American superheroes. The texts themselves participate in the very production of these categories, and ultimately, this essay is interested in this exact discursive process.

Spider-Man and Batman in Kamen Rider

The American superhero appears in *Kamen Rider*, but in a manner that is at once direct and mediated. Meaning, although licensed versions of Spider-Man and Batman do not make an appearance in the series, *Kamen Rider* does feature two characters who are clear references to the American characters. The episodic format of tokusatsu series generally revolves around the introduction of a new villain for each installment; kaiju and kaijin who appear and are vanquished within the half-hour running time. The first two episodes of *Kamen Rider* feature kaijin with eerily familiar names, Kumo Otoko or "Spider Man" and Komori Otoko or "Bat Man." As with the play of English and Japanese in *Kamen Rider*'s title, the two kaijin cleverly invoke their inspirations, and thus subtly link American and Japanese superheroes. As far as the series is concerned, Kumo Otoko and Komori Otoko are significant in their roles as inaugural villains that establish a formal and narrative precedent for the rest of the series, if not the franchise itself.[7] Similarly, the two kaijin are crucial to defining Kamen Rider's role as protagonist; not only do they differentiate themselves as monstrous villains, Kumo Otoko participates on the diegetic level by taking an active part in the creation of Kamen Rider by abducting university student Hongo Takeshi (Fujioka Hiroshi). That act in turn, initiates the series of events that culminate in the transformation of Hongo into the cyborg Kamen Rider.

Hongo's transformation is perhaps the single most important event in *Kamen Rider*. *Kamen Rider* is classified as a henshin hero due to the fact that transformation is central to the character and the franchise. Nearly every character in tokusatsu undergoes some sort of transformation, but what separates the henshin heroes is that the act of transformation itself takes priority (contrast this to the daikaiju who are relatively stable). In the case of *Kamen Rider*, there are two stages to the titular hero's transformation: there is the initial experiment that irrevocably changes him from human to superhuman and the henshin he undergoes in every episode to change from his alter ego of Hongo Takeshi to the cyborg Kamen Rider. The fluidity of these identities is crucial for the henshin heroes. The henshin sequence itself is one of the key set pieces of every *Kamen Rider* episode, both in the initial series and the series since. The sequence emphasizes the tokusatsu special effects particular to the henshin hero, the spectacle of a human becoming posthuman. In addition to the elaborate superimposition and rotoscoping effects, *Kamen Rider* also emphasizes the importance of henshin by having each Rider shout the word in order to initiate the process.

Hongo's transformation into Kamen Rider is part of the machinations of the terrorist organization Shocker, which serves as the series' antagonist. The group's bid for global hegemony revolves around the use of biomechanically engineered personnel. Hongo is just one such Shocker experiment; he is what the series refers to as *kaizo ninken*, or "enhanced human."[8] Through the term, *Kamen Rider* makes very clear that cybernetic augmentation is the source of its protagonist's abilities. In addition, due to the fact that Kamen Rider himself is the result of Shocker experimentation, the series also asserts that by extension, his kaijin nemeses are also cyborgs. Against the kaiju in kaiju cinema, *Kamen Rider* suggests that its villains are not exclusively organic,[9] but more cybernetic in disposition. But what separates Kamen Rider from his adversaries is the fact that he is in reality, *incomplete*. Against Hongo, Kumo Otoko and Komori Otoko are "finished" Shocker products. Hongo, however, is able to escape from the Shocker laboratory before the scientists are able to execute the final procedure of reprogramming his brain. According to the logic of the show, the only thing that separates Hongo from the kaijin then is the fact that the young man is able to retain his own consciousness, which of course entails his sense of morality. As opposed to the kaijin, who are mindless puppets,[10] Hongo maintains his core subjectivity. What further supports this is the recurring villains called Shocker Riders, who appear throughout the franchise. Unlike Hongo, the Shocker Riders are subjects who have successfully undergone the full Shocker procedure. The suit actors wear the identical costume as Kamen Rider and are only differentiated by yellow gloves and boots (as well as their diabolical actions). What we can see in Kamen Rider's relationship to his enemies is the way in which the franchise constantly mediates the range of affinities shared between the characters.

Spider-Man and Batman as Kaijin

As previously mentioned, kaijin differ from daikaiju in that they are neither large, nor do they grow in size.[11] The defining characteristic of kaijin however, is their humanity. While daikaiju tend to emphasize the animality of the creatures (take for example the moth-shaped Mothra or the turtle-shaped Gamera), most kaijin are bipedal and retain a humanoid form. The key importance regarding the kaijin is the issue of degree—what makes the kaijin so frightening is not that they are so unrecognizably monstrous; rather, it is the fact that they remain recognizably human. As opposed to the heroic Kamen Rider, or the American Spider-Man and Batman, Kumo Otoko and Komori Otoko are less human and more creature, but human nonetheless. By placing Kamen Rider in relation to the kaijin (unified by the narrative conceit of biomechanical engineering), the series creates a sliding scale of hybridity. On one end is the human and on the opposite is the modified human. And within the modified human, there is the cyborg hero and the devious kaijin. Corresponding to their degree of hybridity is the moral alignment of each character. Tied closely to morality, humanness in *Kamen Rider* is thus quantifiable, and in the case of the kaijin its presence is bare. In the broader context of tokusatsu, the kaijin of *Kamen Rider* contribute to a taxonomy of monstrosity within a tradition of postwar Japanese visual culture.

A brief return to the taxonomy of Japanese creatures will produce further understanding of the kaijin. By including pre-war Japanese culture into the discussion, the relationship between kaiju and yokai offers further insight. In the same way that Godzilla materializes at the moment that Shintoism recedes, Vartanian points out how the yokai disappears from Japanese culture following World War II (13).[12] Focusing on the corporeal aspect of the kaiju, Vartanian asserts that kaiju are more embodied and destructive as opposed to the ephemeral and psychological terror of the yokai. Vartanian also notes how kaiju and yokai tend to be coded in terms of gender, with the former masculine and the latter feminine (13) although these are of course not exclusive categories. The kaijin in tokusatsu are referred to using a number of terms (especially within the diegesis). In some cases, the kaijin in *Kamen Rider* are called *bakemono*. While the term can be translated into "monster," it is also used to describe a specific class of yokai. And the key characteristic of bakemono is the fact that they can transform. Bakemono thus share another key affinity with the henshin heroes. The relationship between kaiju, yokai, bakemono, and henshin heroes demonstrates not only the regional specificity of Japanese monsters, but also the slippage between the myriad categories. This taxonomy is loose, and the texts themselves constantly play with the borders that separate the creatures.

The kaijin Spider-Man and Batman appear in the first two episodes of *Kamen Rider*, titled *Kaiki kumo otoko*, or "The Mysterious Spider Man" and *Kyofu komori otoko*, "The Terrifying Bat Man." The formal convention where episode titles consist of the featured villains' names is used throughout the series. The titles emphasize the role of the kaijin, demonstrating how the episodes are organized around each villain. Consider also that the first episode's title does not for example, indicate the arrival or creation of a new hero; instead of representing Kamen Rider, it rather signifies his first enemy, Kumo Otoko. Indeed, this could apply to much television in Japan, but in the context of tokusatsu, it is all the more interesting considering that the villains are without exception kaiju and kaijin.

In "The Mysterious Spider Man," university student Hongo Takeshi is training for a motorcycle race when he is intercepted and abducted by Shocker agents. Taken to a hidden Shocker facility, Hongo awakens to find that he is in the middle of their experiment (Hongo wears the Kamen Rider costume from the neck down to indicate that the experiment is still in progress). As the disembodied voice of the Shocker Great Leader, represented by a blinking light on a large eagle crest (just part of the liberally borrowed Nazi iconography), explains the experiment, Hongo escapes with the help of abducted scientist Professor Midorikawa (Nonomura Kiyoshi). Later in the episode Kumo Otoko assassinates the professor, leading Midorikawa's daughter Ruriko (Morigawa Chieko) to mistakenly blame Hongo. Although Hongo manages to defeat the Spider Man, the episode ends on a somber note, a characteristic of tokusatsu cinema (Barr 9) as he must deal with Ruriko's suspicions and his new life as a cyborg. The case of mistaken identity is resolved in the second episode, which centers on a Shocker plot to expand the organization's influence through its new kaijin agent, Komori Otoko. Infecting his victims with a vampiric bite, Komori Otoko produces an army of mindless civilian slaves for Shocker. Kamen Rider confronts Komori Otoko, and upon discovering the cure to the infection, he is able to reverse the effects of the Bat Man's bite after killing the kaijin and taking a single claw that contains the vaccine.

The kaijin villains in "The Mysterious Spider Man" and "The Terrifying Bat Man" perform a number of functions. As noted above, they provide structure to the episodes as the momentary antagonist; this simultaneously allows for the resolution of conflict in a given episode, while a broader structural conflict (the battle with Shocker) undergirds the entire series. Kumo Otoko and Komori Otoko also characterize Shocker, painting a nefarious image of the organization that highlights its attitude towards science and its production of ethically questionable experiments. The kaijin thus invoke the Third Reich as well as the infamous human experiments of Unit 731 of the Imperial Japanese Army. In relation to the Kamen Rider franchise, the kaijin firmly establishes the series within a tokusatsu tradition. For the last forty-five years since, *Kamen Rider* has remained a steady source of kaijin and superheroes.

Perhaps the most significant function of the kaijin is that they are a crucial referent to which the superhero is differentiated. While Kamen Rider himself is something other than human, the kaijin barely retain any sense of humanity. Along these lines, the two episodes of *Kamen Rider* use different formal strategies in presenting the cyborg hero and the kaijin monsters. Horror conventions are used to frame Kumo Otoko and Komori Otoko. Deep contrast, dark shadows, and ominous music cues are deployed in conjunction with the suit actors' menacing performances. The initial *Kamen Rider* series thus demonstrates how tokusatsu includes a number of genres, as the series could be classified as a horror text. Contrast this to the Heisei *Kamen Rider* series which are much more oriented towards children and are ostensibly action-superhero shows. On the other hand, the kaijin in *Kamen Rider* are—as the titles of the episodes suggest—designed to elicit a specific reaction: that of abject horror.

The horror of Kumo Otoko and Komori Otoko is entirely related to their respective American counterparts. Unlike the Toei Spider-Man or the manga Spider-Man and Batman, the Spider Man and Bat Man of *Kamen Rider* bear no resemblance whatsoever to their American counterparts. Indeed, only in considering their names and the premise of the characters, does one realize that these are twists of the iconic heroes from Marvel and DC. While it is clear that the American heroes are men in colorful costumes, the appearances of Kumo Otoko and Komori Otoko do not suggest that the two are merely wearing attire. Instead, the transformation is entirely on the bodily level, as the kaijin are monstrous amalgamations of beast and human (for the viewer of course, it is very clear that the kaijin are suit actors in costumes). In other words, Kumo Otoko and Komori Otoko are a Spider-Man and a Bat-Man in a very literal sense—they are representations of half-beast half-men hybrids. Kumo Otoko's head is large and features three arachnid eyes, fangs, and antennae; Komori Otoko also sports fangs, pointed ears, and large leathery wings under his arms. Hair-like fur covers the heads and bodies of both in order to emphasize their beastly appearances.

In addition to spiders and bats themselves, the cultural significance of both creatures inform the abilities of Kumo Otoko and Komori Otoko. Both display superhuman strength and are able to propel themselves through the air. Kumo Otoko has the ability to spin large webs and is also able to project poisoned darts from his mouth that reduce humans into a bubbling soup. Drawing on the common association between vampires and bats, Komori Otoko can possess other human subjects by biting them in the neck. This also points to the importance of consciousness and agency in *Kamen Rider*, as even though the two kaijin are subordinates in the Shocker organization, they hold a degree of rank that allows them to control other minions. Indeed, kaijin are also referred to as *kanbu* "officers," denoting the military structure of Shocker.

The Monstrosity of the Kaijin, the Horror of World War II

The monstrosity of the kaijin is thus a source of dread for *Kamen Rider*, an anxiety that is in essence concerned with the borders of humanity that are tested through science and technology. Considered within the context of tokusatsu, it thus becomes evident that the horror of *Kamen Rider* aligns with the trauma of postwar Japanese science fiction. Although a television series produced from 1971 to 1973, years removed from the atomic and hydrogen bombs, *Kamen Rider* cannot escape its historical and geographical context. As the Committee for the Compilation of Materials on Damage Caused by the Atomic Bombs in Hiroshima and Nagasaki wrote in 1979, surely the bombings left a lasting impression on the "minds and memories of all its victims" (484–485). I would suggest that a similar mark can be found in Japanese culture. And it is science fiction, if not the very medium of cinema itself, that facilitates a space to consider the inconsiderable, simultaneously allowing the requisite amount of room to allow for the viewers' fetishistic disavowal.

The anxiety of *Kamen Rider* is the dread of nuclear destruction worked through in the context of science fiction television. Kamen Rider himself is not exempt, as he too fears his loss of humanity, exemplified in a scene where he breaks off a knob because he knows not his own strength. While Hongo is able to retain some semblance of humanity, he constantly confronts the kaijin, who are not as fortunate. *Kamen Rider* asks what happens when one retains the shape of a human but loses everything that is understood to be essentially human? That question also happens to be the very same asked by many Japanese following World War II. Victims of the bombings, survivors, educators, and politicians were forced to consider the very question of humanity. Accounts from the victims and survivors describe the fracturing of identity (Dower 116), or how their very humanity was deprived (Committee 485), with "the mediating function of human subjectivity" vanishing in the moments following the explosion, with the people of Hiroshima becoming beastlike as they lost all sense of reason (486). This was the "dehumanizing impact" that robbed the victims of all psychological functions (487). Consider how Hirohito's subsequent surrender was framed as having the stakes of all of humanity at heart (Dower 119–120), or the fact that an entirely new category of people was created, the *hibakusha* or "bomb-affected people."

The question that Japan faced in the middle of the twentieth century concerned the meaning of humanness, and what it means that that humanness could be lost. What was this "new world of terrible and awesome potentialities" (Dower 116) that included "a higher level of consciousness" (Committee 500)? The terrible force that engendered these questions was of course the violent potentiality of science. The traumatic dialectic of science and technology is that it was simultaneously the cause of destruction and the means of liberation. After all, it was the absolute terror of American weaponry, not only in the atomic and hydrogen bombs but also the carpet-bombing and air raids that necessitated absolute concession. And yet, it was only through the development of technology and science that the nation would be able to rebuild in the so-called "postwar miracle" (Allison 56). Of course, postwar pacifism demanded that the nation's efforts focused on consumer and civilian technologies. Read alongside the complete disarmament and dissolution of Japan's standing army (undergirded by the trauma of defeat), the belligerency of Japan does not become erased, but rather repressed, only to recur.

Tokusatsu is one such area where the repressed returns, embodied in the figure of the cyborg hero, performed through the karate of *Kamen Rider* (Allison 99–100). Why is it that the techniques of Kamen Rider, so prominently on display in the opening credits, are named in transliterated English? Instead of *yoko tobi geri*, Kamen Rider's ultimate technique is called the Rider Kick (*Raida kikku*). The militancy of Japanese culture—in this case karate—censored in the years following the war must undergo a mediated dialectic so that it may reappear in an acceptable fashion (and in the language of the former wartime enemy turned political ally). Kamen Rider and the Shocker kaijin thus manifest the complex postwar attitude towards science, dually representing the potentiality of technological advancement. In addition to providing grounds through which to repeat and work through postwar trauma, *Kamen Rider* quite literally participates in the rebuilding process as mass culture was crucial to economic growth (Patten 286).

Even more than their "localized" counterparts, the literal Spider-Man and Bat-Man, Kumo Otoko, and Komori Otoko, reveal the extent to which the horror of World War II haunts Japan, as the dialectic of grappling with the U.S.–Japan relationship points to deeper anxiety regarding technology, subjectivity, and trauma. Read in this light, the presence of a Japanese Spider-Man and a Japanese Batman takes on an additional nuance. As Grady Hendrix and Fred Patten point out, postwar narratives are deeply conservative, and so Kumo Otoko and Komori Otoko also become representatives of American aggression (55; 287).[13]

The brief movement described above, from the original American Batman and Spider-Man to the illustrated Japanese Batman and Spider-Man (and the Toei Spider-Man), back to the Kumo Otoko and Komori Otoko of *Kamen Rider* is in essence a dialectic occurring within the tokusatsu superhero framework. The Other is simultaneously borrowed from and the Self attempts to move away. The Japanese superhero needs the American superhero to become both its counterpart and its enemy. Postwar Japanese mass culture, which is in itself imbricated in the economic and social rebuilding necessitated by the decimation following the war, cannot escape the shadow of the U.S. *Kamen Rider* is born out of the war.

Conclusion

What Kumo Otoko and Komori Otoko demonstrate is the cultural interchange between Japan and the U.S. in regard to superheroes. The Japanese importation of Spider-Man and Batman already illustrates the way in which there was a transnational movement of culture by the middle of the twentieth century. And as the Japanese comic books and the Toei television series make evident, this was not a direct translation so much as a process of mediation. The first two episodes of *Kamen Rider*, with its grotesque versions of Spider-Man and Batman can be seen as a part of this process. As opposed to a reading that prioritizes the idea of Japanization, where international texts are localized through the addition of some sort of indeterminate factor that makes them palatable to Japanese audiences, this essay has approached the movement of superheroes as a dialectic that is constantly changing and entirely historical.

Kamen Rider is a homegrown superhero that is hybrid and contingent, continually moving between human and posthuman. Because he exists in that indeterminate space, he fundamentally inhabits the same continuum as his avowed enemies, who are also at once human and monster. That Kamen Rider would be so close to his enemy is not a necessarily new idea in and of itself—many American superhero narratives are also oriented around the same motif. However, the specificity of *Kamen Rider* is that it is part of a particular film history that is undeniably connected to its place of production and exhibition. As part of the tokusatsu mode, *Kamen Rider* shares a deep connection to the trauma of World War II. In other words, *Kamen Rider*—like *Godzilla* before him—is an unconscious manifestation of Japan attempting to work through World War II. The so-called Japaneseness of *Kamen Rider*, or to be more precise, the Japanese specificity of *Kamen Rider* and its kaiju/kaijin is entirely historical.

This essay has analyzed the two inaugural episodes of *Kamen Rider* as an opportunity to consider a monumentally successful media text that spawned a forty-five-year-long franchise. It has done so as part of a larger effort to seriously consider the role and impact of the kaiju. One of the main concerns of this essay is to dwell in the complex and multifaceted movement of culture, that is not always the lighthearted and uplifting importation and exportation of popular culture. In addition, there is also the oft-neglected yet deeply geopolitical and even disturbing ways in which culture can move. It is not necessarily that the unspoken truth of *Kamen Rider* is that it gets us to consider the atomic bombings of Hiroshima and Nagasaki. Perhaps instead it is that the bombs continue to reverberate throughout culture and history, and the waning but not quite negligible shockwaves move through *Kamen Rider* and beyond, demanding that we turn our attention back towards August 6 and August 9 of 1945.

NOTES

1. The theatrical-release film *Kamen Rider 1* (2016) (Kaneda Osamu) celebrates the forty-fifth anniversary of the franchise and features Fujioka Hiroshi, the star of the original *Kamen Rider* series, reprising his role. The title of the film also refers to the fact that the first Kamen Rider and the initial series is often referred to as Kamen Rider Ichigo, or Kamen Rider 1. Similarly, the 2005 remake film was titled *Kamen Rider: The First* (Nagaishi Takao).

2. Japanese names will be referred to in a conventional order with the family names first and the given names afterwards.

3. The *Super Giant* (1957–1959) series was the first tokusatsu superhero series while Tsuburaya Eiji's *Ultraman* (1966–1967) was an even more crucial predecessor. See Sharp, 263, and Kalat, 132.

4. As Jason Barr notes, the kaiju film moves across several genres and thus in some senses, cannot be "confined" to the genre of science fiction. Kaiju cinema and tokusatsu regularly incorporates elements from horror, fantasy, and even comedy (17). I use "Japanese science fiction" here because of the close association with World War II and the pointed interest in science, specifically technology, biology, and robotics. I do not assert, however, that kaiju appear only in science fiction texts.

5. A second attempt to import *Kamen Rider* occurs in 2008 when the second Heisei series, *Kamen Rider Ryuki* (2002–2003) was imported as *Kamen Rider: Dragon Knight* (2008–2009). Note that the series retains the "Kamen Rider" moniker in favor of the translated "Masked Rider."

6. The connection between Japanese and American superheroes is even more explicit in *Battle Fever J*, as the series was originally conceived as an adaptation of Marvel's *Avengers* (Jiminez-Varea and Perez-Gomez, 87).

7. As the writers of the *Kamen Rider* Wiki page point out, Kumo Otoko and Komori Otoko have become so iconic that many of the *Kamen Rider* series begin with a spider and bat themed villains. See "Spider-Man," *Kamen Rider Wiki*, n.d. http://kamenrider.wikia.com/wiki/Spider_Man, accessed 14 November 2016.

8. Showa era *Kamen Rider* series refer to their heroes as kaizo ninken for the most part, while the term has fallen out of favor in Heisei series. However, the term has recently been reintroduced, especially through the films, which always highlight Kamen Riders from across the entire franchise.

9. Of course, this is not to suggest that kaiju are purely organic. The well-known Godzilla nemesis Mechagodzilla is also a cyborg-kaiju hybrid.

10. The motif of puppets or *ningyo* can be found throughout Japanese mass culture.

11. A notable exception for *Kamen Rider* kaijin is the 1994 film *Kamen Rider J* (Amemiya

Keita). Kamen Rider J holds the distinction of being the only Kamen Rider to grow in size, as do his enemies.

12. The yokai are not completely absent in contemporary Japanese culture, as is evident in their resurgence following the rise of "J-Horror" and films such as *Ring* (*Ringu*) (1998) (Nakata Hideo). More recently, they have enjoyed new popularity following the animated series *Yo-kai Watch* (*Yokai wotchi*) (2014–).

13. Comparable would be Rikidozan's pro wrestling exhibitions against American wrestlers in the middle of the twentieth century. See Lie, 165–166.

Works Cited

Allison, Anne. *Millennial Monsters: Japanese Toys and the Global Imagination*. University of California Press, 2006.
Altman, Rick. "A Semantic/Syntactic Approach to Film Genre." *Cinema Journal*, vol. 23, no. 3, 1984, 6–18.
Anderson, Joseph L., and Donald Richie. *The Japanese Film: Art and Industry*. Expanded edition, Princeton University Press, 1983.
Apostolou, John L. "Introduction." *The Best Japanese Science Fiction Stories*, edited by John L. Apostolou, and Martin H. Greenberg. Dembner Books, 1989, 13–20.
Barr, Jason. *The Kaiju Film*. McFarland, 2016.
Bendazzi, Giannalberto. *Animation: A World History: Volume II: The Birth of a Style—The Three Markets*. CRC Press, 2016.
Burch, Noël. *To the Distant Observer: Form and Meaning in Japanese Cinema*. University of California Press, 1979.
Committee for the Compilation of Materials on Damage Caused by the Atomic Bombs in Hiroshima and Nagasaki. *The Physical, Medical, and Social Effects of the Atomic Bombings*. Translated by Ishikawa, Eisei, and David L. Swain, Basic Books Inc., 1981.
Davis, Grania. "Foreword." *The Best Japanese Science Fiction Stories*, edited by John L. Apostolou, and Martin H. Greenberg. Dembner Books, 1989, 9–12.
Dower, John W. "The Bombed: Hiroshimas and Nagasakis in Japanese Memory." *Hiroshima in History and Memory*, edited by Michael J. Hogan, Cambridge University Press, 1996, 116–142.
Goulding, Jay. "Globalization: Asia." *New Dictionary of the History of Ideas*, edited by Maryanne Cline Horowitz, vol. 3, Thompson Gale, 2005, 941–947.
Hendrix, Grady. "From Nuclear Nightmare to Networked Nirvana: Futuristic Utopianism in Japanese SF Films of the 2000s." *World Literature Today*, vol. 84, no. 3, 2010, 55–57.
Jimenez-Varea, Jesus, and Miguel Angel Perez-Gomez. "Marvel and Toei." *Marvel Comics into Film: Essays on Adaptations Since the 1940s*, edited by Matthew J. McEniry, Robert Moses Peaslee, and Robert G. Weiner, McFarland, 2016, 84–93.
Kalat, David. *A Critical History and Filmography of Toho's Godzilla Series*. McFarland, 1997.
Kidd, Chip, and Chris Burnham. *Bat-Manga!: The Secret History of Batman in Japan*. Pantheon, 2008.
Lie, John. "Pop Multiethnicity." *Race, Ethnicity and Migration in Modern Japan: Indigenous and Colonial Others*, edited by Michael Weiner, Routledge Curzon, 2004.
Masco, Joseph. "Catastrophe's Apocalypse." *The Time of Catastrophe: Multidisciplinary Approaches to the Age of Catastrophe*, edited by Christopher Dole, et al., Routledge, 2016.
Matthew, Robert. *Japanese Science Fiction: A View of a Changing Society*. Routledge, 1989.
Papp, Zília. *Traditional Monster Imagery in Manga, Anime and Japanese Cinema*. Global Oriental, 2011.
Patten, Fred. *Watching Anime, Reading Manga: 25 Years of Essays and Reviews*. Stone Bridge Press, 2004.
Ryfle, Steve. "Godzilla's Footprint." *The Virginia Quarterly Review*, vol. 81, no. 1, 2005, 44–63.
_____. *Japan's Favorite Mon-star: The Unauthorized Biography of "The Big G."* ECW Press, 1998.

Sharp, Jasper. *Historical Dictionary of Japanese Cinema*. Lanham: The Scarecrow Press, 2011.
Shibata, Masako. *Japan and Germany Under the U.S. Occupation: A Comparative Analysis of Post-War Education Reform*. Lexington Books, 2005.
Sontag, Susan. "The Imagination of Disaster." *Commentary*, vol. 40, 1965, 42–48.
Szasz, Ferenc M., and Issei Takechi. "Atomic Heroes and Atomic Monsters: American and Japanese Cartoonists Confront the Onset of the Nuclear Age, 1954–1980." *The Historian*, vol. 69, no. 4, 2007, 728–752.
Tanaka, Motoko. *Apocalypse in Contemporary Japanese Science Fiction*. Palgrave Macmillan, 2014.
Tsutsui, William. *Godzilla on My Mind: Fifty Years of the King of Monsters*. Palgrave Macmillan, 2004.
Vartanian, Ivan. *Killer Kaiju Monsters: Strange Beasts of Japanese Film*. Goliga Books, 2009.

Notes from the Land of Light
Observations on Religious Elements Seen in Ultraman

JUSTIN MULLIS

Despite the increased interest since the turn of the century among western scholars, working in a number of different fields, in the academic analysis of both Japanese popular-culture and western-superhero fiction, only scant attention has been paid to the subject of Japan's robust and storied stable of live-action superhero programs. The reason for this neglect undoubtedly has to do with the fact that even today very little of the Japanese superhero genre has been exported to the West in its original format. For instance, Tsuburaya Production's long-running Ultraman series, the subject of this present essay, has had extremely limited exposure to audiences outside of East Asia. While the original *Ultraman* show was broadcast—in an edited and dubbed format—in the United States by United Artist Television in 1966, it would be nearly 30 years before that show's 1967 follow-up series, *Ultra Seven*, would be broadcast in the U.S. by Turner Program Services—again dubbed and edited—and another six years before the last Ultraman series to receive official U.S. TV distribution, *Ultraman Tiga*, was aired by the Fox Broadcasting Company in 2002; again with a highly irreverent (bordering on parody) dub.

However, even with few markets outside of Asia, Ultraman has still managed to become the third top-selling licensed character in the world.[1] Like many American superheroes, Ultraman is not only popular with children but adults as well. Controversial novelist and Nobel Prize nominee Yukio Mishima identified *Ultraman* as his favorite TV program[2] while Japanese astronaut Doi Takao requested the original *Ultraman* theme song be his personal wake-up call aboard the space shuttle *Columbia* in 1997.[3] The entire city of Shoshigaya-Okura in Setagaya, Tokyo is dedicated to the character[4] and until 2013 Sunshine City, a building complex located in East Ikebukuro,

Toshima, Tokyo, hosted the theme park Ultraman Land.⁵ Ultraman's likeness can be found on such diversified, and in some cases explicitly adult oriented, products as toys, clothes, wrist watches, video games, key chains, golf club covers and even condoms.⁶ In many ways Ultraman has become synonymous with Japan, being seen as an unofficial symbol of country. Case in point: in the wake of the 2011 Tohoku earthquake and tsunami, the Malaysian newspaper *Berita Harian* published a highly controversial political cartoon which depicted Japan *as* Ultraman attempting to outrun an oncoming tidal wave.⁷

Fortunately thanks to the advent of specialty home video labels like Shout! Factory and streaming services like Crunchyroll, it is now possible for non–Japanese audiences to see Japanese superhero shows like *Ultraman*, or Toei's long-running *Super Sentai* series (the basis for Saban's popular Power Rangers franchise), in their original format in Japanese with English subtitles.

An upshot of this newfound accessibility is that it has generated a boom in interest among Americans in the character of Ultraman. American *manga* publisher Viz Media recently licensed the current *Ultraman* (2011–Present) manga series for publication as well as hosting its writer, Eiichi Shimizu, and artist, Tomohiro Shimoguchi, at the 2015 San Diego Comic Con. The original *Ultraman* series is also featured as a key plot point in author Ernest Cline's 2011 best-selling sci-fi novel *Ready Player One*; which is currently being adapted for film by Steven Spielberg. Ultraman is also a lifelong favorite of director Guillermo Del Toro, whose film *Pacific Rim* (2013) was heavily influenced by the franchise—a tip-of-the-hat that was returned when the series *Ultraman X* paid a visit the conspicuously named Planet Guillermo.⁸ Less overt homages include the Ultraman-inspired character Way Big on the popular kid's animated TV series *Ben 10* (2005–Present) and the Eisner Award nominated comic book *Kaijumax* (2015–Present), created by writer/artist Zander Cannon who notes: "A lot of people assume that.... *Kaijumax* is [my] take on Godzilla, but Ultraman is the real inspiration: deliriously fast paced, utterly unconcerned with continuity, and with beautiful monster designs throughout all its incarnations."⁹

While this is not the place to try and make up for the dearth of attention paid by scholars to the subject of Japanese superheroes and how they both reflect and influence Japanese society and popular culture, it will hopefully serve as a start. The goal of this essay then is to shine a light, albeit a limited and non-comprehensive one, on the Japanese superhero genre via an examination of the Ultraman franchise. Because the subject of this volume is *kaiju*, I will be paying special attention to the kaiju that inhabit the world of Ultraman and serve as the hero's principal antagonists. As Anne Allison writes, one of the principal differences between Japanese and American superheroes is that while American superheroes contend chiefly with a rogues gallery of human supervillains, Japanese superheroes spend their time slugging it out with decidedly inhuman monsters and aliens.[10] In doing so I will challenge the popular truism that the monsters of the kaiju genre are principally a commentary on the atomic bomb and its associated dangers,[11] an interpretation which I contend is both wholly inadequate and exegetically crippling, resulting in a myopic view of *kaiju eiga* as a whole and a hair-trigger tendency by some to denounce any film which seems to ignore the supposedly immutable relationship which exists between kaiju and nuclear power.[12]

This will no doubt come as a surprise to many, so let me be clear that I am not saying that kaiju have nothing to do with the dangers of nuclear weapons. Rather as Hidetoshi Chiba of Tokyo's Digital Hollywood University notes, I am simply pointing out that the majority of kaiju movies "do not remind most Japanese audiences of nuclear power or weapons" but rather "are more likely to be linked to causes that existed before the war" for instance "historical natural disasters such as volcanic eruptions, typhoons or earthquakes."[13] My analysis is framed by the academic discipline of religious studies, holding to the contention that we can better understand both the genres of kaiju eiga and Japanese superheroes by first grounding ourselves in the religious traditions which inform Japanese culture. After all, superheroes and religion actually have a lot in common. As Zen Buddhism writer Brad Warner, who also served as Tsuburaya Production's American business liaison for over a decade, succinctly observes "the only place other than … superhero shows for kids where you can find powerful beings who help powerless people out and ask for nothing in return is in the sphere of religion."[14]

Lastly, while my primary subject will be the various Ultraman TV series, and their related media, I will also occasionally cast my analytical net a bit broader by bringing in other superhero shows from the same production company including *Redman* and *Gridman*—both of which ostensibly take place in the same fictive universe as Ultraman. I would also like to, at a key point, incorporate the contemporary Japanese kaiju novel, *MM9* (2007), by acclaimed science fiction writer Hiroshi Yamamoto into my analysis as I see it providing an important insight into the kaiju genre, in addition to the fact that Yamamoto has stated that Ultraman was a key influence on the book.[15]

A Brief History of Ultraman

Ultraman was the brainchild of Japanese special effects artist Eiji Tsuburaya (1901–1970) who for many years served as the head of the special effects department at Toho Company, LTD. Working alongside producer Tomoyuki Tanaka and director Ishiro Honda, Tsuburaya helped to create the now world famous movie monsters Godzilla, Rodan, Mothra, and King Ghidorah among

38   Giant Creatures in Our World

many others as he oversaw the special effects work on nearly all of Toho's science fiction and fantasy films during the 1950s and 60s.

The style of special effects pioneered by Eiji Tsuburaya would come to be known as *tokusatsu* "special filming" and involves the construction of elaborate miniature sets which are then destroyed by actors in rubber monster costumes. Though CGI has made more realistic effects a possibility, such advances have largely been eschewed by the makers of Japanese science fiction films and television since, as *Ultraman Ginga* director Yuichi Abe observes, the "use of real actors, models and even explosives [gives] tokusatsu a level of realism that is not possible with computer graphics."[16] Likewise Yuichi Kikuchi, who oversaw the special effects on the theatrical film *Ultraman: The Next* (2004, Dir. Kazuya Konaka) sees Japan's continued "use [of] costumes instead of going for full CG like they do in America" as a tribute to the legacy of Eiji Tsuburaya who made tokusatsu a "part of Japanese culture."[17]

In addition, writer Phillip Brophy sees a religious dimension at work in tokusatsu, writing that while American cinema has historically placed the filmmaker in the position of Judeo-Christianity's "unseen God ... operating beyond the frame and between the edit; invisible in the act ... yet perceivable through the product," Japanese religious traditions see the divine working through human agents, such as Shinto shrine maidens, leading "Japanese sci fi/fantasy cinema" to embrace "the human figure within the cinematic frame rather than deny its status."[18]

In the early 1960s, Eiji Tsuburaya set out to establish his own studio which would specialize in special effects based science fiction and fantasy series for television. In 1963, Tsuburaya Productions was founded and on January 2, 1966, the studio's first series, *Ultra Q* (1966, 28 Episodes) premiered. *Ultra Q* was a black-and-white science fiction drama modeled after *The Outer Limits* (1963–65, 49 Episodes), but anticipating *The X-Files* (1993–2002, Revived 2016), in which a trio of investigators look into strange phenomena happening throughout Japan. In each episode the protagonists would ultimately discover that the mysterious events were the result of a giant monster, extraterrestrial invaders, or both.

Ultra Q proved extremely popular with adults and children alike and gave Tsuburaya the incentive and financial security to produce a higher budgeted follow-up series, this time to be filmed in color. This new series would also involve paranormal phenomena and giant monsters, but instead of only three investigators, an entire paramilitary team would deal with such threats along with a good giant monster that would fight off the bad ones. Eventually this later idea changed into a giant extraterrestrial superhero: Ultraman.[19] Though this change meant largely abandoning the paranormal *noir* stylings of *Ultra Q* in favor of the science fiction action formula that would define *Ultraman*, Tsuburaya Productions has occasionally revisited the *Ultra Q* format in follow-up series like *Ultra Q: Dark Fantasy* (2004, 26 Episodes) and *Neo Ultra Q* (2013, 12 Episodes) as well as a theatrical film; *Ultra Q The Movie: Legend of the Stars* (1990, Dir. Akio Jissoji).

The first episode of *Ultraman: A Special-Effects Fantasy Series* (1966/67, 39 Episodes), and henceforth referred to simply as *Ultraman*, premiered on July 17, 1966. In the debut episode viewers are introduced to the Science Special Search Party, also known as The Science Patrol, a six-person paramilitary team working for the United Nations and tasked with investigating strange occurrences, combating the giant monsters, and managing alien invaders who threaten mankind. Among The Science Patrol is deputy captain Shin Hayata whose life is forever altered when, while out on patrol, his "Delta VTOL" fatally crashes into a UFO piloted by Ultraman. In order to make amends, Ultraman melds his life force with that of Hayata's, saving the man's life while also bestowing upon him the ability to transform into Ultraman, via a baton-like device called the Beta Capsule, whenever Earth is in danger. The catch is that Hayata can only remain Ultraman for three-minute intervals since, in a reversal of the American Superman myth, Earth's sun actually weakens the superhero.

This setup served as the basis for a typical episode of *Ultraman:* The Science Patrol investigates a mysterious occurrence, discovers its source to be a giant monster and/or extraterrestrial invader, makes a series of failed attempts to combat the unveiled menace thus requiring Hayata, and in the eleventh hour, transforms into Ultraman who then fights and defeats the monster and/or alien, saving the day. Later iterations of the Ultraman series would alter the particulars of this setup—new protagonist, new cast of characters, new paramilitary organization—while keeping the same overall formula.

Likewise Ultraman would be substituted with a similar Ultra hero, whose name would also typically function as the show's title, beginning with *Ultra Seven* (1967/68, 49 Episodes) and then moving onto the more derivatively named Ultraman Jack from *The Return of Ultraman* (1971/72, 51 Episodes) followed shortly by *Ultraman Ace* (1972/73, 52 Episodes), *Ultraman Taro* (1973/74, 53 Episodes), *Ultraman Leo* (1974/75, 51 Episodes) and *Ultraman 80* (1980/81, 50 Episodes). A nearly twenty-year hiatus would separate the Showa-era Ultraman series from the modern Heisei era which began with *Ultraman Tiga* (1996/67, 52 Episodes) and has continued unabated with *Ultraman Dyna* (1997/98, 51 Episodes), *Ultraman Gaia* (1998/99, 51 Episodes), *Ultraman Cosmos* (2000/01, 65 Episodes), *Ultraman Nexus* (2004/05, 39 Episodes), *Ultraman Max* (2005/06, 39 Episodes), *Ultraman Mebius* (2006/07, 50 Episodes), *Ultraseven X* (2007, 12 Episodes), Ultraman Zero—who was introduced in a trilogy of theatrical films as opposed to a weekly TV series[20]— *Ultraman Ginga* (2013/2014, 28 Episodes), and *Ultraman X* (2015/16, 22

Episodes). Last year, Tsuburaya Productions celebrated Ultraman's 50th Anniversary with a new series: *Ultraman Orb* (2016/17, 25 Episodes).[21]

With the same narrative formula first introduced in the original *Ultraman* TV series still being used today, one would be forgiven for imagining that such a repetitive format would quickly grow boring for fans. However, as Brad Warner eloquently puts it, watching Ultraman is like listening to blues music; though there are only three cords involved a surprising number of highly entertaining variations are nevertheless possible, keeping viewers entertained for generations.[22]

It should also be pointed out that the highly structured and predictable nature of such genre entertainment is also indicative of religious rituals, which are repeated yearly until the faithful know them by heart and which use such repetition as a means of bringing comfort to their devotees.[23] This observation, originally made by scholars looking at horror films, is also true of shows like Ultraman. As Japanese-American historian William M. Tsutsui concurs, shows like Ultraman provide their viewers with a worldview which is inherently "optimistic" and "self-healing" since no matter how many times Japan gets destroyed by a different giant monster it will always be restored the following week ready to reenact its ritual destruction all over again.[24] With this final point in place we can begin our analysis of the kaiju which appear in Ultraman and ask what exactly they can tell us about the Japanese conception of the superhero.

Kaiju in Ultraman

Director Akio Jissoji (1937–2006) described the kaiju who appeared in the original *Ultraman* as "symbols of nature" corrupted by "human selfishness," creatures that are in some way the result of human transgressions against nature or one another. Examples include the Godzilla-like Jirass (1966, Ep. 10: "The Mysterious Dinosaur Base") that is driven from its home in Lake Kitayama as a result of heavy fishing depleting its natural food source, or the bizarre bat-starfish hybrid Pestar (1966, Ep. 13 "Oil S.O.S.") whose ocean home has been poisoned by crude oil.[25]

While pollution is one way that humans can demonstrate a disrespect for nature, poaching is another as seen in a two-part story featured in *Ultraman Taro* (1973, Ep. 4: "Big Sea Turtle Monsters Attack Tokyo!" and Ep. 5: "Parent Star, Child Star, First Star") penned by genre veteran Shozo Uehara, in which a group of poachers first capture a pair of kaiju-sized tortoises for profit and then callously devour the pair's eggs in front of them; thereby, enraging the parents who then attack Tokyo.

Of course, imagery of natural and man-made disasters freely mix in the

Japanese imagination as is seen in Nobel prize laureate Kenzaburo Oe's apocalyptic novel *The Floodwaters Have Come Unto My Soul* (1973) in which visions of a devastating flood and nuclear holocaust are deliberately intertwined.[26] Even more terrifying, Japanese citizens experienced such a collision of events in March of 2011 when the devastating Tohoku earthquake and tsunami not only rocked the country but triggered a meltdown at the Fukushima Daiichi Nuclear Power Plant complex. As a result of the 3.11 disasters an episode of the series *Ultra Seven*, (1968, Ep. 26: "Super Weapon R-1"), was temporarily removed from circulation on Japanese TV. The episode involves scientists detonating a fictional super weapon, described as possessing the equivalent power of "8,000 Hydrogen bombs," on a supposedly uninhabited planet. Obviously it turns out the planet was not uninhabited and soon Earth finds itself under attack by the kaiju Gyeron who resembles a kind of mechanized parrot.[27]

Many of the best episodes of the early Ultraman series that address issues dealing with "the vicissitudes of war, invasion and occupation" were scripted by writer Tetsuo Kinjo, a native of the Japanese island of Okinawa which alternately suffered under the thumb of first the Imperial Japanese army during World War II and later an American military occupation which lasted until the mid–1970s.[28] One of Kinjo's most memorable stories occurred in *The Return of Ultraman* (1971, Ep. 11: "Poison Gas Monster Appears") in which MAT team member Fumio Kishida learns that his father had been responsible for the development of chemical weapons used by the Japanese army during World War II. Now these same weapons have given rise to a spiny lizard-like kaiju called Mognezun that exhales the very same poison gas.

Another outstanding pair of episodes penned by Kinjo come from *Ultra Seven* (1968, Ep. 14: "The Ultra Garrison Goes West, Part 1" and Ep. 15: "The Ultra Garrison Goes West, Part 2") and introduces the now iconic kaiju robot King Joe, whose name is actually an homage to the writer. In this two-part story an American scientific investigation to the planet Pedan is mistaken by the planet's inhabitants as a declaration of war, to which the Pedan aliens respond by sending King Joe to attack the United Nations. In other cases the relationship between a kaiju and weapons of mass destruction needs no explanation, such as the hybrid crocodilian-battleship kaiju Yamaton from Daiji Kazumine's *Ultraman* (1966–67) manga or the self-explanatory Dinosaur Tank from *Ultra Seven* (1968, Ep. 28: "Dash The 700 Kilometers!").

But weapons of war are not the only technological dangers dealt with in *Ultraman*. In one episode of *Ultraman* (1966, Ep. 20: "Terror on Route 87") the griffin-like kaiju Hydra attacks cars on the freeway. It is eventually revealed that the monster is the manifestation of the angry spirit of a child who died in a hit-and-run automobile accident.[29] Such a kaiju recalls the Buddhist notion of "hungry ghosts," terrible "wraith-like creatures" whom a human with unresolved earth-bound desires, such as need for revenge, can be reborn as after death.[30] In another unforgettable episode of *Ultraman* (1966, Ep. 23 "My Home Is Earth") directed by Akio Jissoji addressed the dangers of space travel in which "a brave astronaut [is] mutated by extraterrestrial contact" into a misshapen monster called Jamila. Shin-ichi Ooka, the current president of Tsuburaya Productions, describes this episode as "quite tragic" noting that "after Ultraman defeats the rampaging creature, the Science Patrol begs Jamila's forgiveness, solemnly unveiling a plaque in the astronaut's memory."[31]

The Return of Ultraman (1971, Ep. 34: "The Life That Can't Be Forgiven") even touched on the dangers of genetic engineering, nearly two decades before films like *Jurassic Park* (1992, Dir. Stephen Spielberg) would. In this story a mad scientist splices the DNA of a plant and a reptile creating the terrifying vegetable-animal hybrid kaiju Leogon—and if this plotline sounds familiar to Godzilla fans it's because it was penned by writer Shinichiro Kobayashi, the same writer who would later compose the initial story treatment for *Godzilla vs. Biollante* (1989, Dir. Kazuki Omori) by essentially recycling one of his old Ultraman storylines.[32]

Tsuburaya Production's *Gridman* (1993/94, 39 Episodes) updated the concept of Ultraman "for the electronic age" moving the action from the streets of Tokyo to those of the internet's information superhighway.[33] *Gridman*'s kaiju personify computer viruses and other cyber threats but for the most part look and act just like their Ultraman counterparts. In the debut episode (1993, Ep. 1: "New Century Hero Birth!") the crystalline virus kaiju Gilarus attacks the computers in a hospital, shutting down the facility and endangering the lives of the patients.[34] One key difference between *Gridman* and Ultraman though is that Gridman is not assisted by a Science Patrol-style team of battle-hardened adults but instead a trio of "child technocrats" whose parents remain utterly oblivious to what their children are doing online.[35]

Lastly, kaiju can also serve as symbols of "social ostracism" as seen in several episodes of *Ultra Q* (1966, Ep. 2: "Goro and Goroh" and Ep. 12: "I Saw a Bird.")[36] In the episode "Goro and Goroh," a deaf-mute man named Goroh works as a custodian at a research facility located near Amagi Mountain and befriends a monkey he dubs Goro. Goroh begins feeding walnuts to Goro, only to discover the walnuts are laced with chemicals from the research facility. This causes Goro to grow 50 meters tall and develop a nearly insatiable appetite; desperate not to lose his only friend, Goroh begins robbing stores in order to try and provide Goro with enough food. When Goroh is eventually caught by police and imprisoned, Goro heads into the city to try and rescue his human friend causing a panic. Likewise in "I Saw a Bird," a young homeless boy named Saburo, who lives in a ramshackle shack on the beach, befriends the prehistoric bird kaiju Larugeus. When Saburo is harassed by the locals, Larugeus comes to his rescue by beating up gale-force winds and reigning down considerable destruction on the town.

But perhaps no episode of Ultraman deals with the dangers of social alienation better than the saga of alien Mates as recounted in *The Return of Ultraman* (1971, Ep. 33: "The Monster Tamer and the Boy"). In this story, Mates visits Earth with the intent of studying our planet's weather patterns; however, Mates soon becomes ill as a result of earth's pollution and is forced to extend his stay while he recuperates. While on Earth, Mates finds an orphaned boy named Ryou Sakuma and he chooses to raise him as his son. Despite being utterly benevolent, Mates is eventually gunned down by a scared police officer simply because he is an alien. The incident causes Mates' ship to release the dormant salmon-like kaiju Muruchi who is then subsequently defeated by Ultraman Jack.[37]

It is also possible for storylines in the Ultraman series to hit a little too close to home when it comes to sensitive topics. This was the case regarding the now infamous banned episode of *Ultra Seven* (1967, Ep. 12: "From a Planet With Love"), written by Mamoru Sasaki and directed by Akio Jissoji. In this story a group of all-male aliens from the planet Spehlia arrive in Japan seeking refugee status after their home world was annihilated via nuclear war. The Japanese members of the Ultra Guard are sympathetic to the Spehlians until it later comes to light that the aliens, who are depicted as manikin-like humanoids covered in keloid scars, are vampiric by nature and already in the process of draining the blood of several young Japanese women. Though the episode aired without any initial objections, it later came to the attention of the Tokyo Branch of the Confederation of A- and H-Bomb Sufferers Organization who interpreted it as a slight against *Hibakusha*: survivors of the atomic bombings of Hiroshima and Nagasaki. After being lambasted by the *Asahi Shimbun* newspaper, Tsuburaya Productions put the episode into self-imposed exile, removing it from circulation on TV and striking it from all future home video releases of *Ultra Seven*.[38]

Kaiju and Chaos

One of the most important artists in the history of the kaiju genre is Tohl Narita (1929–2002), who designed the first several iterations of Ultraman as well as a number of iconic kaiju for both Toho Studios and Tsuburaya Productions. Narita saw kaiju as "expressions of chaos in the space age" and felt that "such monsters" could only be "achieve[d] in abstraction."[39] As a result, Narita worked very closely with surrealist painter Taro Okamoto and artist Ryosaku Takayama on the Ultraman series, incorporating elements of surrealism, primitivism and Dadaist influences into the show's monster designs.[40]

One kaiju, the evil space alien Dada, who first appeared in *Ultraman* (1967, Ep. 28: "Human Specimens 5 & 6"), even draws his *nom de plume* from the European art movement of the same name.

Avant-garde pop artist Takashi Murakami, whose work is heavily influenced by Narita, notes that Narita had a set of "self-imposed rigorous principals" when it came to designing kaiju which included an avoidance of both the "simpleminded enlargement of animals, insects, and the like" and the depiction of bodily "deformity or disfigurement." Narita dismissed such conventions because he saw them as counterproductive to the portrayal of kaiju as symbols of primordial chaos, a concept which could be better conveyed via "abstraction, unusual proportions, and inventive transformations."[41]

As personifications of primordial chaos, Biblical scholars Timothy K. Beal and Robert M. Price both see kaiju fitting nicely into a category of mythical beings known as "Chaos Monsters" which were first identified in the late 1800s by German scholar Hermann Gunkel and chiefly known from the religious traditions of the Ancient Near East with notable examples including the dragon-goddess Tiamat from the Mesopotamian creation epic *Enuma Elish* and the fire-spitting sea serpent Leviathan of the Hebrew Bible, whose scaly skin cannot be pierced by conventional weaponry (Job 41).[42]

The most exhaustive study to date on Chaos Monsters is Neil Forsyth's *The Old Enemy* (1987) which profiles the classical Chaos Monsters as not only colossal in size but also reptilian in nature, chimera-like in appearance and having a close association with "the chaotic, disintegrating power of water, whether as raging sea or flooding river"[43]; an association which Patrick Macias, editor-in-chief at Crunchyroll, notes that many kaiju also share "as a mythic personification of natural destructive forces: the earthquakes, tsunami and typhoons that have regularly struck Japan over the centuries."[44] A smattering of examples include the rhinoceros-like kaiju Seamons from the two-part story from *The Return of Ultraman* (1971, Ep. 13: "Terror of the Tsunami Monsters, Tokyo's Big Pinch" & Ep. 14: "Terror of The Two Tsunami Monsters, Tokyo's Dalong Reel") who appears on the island of Hachijojima with the intent of building a nest. When MAT attacks Seamons, she summons her mate Seagorath and the two create a massive tsunami. Other kaiju with destructive environmental powers includes the jellyfish-like Varricane, also from *The Return of Ultraman* (1971, Ep. 28: "Ultra Special Operation"), who could generate devastating typhoons, and more recently the bird-like kaiju Maga-Basser from *Ultraman Orb* (2016, Ep. 1: "The Wanderer from Sunset") capable of wiping up destructive tornados.

Japan has its own variation on the Chaos Monster myth in the story of the *Yamata-no-Orochi* as recounted in the nineteenth chapter of the *Kojiki* "Records of Ancient Matters," a Shinto work which dates from 712 C.E. the *Kojiki* describes the Orochi as a gigantic serpent possessing "eyes like red ground cherries; his one body has eight heads and eight tails. On his body grow moss and cypress and cryptomeria trees. His length is such that he spans eight valleys and eight mountain peaks. If you look at his belly, you see that blood is oozing out all over it" (1.19.10).[45] Initially Orochi's reign of terror goes unchecked until the Shinto storm god Susanoo comes to earth with his "sword ten hands long" with which he hacks "the dragon to pieces, so that the Pi river ran with blood." (1.19.19) Today the Orochi remains an important part of Japanese popular-culture, including in Ultraman, whose 50th-Anniversary series, *Ultraman Orb*, featured an significant kaiju modeled off the legendary beast (2016, Ep. 11 "Trouble! Mama's Here!" and Ep. 12 "The Dark King's Blessing").

Like Chaos Monsters, kaiju embody a type of ontological disorientation that results in an inability to easily categorize them or process their existence on an empirical level. In terms of appearance alone, kaiju—especially those which have appeared on the various Ultraman programs over the years—come in a variety of shapes so teratologically fabulous as to stun the mind, often employing "the same technique of pasting together features of disparate creatures to form multi-headed, many-winged, etc., chimeras" as that of "ancient apocalyptic books" such as the Bible's *Book of Daniel* and *Book of Revelation*.[46]

These "hybrid monsters indicate the liminality of the situation, the impending passage into a different order of being and meaning, the dissolution of the worldview rather than of the world itself," writes Price, "When I face the neither-both-fish-nor-fowl creatures of the apocalyptic genre, I know the end of sweet reason is at hand. The world does not make anything like the sense I once thought it did."[47] Seen from this vantage point, the appearance of a kaiju denotes more than the presence of a large and extraordinary animal—as is often the case in American giant monster movies—but is rather a signpost that a transformation of the world itself has taken place as well as our understanding of it.

As a result, the very existence of kaiju thrusts our world back into primordial chaos. Not only in the material realm where kaiju crush cars and smash skyscrapers but also in the existential realm as well. There is no way such creatures could exist, and yet they do. The crisis of understanding this creates is expressed well by the protagonist Ryo Haida in the opening chapter of writer Hiroshi Yamamoto's Ultraman influenced kaiju novel *MM9*:

> No creature weighing a hundred tons could possibly stand up straight and walk itself across the surface of the earth. Not while following the laws of science anyway. No matter how the numbers were crunched, bones and muscles of that size just wouldn't be capable of supporting their own weight. And yet kaiju appeared all over the world, and on a regular basis. Even dissection and anatomical analysis had never been able to solve that mystery. Moreover, in previous encounters with kaiju, tank and battle-crusier cannon fire were less effective than projections would have suggested—an

indication that the laws of physics were broken by not only the strength of kaiju bones and muscle, but likely their skin as well.[48]

This sensation that "the laws of physics are broken" by the very existence of kaiju emphasize their monstrosity and role as harbingers of chaos. It is an idea which is also highlighted effectively in the form of the surreal kaiju Gan Q from *Ultraman Gaia* (1998, Ep. 6: "The Ridiculing Eye") who initially appears as a giant eyeball staring unblinkingly out of the Earth's surface and, somehow, laughing manically, though no discernible mouth is present. Even more troubling, attempts by young science whiz Gamu Takayama to analyze Gan Q's biological and physical makeup come up negative, leading Takayama to declare that Gan Q's very "existence itself is irrational"; a realization which causes Takayama to suffer a nervous breakdown during the heat of battle with the monster.

Ultraman Gaia was one of several Ultraman series, including *Ultraman Max* and *Ultra Q: Dark Fantasy*, which featured episodes penned by prolific Japanese horror author Chiaki J. Konaka, whose work is heavily influenced by American horror icon H.P. Lovecraft (1890–1937). Lovecraft's hallmark was the development of what he called "cosmic horror"; stories which presented the reader with "a certain atmosphere of breathless and unexplainable dread of outer, unknown forces" and which dealt foremost with "that most terrible conception of the human brain—a malign and particular suspension or defeat of those fixed laws of Nature which are our only safeguard against the assaults of chaos and the daemons of unplumbed space."[49]

In this way, Lovecraft's notion of "cosmic horror" aligns well with Price and Yamamoto's idea of kaiju as beings which break the laws of nature thereby ushering in a new understanding of a world governed by chaos and destruction as seen in the two-part series finale for *Ultraman Tiga* (1997, Ep. 51: "Master of Darkness" and Ep. 52: "To the Shining Ones") in which Tiga confronts the kaiju Gatanozoa who is based on one of Lovecraft's alien god-monsters, Ghatanothoa, from the 1933 short story "Out of the Aeons."[50]

We must remember that Japanese kaiju are more than mere objects of raw terror and abjection; however, kaiju fulfill a variety of roles, serving as both heroes and villains, and as warnings for when humankind has transgressed in their relationship to both nature and society. In this capacity, kaiju also invoke another important monster from Japanese mythology; the giant catfish *Namazu*, often depicted as possessing a combination of cetacean and draconian features, is believed to be responsible for earthquakes caused by its attempts to burrow its way under Japan.[51]

Though depictions of the Namazu go back as far as the 15th-Century, the giant catfish only achieved true celebrity status after the great Edo Earthquake of 1855 rocked the country. At the time many people in Japan felt that the Edo aristocracy had become corrupt, hoarding their accumulated wealth, while the common people fell into poverty and misery. The Edo Earthquake conversely loosened the purse strings of the capital aristocrats and resulted in a more even distribution of resources among the city's denizens. As a result the earthquake was widely interpreted as the Namazu punishing the Japanese people for succumbing to avarice and acrimony.[52] Consequently, woodblock prints, the most popular media of the day, featuring Namazu became popular items in the Edo marketplace. Today art historians have documented over 300 different kinds of *namazu-e* prints.

According to religious studies scholar Takashi Miura, the view of the Namazu as a veritable karmic barometer by which humankind's relationship with the Earth and each other can be gauged places it in the company of a special class of seldom remarked upon Japanese deities known as "Yonaoshi Gods," or "gods of world renewal." They were invested with special authority to rectify the various evils at work in the world. To accomplish this, the Yonaoshi Gods were believed to unleash apocalyptic cataclysms, often as natural disasters but sometimes as wars and riots, literally tearing down the current corrupt infrastructure so as to provide the necessary rejiggering needed for a new more equitable society to start over.[53]

Like the Namazu, kaiju are also harbingers of chaos and destruction, personifications of disaster, both natural and man-made, who serve as a warning that humanity has upset the delicate balance, which is the natural order of things. More than mere atomic scarecrows, we can now see that kaiju are polyvalent creatures embodying, as Japanese film historian Jerome F. Shapiro notes, a wide variety of themes including "tradition, family, harmony with nature, and the centrality of women in Japanese society. Other themes focus on a broader social context, including the dangers of modernity, technology, or capitalism, and the role of the military. The most important theme, however, is the restoration of balance and harmony."[54]

Sympathy for Kaiju

Despite serving as heralds of devastation and cosmic unrest, kaiju nevertheless remain beloved figures by the Japanese. Science fiction critic Mari Kotani writes that the earliest manifestations of the Japanese *otaku* (i.e. geek) subculture began with individuals who obsessively catalogued the kaiju from the various Ultraman TV series.[55] Director Ishiro Honda, best known for helming such kaiju classics as *Godzilla* (1954), *Rodan* (1956), and *Mothra* (1961) but who also directed a number of episodes for *The Return of Ultraman* as well[56] undoubtedly summed up Japanese audience's capacity to become emotionally attached to kaiju best in an October 1968 interview with *Midi/Minuit Fantastique* magazine when he said:

Monsters are tragic beings. They are born too tall, too strong, too heavy. They are not evil by choice. That is their tragedy. They do not attack people because they want to, but because of their size and strength, mankind has no other choice but to defend himself. After several stories such as this, people end up having a kind of affection for the monsters. They end up caring about them.[57]

Tsuburaya Production's Shin-ichi Ooka puts it another way: "One of the secrets to the popularity of the 'Ultra' series is that the kaiju and aliens, who you'd think would be the enemies, are actually the stars."[58] Responding to the popularity of the Ultraman kaiju early on, Tsuburaya began having some of them serve as allies for the franchise's various heroes. Beginning with *Ultra Seven*, viewers were introduced to the concept of Capsule Monsters which were kaiju who inhabited tiny containers that protagonist Dan Moroboshi wore on his utility belt and who could be summoned to battle alongside the hero when needed; a concept which started the Japanese subgenre of "Battle Monster" games which continue to this day with such multimedia juggernauts as Nintendo's Pokémon and Toei's Digimon.[59]

The tendency for Japanese people to view kaiju with both affection and sympathy is, oddly enough, perhaps best seen in the Tsuburaya Productions series which, without a doubt, treats them the most inhumanely: *Redman* (1972, 138 Episodes). Originally airing as part of the children's variety program, *Ohayo! Kodomo Show,* on Nippon TV—with each episode lasting less than five-minutes and "made on an extremely low budget"—*Redman* featured no elaborate miniature sets, cut-rate monster costumes and no discernible narrative, being essentially "little more than two suit actors in costume fighting each other with little choreography involved."[60]

Almost every episode of *Redman* opens with one or two kaiju strolling through a field or wooded area, seemingly minding their own business, when Redman abruptly appears and attacks them. In many episodes the kaiju actually attempt to flee from Redman only to have the would-be hero give chase, running them down before brutally slaying them. While Tsuburaya Productions may have hoped that young undiscriminating viewers would see *Redman* as Ultraman boiled down to its most basic fundamentals—superhero vs. kaiju—the show had the exact opposite effect. Rather than cheering for Redman as he cut down each monster with his signature "Red Knife," the show instead became "notorious among Japanese viewers for its 'cruelty' toward [the] monsters."[61] It is important to stress here that all of the kaiju that appeared on *Redman* were well-known beasts recycled from prior Ultraman series; monsters and aliens which, in many cases, had been responsible for wholesale death and destruction. Nevertheless, Japanese audiences still saw these kaiju as fundamentally innocent by nature and without any context to account for Redman's (over)zealous punishment of them, came to see Redman as a "Serial Killer" rather than a superhero.[62]

Part of what could explain the Japanese's willingness to view kaiju with a sympathetic eye despite their status as literal aliens may be sociolinguist Suzuki Takao's observation "that the Japanese language, unlike Indo-European languages, does not have a long or consistent history of personal pronouns to distinguish between 'I' and 'You,' 'We' and 'Them'" and other such terms that make it easy to ostracize others.[63] The result of this has been a culture in which the dominant group inevitably ends up identifying with "the Other" rather than seeking to destroy it. Nevertheless, Suzuki adds a caveat noting that this "Other-oriented self-designation" only operates so long as "the Other" is seen as an honorary member of Japanese culture.[64] Of course as modern day legendary figures of Japan, personifications of primordial chaos akin to the mythical Orochi and Namazu, the Japanese identity of kaiju need not be questioned. Clearly kaiju have "always-already-been Japanese" by definition.[65] But if kaiju aren't all-bad then where does this leave our superhero Ultraman?

Conclusion: Here Comes Ultraman!

Sympathetic or not, another fact about kaiju also remains true: when left to their own devices, kaiju are just as likely to level a city whether its denizens have transgressed or not. The same is also true of the Namazu, which is why popular folklore tells of the giant catfish, like the Orochi, requiring some additional divine intervention; in this case from the thunder god *Kashima* who would "immobilize" the Namazu through a combination of sumo wrestling moves and "a heavy capstone" (or possibly a sword) with which he would pin the fearsome fish to the ground.[66] If the kaiju in Ultraman are then best understood as contemporary analogs to Japanese Chaos Monsters like Orochi and Yonaoshi Gods like Namazu then following the same logic would lead one to conclude that Japanese superheroes like Ultraman correspond to Japanese divinities like Kashima.

Japan is a country with a long and complex religious history, where the disparate faiths of Shinto, Buddhism, Confucianism and, since the mid–16th Century, Christianity have each played a crucial role in shaping the Japanese conception of life, death, morality and cosmology. Nevertheless, religious affiliation remains surprisingly low in contemporary Japan with only around 30 percent of the population identifying themselves as religiously affiliated—to help put that into perspective only around 22 percent of the U.S. population identifies themselves as religiously *un*affiliated.[67] Even more surprising is that in spite of this, participation in religious practices in Japan is extremely high with upwards of 90 percent of Japanese people claiming that they regularly visit Shinto shrines, pray at Buddhist altars and will consult a priest to spiritually purify their home or business, while between 60–50 percent of Japanese claim to believe in Shinto gods or the Buddha.[68] What this suggests is that religion in contemporary Japan serves a primarily theatrical role with different traditions swapped in and out depending on the circumstances. Patrick Drazen distills modern Japanese religiosity down into the following adage: "Born Shinto, marry Christian, die Buddhist."[69]

The impact that this kind of religious syncretism has had on Japanese pop-culture is appreciable. In contrast to American superheroes, which Richard Reynolds characterizes as largely "socially conservative," and in which scholar Marco Arnaudo finds the subject of religion, though abundant, often treated with kid gloves, Jolyon Baraka Thomas has demonstrated that the use of religion in Japanese *anime* and *manga*—and I would add tokusatsu— is not only fast and loose but often extremely creative and thus highly irreverent.[70] For example, Japanese artists have few hesitations about reimaging the angels of the Judeo-Christian apocrypha as extraterrestrial kaiju bent on humanity's ultimate destruction as seen in Hideaki Anno's acclaimed—and heavily Ultraman influenced—series *Neon Genesis Evangelion* (1995/96, 26 Episodes)—or about "removing religions like Buddhism from their institutional and doctrinal contexts in the service of adventure stories."[71]

Of the multiple religions which makeup Japan's spiritual topography it is Buddhism which has had the most overt influence on the character of Ultraman. In many respects Ultraman resembles a science fictional take on the Buddhist concept of a bodhisattva, individuals on the path to becoming a Buddha who succeeded in attaining enlightenment but who, rather than moving on to Nirvana, vow to remain on Earth over countless lifetimes in order to help the rest of humanity. As bodhisattvas, these individuals often leave behind their physical earthly bodies, *Nirmanakaya*, and acquire a new "heavenly body," *Sambhogakaya*, along with various supernatural powers that lead to their association with certain ideals or attributes, making them similar in some ways to Catholic Saints.[72]

As discussed above, Ultraman also goes through a bodily transformation, as he leaves behind his form as an androgynous silver-skinned giant and takes on a diminutive fleshly human body in order to assist mankind. The Japanese word used for this transformation is *henshin* "changing body" and has become synonymous with the superhero genre in Japan. Not surprisingly, according to Anne Allison, the term henshin is derived from Japanese Buddhism and originally referred to "the Buddhist transmutation of deities into human shape in order to better teach Buddhism to mortals."[73] Likewise, artist Tohl Narita saw in Ultraman an "expression of 'order'" in the cosmos, in opposition to the kaiju who symbolized chaos, and as a result chose the much-loved bodhisattva of compassion, Kannon, and the legendary Zen Buddhist master and "warrior of the universe.... Miyamoto Musashi" as his models for Ultraman.[74] Moreover, Takashi Murakami also sees in "Ultraman's serene face ... the perfected features of Buddhist divinities" particularly "the bodhisattva Maitreya."[75] In East Asian Buddhist belief Maitreya is identified as the "future-Buddha"; a messianic figure who will descend to this world in the distant future as the Buddha of the next great age bringing enlightenment to the multitudes.[76]

Murakami also notes the recurring theme of "light" in the Ultraman series. Ultraman hails from a crystalline planet called The Land of Light and is frequently referred to by humans as a "Giant of Light." Ultraman also "needs to bathe in a beam of light emitted by the Beta Capsule in order to reclaim his alien body," an idea which Murakami sees as "not so far from the Buddhist belief in renewal through rebirth."[77] It is also worth noting that Ultraman's Beta Capsule, or equivalent transformation device, essentially functions as a religious talisman and that in several series, including *Ultraman Tiga*, *Ultraman Nexus* and *Ultraman Ginga*, the protagonist discoveries the device housed inside a shrine or temple.

True to Japan's pluralistic nature, Buddhism is not the only religion interwoven into Ultraman's identity. For instance, though Eiji Tsuburaya claimed that Ultraman's red and silver color scheme was chosen because he felt it reflected the Space Age,[78] scholar Tom Gill points out that it is also highly reminiscent of the red and white color combination frequently seen in Shinto religious rites where the pairing is considered auspicious and thought to ensure good luck.[79]

In addition, in an early episode of the original *Ultraman* (1966, Ep. 7: "The Blue Stone of Baraj") The Science Patrol travels to the fictitious Middle Eastern city of Baraj in which they discover an ancient temple housing a statue of Ultraman who the locals identify as somehow corresponding with the Biblical character of Noah. Furthermore beginning with the two-part *Ultra Seven* story (1968, Ep. 39: "The Seven Assassination Plan Pt. 1" and Ep. 40: "The Seven Assassination Plan Pt. 2") the Ultraman series began regularly featuring episodes in which Ultraman would be crucified and subsequently resurrected, including the now famous *Ultraman Ace* two-parter (1972, Ep. 13: "Execution! The Five Ultra Brothers" and Ep. 14: "The Five Stars that Scattered Throughout the Galaxy") in which Ultraman, Ultraman Zoffy, Ultra Seven and Ultraman Jack are lured to the planet Golgotha—named after the hill on which Christ was killed (Mark 15:22; John 19:17)—and crucified simultaneously by robot assassin Ace Killer.[80]

Though decidedly subtle, this mixture of various religious elements that inform Ultraman's internal mythology is still overt enough that they can be easily recognized by anyone familiar with the respective traditions or curious enough about the origin of such ideas and imagery. These elements also indicate that despite its science-fictional trappings—the titular hero is explicitly identified as an extraterrestrial from outer space—the Ultraman franchise has long carried a number of notable religious connotations and subtexts which easily support the conclusion that Ultraman is intended to be understood by

52   Giant Creatures in Our World

viewers as not only superhuman but supernatural; a veritable deity in his own right.

Our exploration of the role of kaiju in *Ultraman* has worked to illuminate a very different conception of the superhero, one unique to Japanese culture. As complex characters and arbiters of social change rather than simple unambiguously evil aberrations, kaiju function less as foes and more as foils for the human protagonists in Ultraman to try and work out the various complex problems facing humanity. Where this leaves the figure of *Ultraman* then is as a hero whose role is not so much to overt disaster as it is to restrain it, whose job is not saving the world but rather society.

Notes

1. "After Mickey Mouse and Charlie Brown," Brad Warner, *Hardcore Zen* (Somerville, MA: Wisdom Publications, 2003), 44.

2. Frederik L. Schodt, *The Astro-Boy Essays* (Berkley, CA: Stone Bridge Press, 2007), 136.

3. August Ragone, *Eiji Tsuburaya: Master of Monsters* (San Francisco: Chronicle Books, 2007), 120.

4. Daisuke Ishizuka, "Shoshigaya-Okura is still the Ultraman City" *SciFi Japan* (01/25/2012), http://www.scifijapan.com/articles/2012/01/25/soshigaya-okura-is-still-the-ultraman-city/http://www.scifijapan.com/articles/2012/01/25/soshigaya-okura-is-still-the-ultraman-city/.

5. "Ultramanland Theme Park Closes After 17 Years," *Anime News Network* (09/02/2013), http://www.animenewsnetwork.com/news/2013-09-02/ultramanland-theme-park-closes-after-17-years.

6. Brad Warner, *Hardcore Zen* (Somerville, MA: Wisdom Publications, 2003), 44.

7. "Uproar brings apology for BH tsunami cartoon," uppercaise.wordpress.com (03/13/2011), http://uppercaise.wordpress.com/2011/03/13/uproar-bh-tsunami-cartoon/.

8. Matt Alt, "Ultraman: Ultracool at 50," *The Japan Times* (07/16/2016), http://www.japantimes.co.jp/culture/2016/07/16/tv/ultraman-ultracool-50/#.V9ilUTWGMg4.

9. Zander Cannon, *Kaijumax Season 2 #2* (Oni Press, 2016).

10. Anne Allison, "Sailor Moon: Japanese Superheroes for Global Girls," in *Japan Pop!: Inside the World of Japanese Popular Culture*, Ed. Timothy J. Craig (New York: Routledge, 2000), 263.

11. David Kalat, *A Critical History and Filmography of Toho's Godzilla Series*. 2nd Edition. (Jefferson, NC: McFarland, 2010), 16.

12. See J.F. Sargent, "How 'Pacific Rim' Got Kaiju Wrong," *Film School Rejects* (08/01/2013), https://filmschoolrejects.com/how-pacific-rim-got-kaiju-wrong-c154c1499531#.kaxn55pfr, and Steve Ryfle, "Godzilla, Whitewashed: A Special Report," *World Cinema Paradise* (05/18/14), http://worldcinemaparadise.com/2014/05/18/special-report-whitewashing-godzilla/ for two examples of American commentators chastising recent kaiju movies for veering away from the supposedly immutable relationship which exists between kaiju and nuclear power.

13. Michael Fitzpatrick, "Godzilla: Why Japan loves monster movies" *BBC Culture* (05/16/14), http://www.bbc.com/culture/story/20140516-giant-lizard-on-the-loose.

14. To be clear, it should be noted that Warner makes this analogy only as part of a theologically motivated polemic in which he is attempting to assert that Zen Buddhism is not a religion and does not adhere to a belief in the intervention of powerful god-like beings in human affairs, a claim that this author disputes. Brad Warner, *Hardcore Zen* (Somerville, MA: Wisdom Publications, 2003), 60.

15. Hiroshi Yamamoto, "The World of MM9" trans. Nathan Collins, Haikasoru.com (01/24/12), http://www.haikasoru.com/mm9/the-monsters-of-mm9/.

16. Martin Fackler, "Rubber-Suit Monsters Fade. Tiny Tokyos Relax." *The New York Times* (09/01/2013), http://www.nytimes.com/2013/09/02/world/asia/japan-films-shed-rubber-suits-godzilla-roars.html.
17. "Ultraman: The Next," *SciFi Japan* (05/15/2010), http://www.scifijapan.com/articles/2010/05/15/ultraman-the-next/.
18. Phillip Brophy, "Monster Island: Godzilla & Japanese Sci-Fi/Horror/Fantasy," in *Asian Cinemas*, eds. Dimitris Eleftheriotis, and Gary Needham (University of Hawaii Press, 2006), 57–58.
19. August Ragone, *Eiji Tsuburaya: Master of Monsters* (San Francisco: Chronicle Books, 2007), 114.
20. These films were: *Mega Monster Battle: Ultra Galaxy Legend The Movie* (2009, Dir. Koichi Sakamoto), *Ultraman Zero: The Revenge of Belial* (2010, Dir. Yuichi Abe); *Ultraman Saga* (2012, Dir. Hideki Oka).
21. This is not intended to be a complete or exhaustive list of every show, movie, anime, or spin-off which makes up the Ultraman franchise. Rather it is a selective list of what I consider to be the major installments and focusing on those works which are live-action, filmed in Japanese, and introduce a new Ultraman. All show and film titles have been checked against Tsuburaya Productions' Official English Title List found here: http://www.scifijapan.com/articles/2014/01/30/tsuburaya-productions-official-english-title-list/.
22. Brad Warner, *Hardcore Zen* (Somerville, MA: Wisdom Publications, 2003), 59.
23. See Douglas E. Cowan, *Sacred Terror* (Waco, TX: Baylor UP, 2008), 12; Andrew Britton as quote by Carol J. Clover in *Men, Women, and Chainsaws: Gender in the Modern Horror Film* (Princeton: Princeton University Press, 1992), 9.
24. Jenny Lawton, "Japan: The Imagination of Disaster," *Studio 360* (18 March, 2011), http://www.studio360.org/2011/mar/18/japan-imagination-disaster/.
25. Mark Schilling, *The Encyclopedia of Japanese Pop Culture* (NY: Weatherhill, Inc., 1997), 278.
26. Susan J. Napier, *Anime from Akira to Howl's Moving Castle*, 2nd Ed. (NY: Palegrave Macmillan, 2005), 251.
27. Kevin Derendorf, "Happy 50th to Ultraman! (also, weekly news recap)" *Maser Patrol* (07/09/2016), https://maserpatrol.wordpress.com/2016/07/09/happy-50th-to-ultraman-also-weekly-news-recap/.
28. August Ragone, "The Making of Ultra Seven" liner notes with *Ultra Seven: The Complete Series* DVD (Shout! Factory, 2012).
29. Jose Luis Sanz, *Now Starring T. Rex!* (Bloomington, IN: Indiana UP, 2002), 120. This is actually only one explanation proffered in the episode, another being that Hydra is a god who avenges the untimely death of children.
30. Damien Keown, *Buddhism: A Very Short Introduction* (New York: Oxford UP, 1996), 36.
31. Matt Alt, "Ultraman: Ultracool at 50," *The Japan Times* (07/16/2016), http://www.japantimes.co.jp/culture/2016/07/16/tv/ultraman-ultracool-50/#.V9ilUTWGMg4.
32. "When Roses Attack: 25 Years of Godzilla vs. Biollante with Ed Godziszewski," Scified.com (01/22/2015), http://www.scified.com/news/when-roses-attack-25-years-of-godzilla-vs-biollante-with-ed-godziszewski.
33. Tom Gill, "Transformational Magic: Some Japanese super-heroes and monsters" in *The Worlds of Japanese Popular Culture* (Cambridge, MA: Cambridge UP, 1998), 37.
34. Bob Johnson, "Gridman: Hyper Agent vs. Computer Virus Monsters!" *Monster Attack Team* #7, 42.
35. Tom Gill, "Transformational Magic: Some Japanese super-heroes and monsters," in *The Worlds of Japanese Popular Culture* (Cambridge, MA: Cambridge UP, 1998), 38.
36. Peter Lovold, "Female Characters in Kaiju Films," *G-Fan* #109, 23.
37. Edward Holland, "Ultraman, Path Towards Resurrection." *Monster Attack Team* #8, 124–126.
38. August Ragone, "The Making of 'Ultra Seven,'" liner notes, *Ultra Seven: The Complete Series* DVD (Shout! Factory, 2012).
39. Tohl Narita, *Works by Tohl Narita: Ultra Monsters* (1983) quoted by Takashi

Murakami, *Little Boy: The Arts of Japan's Exploding Subculture* (New Haven, CT: Yale University Press, bilingual edition, 2005), 30.

40. Zilia Papp, *Traditional Monster Imagery in Manga, Anime and Japanese Cinema* (Global Oriental, 2010), 130–131.

41. Takashi Murakami, *Little Boy: The Arts of Japan's Exploding Subculture* (Yale UP; Bilingual edition, 2005), 30. It is important to note however that not all artists and directors working in the kaiju genre have chosen to follow Narita's model. For more on this see my remarks in the roundtable discussion "What is Kaiju?" at the beginning of this collection.

42. Timothy K. Beal, *Religion and Its Monsters* (New York: Routledge, 2001), 161–162; Robert M. Price, "Cthulhu verses Godzilla," in *Lairs of the Hidden Gods Vol. 3: Straight to Darkness*, ed. Ken Asamatsu (Fukuoka, Japan: Kurodahan Press, 2006), 8. See also Hermann Gunkel, *Creation and Chaos in the Primeval Era and the Eschaton* (Eerdmans; Tra edition, 2006).

43. Neil Forsyth, *The Old Enemy* (NJ: Princeton UP, 1987), 47.

44. Michael Fitzpatrick, "Godzilla: Why Japan loves monster movies," *BBC Culture* (05/16/14), http://www.bbc.com/culture/story/20140516-giant-lizard-on-the-loose.

45. All citations come from *Kojiki*, trans. Donald L. Philippi (University of Tokyo Press, 1968).

46. Robert M. Price, "Cthulhu versus Godzilla," in *Lairs of the Hidden Gods Vol. 3: Straight to Darkness*, ed. Ken Asamatsu (Fukuoka, Japan: Kurodahan Press, 2006), 8.

47. Ibid., 8.

48. Hiroshi Yamamoto, *MM9*, trans. Nathan Collins (San Francisco: Haika Soru, 2012), 24–25.

49. H.P. Lovecraft, *Supernatural Horror in Literature*, http://www.hplovecraft.com/writings/texts/essays/shil.aspx.

50. Justin Mullis, "The Cthulhu Mythos in Japan," *The Lovecraft eZine* (01/09/2013), https://lovecraftzine.com/2013/01/09/the-cthulhu-mythos-in-japan/. Koanaka is also not the only writer to incorporate elements of Lovecraft's Cthulhu Mythos into Ultraman. The first was veteran tokusatsu actor Shin Kishida, writing under the pseudonym Shin Akekawa, who penned an episode of *The Return of Ultraman* (1971, Ep. 35: "Cruel! The Light-Monster PrizMA") based primarily on Lovecraft's short story "The Color Out of Space," but to a lesser extent his novella At the Mountains of Madness as well. Writer Keiichi Hasegawa also wrote a two-part *Ultraman Dyna* story (1997, Ep. 25: "The Kraakov Won't Surface Pt. 1" and Ep. 26: "The Kraakov Won't Surface Pt. 2") in which Dyna faces off against the kaiju Deegon and Suhume; who are clearly based on Lovecraft's Dagon and Cthulhu.

51. Gregory Smits, "Shaking Up Japan: Edo Society and the 1855 Catfish Picture Prints," *Journal of Social History* Vol. 39, No. 4 (Summer 2006): 1045–1078.

52. David Bressan, "Namazu the Earthshaker" *Scientific American* (03/10/2012), http://blogs.scientificamerican.com/history-of-geology/namazu-the-earthshaker/.

53. Takashi Miura, *Renewing the World: The Rise of Yonaoshi Gods in Japan* (Princeton, NJ : Princeton University, 2015).

54. Jerome F. Shapiro, *Atomic Bomb Cinema* (NY: Routledge, 2001), 272.

55. Patrick W. Galbraith, *Moe Manifesto: An Insider's Look at the Worlds of Manga, Anime, and Gaming* (Ruthland, VT: Tuttle Publishing, 2014), 34–35. Readers are encouraged to seek out the full interview found in this book with Mari Kotani, who goes on to establish a provocative link between old-school kaiju otaku and contemporary moe otaku who obsessively catalogue and collect images related to cute female anime characters, suggesting that otaku view both kaiju and moe girls interchangeably. As if to further validate this contention in September of 2016 Tsuburaya Pro. released the web-anime series *Kaiju Girls* (2016—Present) in which popular kaiju from the Ultraman series have been reborn as nubile high school girls who must contend not only with the sundry problems of adolescence but also with the occasionally overwhelming desire to wreck major metropolises. Patrick Macias, "Crunchyroll Adds 'KAIJU GIRLS' to Fall Simulcasts," Crunchyroll.com (09/26/2016), http://www.crunchyroll.com/anime-news/2016/09/26-1/crunchyroll-adds-kaiju-girls-to-fall-simulcasts.

56. Kevin Derendorf, "A Guide to Ultraman's Celebrity Guest Directors" *Maser Patrol* (02/02/2016), https://maserpatrol.wordpress.com/2016/02/02/a-guide-to-ultramans-celebrity-guest-directors/.

57. Peter H. Brothers, *Of Mushroom Clouds and Mushroom Men* (CreateSpace Independent Publishing Platform; 2nd Ed., 2009), 20.
    58. Matt Alt, "Ultraman: Ultracool at 50" *The Japan Times* (07/16/2016), http://www.japantimes.co.jp/culture/2016/07/16/tv/ultraman-ultracool-50/#.V9ilUTWGMg4.
    59. Kevin Derendorf, "Ultra-Inspired: Japan's major entertainment franchises take cues from M78" *Maser Patrol* (01/01/2016), https://maserpatrol.wordpress.com/2016/01/01/ultra-inspired-japans-major-entertainment-franchises-take-cues-from-m78/ Later installments in the *Ultraman* franchise such as *Ultraman Ginga* and *Ultraman X* would revamp the idea of the Capsule Monsters by swapping out capsules for more marketable items like trading cards and "Spark Dolls" (vinyl action figures) while the Capsule Monsters would eventually get their own two season spin-off series: *Ultra Galaxy Mega Monster Battle* (2007/2009, 26 Episodes).
    60. Jorge Salas, "Redman: The Tokusatsu Show Taking the Internet By Storm," *The Tokusatsu Network* (05/09/2016), http://tokusatsunetwork.com/2016/05/redman-tokusatsu-show-taking-internet-storm/.
    61. *Ibid.*
    62. *Ibid.*
    63. Chon Noriega, "Godzilla and the Japanese Nightmare: When THEM! is U.S." *Hibakusha Cinema Journal* 27, No. 1 (1987), 67.
    64. *Ibid.*, 68.
    65. *Ibid.*, 68.
    66. David Bressan, "Namazu the Earthshaker" *Scientific American* (03/10/2012), http://blogs.scientificamerican.com/history-of-geology/namazu-the-earthshaker/.
    67. Jolyon Baraka Thomas, *Drawing on Tradition: Manga, Anime, and Religion in Contemporary Japan* (Honolulu: University of Hawaii Press, 2012) 9–11. Statistics regarding the number of religiously unaffiliated people in the United States comes from the 2014 Pew Religious Landscape survey which can be reviewed here: http://www.pewforum.org/2015/05/12/americas-changing-religious-landscape/.
    68. Mary Pat Fisher, *Living Religions* (Saddle River, NJ: Pearson Education, Inc., 9th Edition, 2014), 222.
    69. Patrick Drazen, *Anime Explosion!* (Berkley, CA: Stone Bridge Press, 2003), 153–154. My description of Japanese religiosity as "theatrical" also comes from Drazen.
    70. See Richard Reynolds, *Super Heroes: A Modern Mythology* (Jackson: University Press of Mississippi, 1994) for more on the conservative nature of American superhero fiction; and Marco Arnaudo, *The Myth of the Superhero* (Baltimore, MD: Johns Hopkins UP, 2013), for an excellent overview on the subject of American superheroes and religion. In particular Arnaudo writes that though American superhero comics are full of "pagan divinities and beings with godlike powers" as well as strong allusions to biblical personages such as Moses and Christ, the highly volatile nature of American religiosity often necessitates that the writers and publishers of superhero stories issue "disclaimer(s) to reassure readers (and sometimes their parents)" that such stories are not attempting to demean or undermine their reader's faith (27).
    71. Jolyon Baraka Thomas, *Drawing on Tradition: Manga, Anime, and Religion in Contemporary Japan* (Honolulu: University of Hawaii Press, 2012), 64.
    72. Damien Keown, *Buddhism: A Very Short Introduction* (New York: Oxford UP, 1996), 58–61.
    73. Anne Allison, *Millennial Monsters* (Berkley: University of California Press, 2006), 288.
    74. August Ragone, *Eiji Tsuburaya: Master of Monsters* (San Francisco: Chronicle Books, 2007), 117.
    75. Takashi Murakami, *Little Boy: The Arts of Japan's Exploding Subculture* (New Haven, CT: Yale University Press, bilingual edition, 2005), 26.
    76. Damien Keown, *Buddhism: A Very Short Introduction* (New York: Oxford UP, 1996), 65.
    77. Takashi Murakami, *Little Boy: The Arts of Japan's Exploding Subculture* (Yale UP; Bilingual edition, 2005), 26.

78. August Ragone, *Eiji Tsuburaya: Master of Monsters* (San Francisco: Chronicle Books, 2007), 117.

79. Tom Gill, "Transformational Magic: Some Japanese super-heroes and monsters" in *The Worlds of Japanese Popular Culture* (Cambridge, MA: Cambridge UP, 1998), 34. This is also the reason why the Red Ranger is always the default leader on Super Sentai/Power Rangers.

80. Brian Ashcraft, "The Crucifixion of Japan's Greatest Super Hero," Kotaku.com (11/08/2012), http://kotaku.com/5958760/the-crucifixion-of-japans-greatest-super-hero. Also a special thanks to friend and fellow Japanese superhero addict Connor Anderson for his tireless and ongoing efforts to catalogue every crucifixion presented in a Japanese superhero show and for providing me with a list of every Ultraman episode featuring one.

Works Cited

Allison, Anne. "Sailor Moon: Japanese Superheroes for Global Girls" in *Japan Pop!: Inside the World of Japanese Popular Culture*. Ed. Timothy J. Craig. New York: Routledge, 2000.
Alt, Matt. "Ultraman: Ultracool at 50." *The Japan Times*, 16 July 2016. http://www.japantimes.co.jp/culture/2016/07/16/tv/ultraman-ultracool-50/#.V9ilUTWGMg4.
"America's Changing Religious Landscape." *Pew Research Center*. May 12, 2015. http://www.pewforum.org/2015/05/12/americas-changing-religious-landscape/.
Arnaudo, Marco. *The Myth of the Superhero*. Baltimore, MD: Johns Hopkins University Press, 2013.
Ashcraft, Brian. "The Crucifixion of Japan's Greatest Super Hero." Kotaku.com. November 8, 2012. http://kotaku.com/5958760/the-crucifixion-of-japans-greatest-super-hero.
Beal, Timothy K. *Religion and Its Monsters*. New York: Routledge, 2001.
Bressan, David. "Namazu the Earthshaker." *Scientific American*, 10 March 2012. http://blogs.scientificamerican.com/history-of-geology/namazu-the-earthshaker/
Brophy, Phillip. "Monster Island: Godzilla & Japanese Sci-Fi/Horror/Fantasy" in *Asian Cinemas*. Eds. Dimitris Eleftheriotis & Gary Needham. University of Hawaii Press, 2006.
Brothers, Peter H. *Of Mushroom Clouds and Mushroom Men*. 2nd ed. CreateSpace Independent Publishing Platform, 2009.
Clover, Carol J. *Men, Women, and Chainsaws: Gender in the Modern Horror Film*. Princeton: Princeton University Press, 1992.
Cowan, Douglas E. *Sacred Terror*. Waco, TX: Baylor University Press, 2008.
Derendorf, Kevin. "A Guide to Ultraman's Celebrity Guest Directors." *Maser Patrol*. February 2, 2016. https://maserpatrol.wordpress.com/2016/02/02/a-guide-to-ultramans-celebrity-guest-directors/.
_____. "Happy 50th to Ultraman! (also, weekly news recap)." *Maser Patrol*. July 9, 2016. https://maserpatrol.wordpress.com/2016/07/09/happy-50th-to-ultraman-also-weekly-news-recap/.
_____. "Ultra-Inspired: Japan's Major Entertainment Franchises Take Cues from M78." *Maser Patrol*. January 1, 2016. https://maserpatrol.wordpress.com/2016/01/01/ultra-inspired-japans-major-entertainment-franchises-take-cues-from-m78/.
Drazen, Patrick. *Anime Explosion!* Berkley, CA: Stone Bridge Press, 2003.
Fackler, Martin. "Rubber-Suit Monsters Fade. Tiny Tokyos Relax." *The New York Times*, 1 September 2013. http://www.nytimes.com/2013/09/02/world/asia/japan-films-shed-rubber-suits-godzilla-roars.html.
Fisher, Mary Pat. *Living Religions*. 9th ed. Saddle River, NJ: Pearson Education, Inc., 2014.
Fitzpatrick, Michael. "Godzilla: Why Japan loves monster movies." *BBC Culture*. May 16, 2014. http://www.bbc.com/culture/story/20140516-giant-lizard-on-the-loose.
Forsyth, Neil. *The Old Enemy*. NJ: Princeton University Press, 1987.
Galbraith, Patrick W. *Moé Manifesto: An Insider's Look at the Worlds of Manga, Anime, and Gaming*. Ruthland, VT: Tuttle Publishing, 2014.
Gill, Tom. "Transformational Magic: Some Japanese Super-Heroes and Monsters" in *The Worlds of Japanese Popular Culture*. Cambridge, MA: Cambridge University Press, 1998.
Gunkel, Hermann. *Creation and Chaos in the Primeval Era and the Eschaton*. Eerdmans, 2006.

Holland, Edward. "Ultraman, Path Towards Resurrection." *Monster Attack Team* 2, no. 8 (2010).
Ishizuka, Daisuke. "Shoshigaya-Okura Is Still the Ultraman City." *SciFi Japan*, 25 January 2012. http://www.scifijapan.com/articles/2012/01/25/soshigaya-okura-is-still-the-ultraman-city/.
Johnson, Bob. "Gridman: Hyper Agent vs. Computer Virus Monsters!" *Monster Attack Team* 1, no. 7. publication date unknown.
Kalat, David. *A Critical History and Filmography of Toho's Godzilla Series*. 2nd ed. Jefferson, NC: McFarland, 2010.
Keown, Damien. *Buddhism: A Very Short Introduction*. New York: Oxford University Press, 1996.
Kojiki. Trans. Donald L. Philippi. Japan, Tokyo: University of Tokyo Press, 1968.
Lawton, Jenny. "Japan: The Imagination of Disaster." *Studio 360*. 18 March 2011. http://www.studio360.org/2011/mar/18/japan-imagination-disaster/.
Lovecraft, H.P. "Supernatural Horror in Literature." *The H.P. Lovecraft Archive*. October 20, 2009. http://www.hplovecraft.com/writings/texts/essays/shil.aspx.
Lovold, Peter. "Female Characters in Kaiju Films." *G-Fan* 1, no. 109 (Summer 2015).
Macias, Patrick. "Crunchyroll Adds 'KAIJU GIRLS' to Fall Simulcasts." Crunchyroll.com. September 26, 2016. http://www.crunchyroll.com/anime-news/2016/09/26-1/crunchyroll-adds-kaiju-girls-to-fall-simulcasts.
Miura, Takashi. *Renewing the World: The Rise of Yonaoshi Gods in Japan*. Princeton, NJ: Princeton University, 2015. http://dataspace.princeton.edu/jspui/handle/88435/dsp01x920g0243.
Mullis, Justin. "The Cthulhu Mythos in Japan." *The Lovecraft eZine*. January 9, 2013. https://lovecraftzine.com/2013/01/09/the-cthulhu-mythos-in-japan/.
Murakami, Takashi. *Little Boy: The Arts of Japan's Exploding Subculture*. Bilingual ed. New Haven, CT: Yale University Press, 2005.
Napier, Susan J. *Anime from Akira to Howl's Moving Castle*. 2nd ed. NY: Palegrave Macmillan, 2005.
Noriega, Chon. "Godzilla and the Japanese Nightmare: When THEM! Is U.S." *Hibakusha Cinema Journal* 27, no. 1 (1987).
Papp, Zilia. *Traditional Monster Imagery in Manga, Anime and Japanese Cinema*. Folkestone, Kent, UK: Global Oriental, 2010.
Price, Robert M. "Cthulhu verses Godzilla" in *Lairs of the Hidden Gods Vol. 3: Straight to Darkness*. Ed. Ken Asamatsu. Fukuoka, Japan: Kurodahan Press, 2006.
Ragone, August. *Eiji Tsuburaya: Master of Monsters*. San Francisco: Chronicle Books, 2007.
_____. "The Making of 'Ultra Seven'" Liner Notes Issued with *Ultra Seven: The Complete Series* DVD. Shout! Factory, 2012.
Ryfle, Steve. "Godzilla, Whitewashed: A Special Report." *World Cinema Paradise*. May 18, 2014. http://worldcinemaparadise.com/2014/05/18/special-report-whitewashing-godzilla/
Salas, Jorge. "Redman: The Tokusatsu Show Taking the Internet by Storm." *The Tokusatsu Network*. May 9, 2016. http://tokusatsunetwork.com/2016/05/redman-tokusatsu-show-taking-internet-storm/.
Sanz, Jose Luis. *Now Starring T. Rex*! Bloomington, IN: Indiana University Press, 2002.
Sargent, J.F. "How 'Pacific Rim' Got Kaiju Wrong." *Film School Rejects*. August 1, 2013. https://filmschoolrejects.com/how-pacific-rim-got-kaiju-wrong-c154c1499531#.kaxn55pfr.
Schilling, Mark. *The Encyclopedia of Japanese Pop Culture*. NY: Weatherhill, Inc., 1997.
Schodt, Frederik L. *The Astro-Boy Essays*. Berkley, CA: Stone Bridge Press, 2007.
Shapiro, Jerome F. *Atomic Bomb Cinema*. NY: Routledge, 2001.
Smits, Gregory. "Shaking Up Japan: Edo Society and the 1855 Catfish Picture Prints." *Journal of Social History* 39, no. 4 (Summer 2006).
Thomas, Jolyon Baraka. *Drawing on Tradition: Manga, Anime, and Religion in Contemporary Japan*. Honolulu: University of Hawaii Press, 2012.
"Tsuburaya Production's Official English Title List." *SciFi Japan*. January 30, 2014. http://www.scifijapan.com/articles/2014/01/30/tsuburaya-productions-official-english-title-list/.

"Ultraman: The Next." *SciFi* Japan, 15 May 2010. http://www.scifijapan.com/articles/2010/05/15/ultraman-the-next/.

"Ultramanland Theme Park Closes After 17 Years." *Anime News Network*, 9 February 2013. http://www.animenewsnetwork.com/news/2013-09-02/ultramanland-theme-park-closes-after-17-years.

"Uproar brings apology for BH tsunami cartoon." uppercaise.wordpress.com. March 13, 2011, at http://uppercaise.wordpress.com/2011/03/13/uproar-bh-tsunami-cartoon/.

Warner, Brad. *Hardcore Zen*. Somerville, MA: Wisdom Publications, 2003.

"When Roses Attack: 25 Years of Godzilla vs. Biollante with Ed Godziszewski." Scified.com. January 22, 2015. http://www.scified.com/news/when-roses-attack-25-years-of-godzilla-vs-biollante-with-ed-godziszewski.

Yamamoto, Hiroshi. *MM9*, trans. Nathan Collins. San Francisco, CA: Haika Soru, 2012.

_____. "The World of MM9" trans. Nathan Collins. Haikasoru.com. January 24, 2012. http://www.haikasoru.com/mm9/the-monsters-of-mm9/.

Monsters of the Rift
Kaiju as Ciphers of Unbalance

Jase Short

How do we, as human beings, imagine our relationship to the natural world upon which our very existence is predicated? Further, how do we represent this imagination in the form of art, particularly given the state of what some have called a *metabolic rift* between human societies and the natural world? One such way that we have represented this imagined version of our relationship is through the peculiar genre of fantastic film known as kaiju eiga. From the very beginning of the kaiju genre something has set these fantasy creations apart from their gargantuan siblings. Whereas films like *The Beast From 20,000 Fathoms* (1953) portrayed their gigantic antagonists as wild animals set loose in strange environments, kaiju have always been defined by a certain spiritual quality that marks them as forces of nature. There is a mythic quality to kaiju that is absent from their siblings, a quality that allows them to effortlessly slip between the genres of science fiction, fantasy, and horror.

The genre has as its cornerstone a conception of nature as out of balance, or *unbalanced*, a notion that is profoundly illuminating for our contemporary situation. It is my contention that this equation of kaiju with the sensibility of unbalance forms a kind of *cultural cipher*, a symbol which can be immediately recognized by millions of untrained eyes to represent something. There is something inherently disturbing and disorienting about the aesthetic underlying kaiju that strikes a chord with audiences across borders and time.

This is not to say that these peculiarly modern fantasies are timeless, for they are in fact the products of what we might call *modernity*, or more poignantly, *late capitalism*. The emergence of peculiarly modern monstrosities is a topic too vast for the present work, but we can see the contours of a modern teratology emerging in scholarship today. Works including David McNally's

Monsters of the Market: Zombies, Vampires, and Global Capitalism or Annalee Newitz's *Pretend We're Dead: Capitalist Monsters in American Pop Culture* have located the origin of these mythologies not with hangovers from a pre-modern era of superstition, but rather within the contemporary world as human beings try to come to terms with the profound effects of modern civilization.

Rapid industrialization, social isolation, profound disruptions of tradition and communal continuity have led to an era defined by extreme alienation and atomization among billions of human beings. In the midst of this, rapacious destruction of local ecologies by "business as usual" industry and extraordinarily destructive warfare have led many to grasp for new symbols adequate for a new world. Among these symbols we have zombies, vampires, robots, alien invaders, giant monsters, and more. In *Colonialism and the Emergence of Science Fiction*, John Rieder argues that the best way to read just figures is, "…symptomatically and socially … to regard them as "mythic," not in the interest of seeing some kind of persistence of the Eternal in popular culture, but in Claude Levi-Strauss' sense of myths as imaginary resolutions to real social contradictions" (20).

The anxiety provoked by these fictional entities is a decidedly modern one predicated upon profound experiences of social dislocation, mass devastation, and the transformation of the natural world into a decidedly human habitat. Accompanying this anxiety is a sense of awe and fascination predicated on a certain sublimity built into these fantasy creations. This duality or dialectic at the heart of these artistic representations is made possible by the function of kaiju as fantastical embodiments of the social sensibility of unbalance.

Metabolic Rift and the Anthropocene

Toho's famous producer, Tomoyuki Tanaka, claimed that "Godzilla is the son of the atomic bomb, the sacred beast of the apocalypse." Ishiro Honda himself said of kaiju that they are born "too tall, too strong, too heavy, that is their tragedy." From their inception in the 1954 *Gojira*, the team responsible for the production of these soon-to-be international icons understood them to be something more than flashy entertainment. They were in fact amalgamations of social anxieties brought on by a brave new world that had overtaken the old agrarian societies marked by relative stability and generational continuity.

A defining feature of contemporary civilization is the fact of the capitalist world market and its concomitant disruptions of humanity's already complicated relationship with the rhythms and processes of the natural world. Our peculiar relationship to the world is one of a dialectical emergence from that world, which is to say that human beings emerged from the natural world and yet enjoy certain properties—notably consciousness—which separate them from the source of their emergence. Humanity is made by the natural world and in turn makes over nature, producing tools both physical and mental which supervene on the rhythms and patterns of natural systems. Marx described these technologies as "natural material transformed into organs of the human will over nature, or of human participation of nature. They are organs of the human brain, created by the human hand; the power of knowledge, objectified" (Marx).

Consequently, a condition of human existence is the maintenance of a healthy metabolic exchange between particular societies and the natural world. The act of making and remaking the world carries with it the risk of upsetting the processes which guarantee human life itself—which is to say, we are always at risk of engineering a metabolic rift. While humans have always made profound impacts on the natural world, particularly after the development of sedentary agricultural societies during the Holocene epoch, a qualitative jump in the severity of this impact has taken place over the period of the last century or so.

In the early 2000s, the International Commission on Stratigraphy, the committee of the International Union of Geological Sciences tasked with developing the geological time scale, convened an Anthropocene Working Group (AWG) to formally define "the Anthropocene" as a new geological epoch distinct from the Holocene, the period beginning 11,000 years ago stretching through the contemporary period encompassing the entirety of human civilization. Two-thirds of the working group signed onto a January 2015 article which made the following case for a new geological epoch initiated by humanity's impact on the natural world:

> Humans started to develop an increasing, but generally regionally and highly diachronous, influence on the Earth System thousands of years ago. With the onset of the Industrial Revolution, humankind became a more pronounced geological factor, but in our present view it was from the mid–20th century that the worldwide impact of the accelerating Industrial Revolution became both global and near-synchronous [Angus 55].

The AWG presented its findings to the International Geological Congress in Cape Town South Africa in August of 2016. Whether the concept of the Anthropocene is ratified and becomes the stuff of textbooks is an open question, but it is not insignificant that a number of world renowned scientists working on the issue for years have concluded—with almost no dissensions—that a new epoch has been initiated by human activity in the world.

This Anthropocene is characterized by what social theorist John Bellamy Foster has called a "metabolic rift" between humanity and nature. This concept emerged from his scholarly treatment of Karl Marx's conception of nature, in particular his work on early capitalist agriculture in England. Marx, Foster argues, places the notion of metabolism at the center of his work in order to theorize processes *within* human society and *between* particular societies and the natural world. Foster writes:

> The key conceptual category in Marx's theoretical analysis ... is the concept of metabolism (*Stoffwechsel*). The German word "*Stoffwechsel*" directly sets out in its elements the notion of "material exchange" that underlies the notion of structured processes of biological growth and decay captured in the term "metabolism." ... Marx utilized the concept of metabolism to describe the human relation to nature through labor [Foster 157].

What Foster contends is that a thoroughly Marxist theory of nature is predicated upon this notion of metabolic exchange within a given society and between that society and nature. Internal to a society, patterns of exploitation, domination, and oppression central to the maintenance of class society upset this metabolism, leading to condition of unbalance that tend to provoke hostility and social struggle between competing powers. Furthermore, the conditions necessary to maintain this state of affairs within a given society provide the foundation for a rift between that society and the natural world, as the short term needs of the system's beneficiaries tend to outweigh the long term conditions of a healthy metabolic exchange.

In short, in order for unequal relations to be maintained within a society an unequal relationship between that society and the natural world becomes necessary. Foster uses this concept to explain the rise of modern capitalism, a system predicated on exponential growth and the transformation of living nature into artificial commodities not according to human need, but according to the need to maintain rates of profit for the system beneficiaries. Foster sums up Marx's social and ecological thought:

> Marx therefore employed the concept both to refer to the actual metabolic interaction between nature and society through human labor (the usual context in which the term was used in his works), and in a wider sense (particularly in the *Grundrisse*) to describe the complex, dynamic, interdependent set of needs and relations brought into being and constantly reproduced in alienated form under capitalism, and the question of human freedom it raised—all of which could be seen as being connected to the way in which the human metabolism with nature was expressed through the concrete organization of human labor. The concept of metabolism thus took on both a specific ecological meaning and a wider social meaning [158].

The story of how humanity's metabolic rift with nature began and all its specific conditions and manifestations is too complex a topic for the limits of the present work. I take it as relatively non-controversial at this stage in human history, as the overwhelming body of scientific evidence points to profound ruptures in the Earth System in the form of mass deforestation, the rising toxicity of air and soil, the devastating effects of industrial agriculture on soil systems, as well as the unprecedented impact of anthropogenic climate change brought about by the widespread use of fossil fuels. What is less apparent is the ways in which artistic expression have expressed the social imagination of this condition. Whereas many scholars recognize zombies and vampires as broadly symbolic of capitalism's labor cycles (McNally) alien invaders as stand-ins for colonial adventurism (Rieder), and robots as metaphors for the inhuman conditions of capitalist modernity (Newitz), kaiju have not enjoyed the same attention as rich objects of theoretical analysis.

Unbalance

How human beings imagine this metabolic rift is the subject of this essay. With confidence one can agree that human beings generally agree that something unsettling is happening with our relationship to the natural world, and there are a number of contemporary fantastical narratives that attempt to reflect on this. I call the sensibility, or imagined relation, to this metabolic rift unbalance. The term originated with Tsuburaya Productions' initial title for its hit 1966 show *Ultra Q*, which has been described as a hybrid between *The Twilight Zone* and Toho's Godzilla films. Unbalance refers here not only to our unease with this rift, but a recognition that it represents a new normality. Unbalance is the sensibility of the normalization of our metabolic rift, and carries with it the ideological propensity to promote either acquiescence to this state of affairs or a drive to mitigate its worst effects in order for humanity to find a new way of being that can sustainably exist in these circumstances.

Ultra Q is broadly representative of this normalization, as the characters must continually revolutionize their sense of what is possible when exposed to what seem to be strange aberrations, but upon further investigation are merely symptoms of a universe that can only be described as weird. This is most apparent in the episode "The Gift From Space" in which the closing scene shows the character unknowingly wearing a necklace containing the egg of another Namegon, the monster that had just been vanquished. This cyclical sensibility cuts against the tendency of modern narratives to operate in a linear fashion, and sets the world of kaiju apart from Anglo-American giants who usually end up dead at the end of their films. This is a marker of the sensibility of unbalance, which portrays characters that must adapt to a new weird world rather than exorcise the current one of its evils.

This relationship between kaiju and unbalance predates the series. Thematically, unbalance has been central to the kaiju genre running from the original *Gojira* (1954) to both contemporary re-imaginings of the monster by both Hollywood in 2014 and Toho Studios with its much-lauded *Shin Godzilla* (2016). In virtually every film of the genre the objective conditions of metabolic rift are embodied in fantastic figures pregnant with allusion and meaning. Indeed we must assert that art is never produced in a vacuum and that it required appropriation and reconfiguration of input from the world in order to be intelligible to an audience. In the case of kaiju, the prevailing sensibility has been that these creatures are emerging not as one off events, but as part of an emerging new pattern.

At the end of *Gojira* (1954), Dr. Yamane reflects that more atomic tests will yield new monsters. Mothra survives the end of her film, opening up for a sequel in the form of *Mothra vs Godzilla* (1964) in which human society has come to terms with the existence of these strange creatures as a matter of course. By *Invasion of Astro-Monster* (1965), what is peculiar is not the kaiju themselves, but the appearance of alien invaders. Kaiju have become such a regular part of the scenery that they are seemingly side characters to the broader narrative.

Kaiju are constituted by reference and allusion to events—particularly crises—contemporary to each production. In his infamous work of literary theory, *The Political Unconscious*, Fredric Jameson argues for a distinction between "empirical texts"—the very works of fiction under discussion, such as specific films or novels—and the "master narrative" underlying them. In these formulations individual "empirical" texts ought to be utilized to construct "master narratives of the political unconscious." Elsewhere I have summarized this reading of Jameson's literary theory:

> It is the task of the literary theorist to detect and to reveal ... "the outlines of some deeper and vaster narrative movement" which corresponds to the broader social structures from which the "empirical text" derives its meaning. This is to say that, whatever the artist's intent in producing such a text, there is underlying it a social knowledge and perspective on the artist's social context. Thus, all texts are inherently political, and contain at least some degree of social critique [Short, "The Theory and Appeal of Giant Monsters"].

The unconscious narrative underlying kaiju fiction can be illustrated by the case of Japanese audiences' response to the original 1954 film. Japan had experienced a self-imposed isolation from the developments of world colonialism as late as the 1850s, and only after having its trade relations imposed from the outside did its rulers seek to join other nations at the center of global power. The Meiji Restoration was actually a revolution from above imposed by Japan's ruling class on the entire country, a revolution in relations of production and consequently in social relations generally speaking. In one generation a nation of farmers living in civilized but preindustrial conditions became a powerful modern industrial power complete with massive cities and a colonial reach spanning the entire Pacific Ocean.

Through incentives and more direct means farmers were compelled to leave behind their rural way of life (or at least their children were) to head to the cities in order to work for wages. Their entire world was upended, but nonetheless the cult of the Emperor held the cultural fabric of the country together until the vast and terrible Second World War upended the entire arrangement, demystified the Emperor's divine status, and resulted in the wholesale destruction of the country at the hands of a merciless bombing campaign which culminated in the horrifying use of atomic weapons on Hiroshima and Nagasaki.

The sense of being rapidly thrown into a new world, of being estranged from what one takes for granted as normal, pervaded Japan in the years leading to and following the Second World War. The devastation experienced was so utterly thorough and without analog that for millions of ordinary Japanese something like an apocalypse had occurred. Under the conditions of the U.S. military occupation of Japan, serious criticism of the United States was barred via a strict censorship regime. Immediately following the formal end of the occupation, the pioneering team of Tomoyuki Tanaka, Ishiro Honda, and Eiji Tsuburaya set out to create a work of fantasy that could tap into this pent up sense of dislocation, alienation, and bewilderment. The result of this creative process was the now iconic film *Gojira*, released in a heavily edited form as *Godzilla, King of the Monsters* to international audiences in 1956.

Gojira *and the First Sequence of Kaiju Eiga 1954–1966*

Shot in a somber documentarian style, *Gojira* (1954) is in many ways a work of art that has never been surpassed within the genre. Playing on themes resonant from the devastation of the war and the recent *Lucky Dragon* No. 5 incident, the film captures the mood of an era experiencing the peculiar sense of unbalance which accompanies an uncertain recovery from a time of absolute devastation. Prosperity returned to Japan as it developed a symbiotic relationship with the U.S. war effort on the Korean peninsula, and the U.S. leadership very quickly realized that it had much to gain and little to lose by a reindustrialized and powerful Japan.

Unease with this new sensibility became a central theme in later works within the genre, as many in Japanese society felt that the nightmare of the war had passed without meaningful reflection. The love triangle between the characters of Ogata, Emiko, and Dr. Serizawa is a perfectly illustration of this anxiety. Emiko had been set to marry the war veteran Serizawa from a young age, but had found herself in a love affair with the younger Ogata who had never experienced the trauma of war. Serizawa's unexplained eye patch visually references this dark past. The film is peppered with other references, from train car discussions of air raids to scenes of rapid and intense civilian evacuation.

Godzilla himself emerges in the film as a kind amalgamation of the war and its aftermath. All of the anxieties and horror of that period were too much to be directly addressed, both because of official censorship and the inherent difficulty of discussing complex socio-economic trauma. A creature with fantastic origins in local folklore of Pacific Islanders which has undergone a thorough science fictionalization at the hands of atomic testing became for the Japanese public a *cultural cipher*, or a symbol which could be readily understood as representative of something too vast and complex for a more realistic-oriented narrative.

This popular culture object—Godzilla—inaugurated an entire genre. One cannot properly situate kaiju eiga under the rubrics of something more specific, like science fiction or horror. Indeed, elements of science fiction and horror are vital components to the alchemical processes that produce this unique aesthetic, but the genre is not reducible to these. The unique sensibility of kaiju are produced via a routinized shift between different registers for interpreting fantastic symbols. The films and other products of the genre move freely between science fictional, mythic, magical, and other genre tropes. The implausible giant monster is rendered plausible precisely through these slippages that undermine any attempt to reduce them to other genres.

The films which followed *Gojira* (1954) included *Rodan* (1956), *Varan* (1958), and the seminal *Mothra* (1961). These early films carried the cultural imprint of the American atomic horror movies that they in part sought to emulate. A pattern of monster emergence followed by the destruction of the monster at the end took hold until *Mothra*, which represented a dialectical folding inward of the genre. That is to say, with *Mothra* the genre took the first step of emphasizing those elements that made it distinct from the atomic horror films its sought to emulate.

This process of an aesthetic work coming to resemble itself more precisely took the form of generating kaiju which were inherently *indestructible* and situating them in a world in which they were not one off aberrations, but rather belonged to a world which was itself weird. Until *Mothra* (1961), each film began with a monster's emergence and concluded with its exorcism from the world. In *Gojira* (1954) the seeds of the new sensibility were born with Dr. Yamane's prophetic claim that new monsters would soon emerge, but we get nothing of this at the conclusion of *Rodan* (1956) and *Varan* (1958), which share a narrative structure with many Anglo-American giant monster films.

Kaiju as Embodiments of a Weird World

The "giant monsters on the loose" of atomic horror were primarily interstitial beings; that is, "creatures in whom two distinct, sometimes even contradictory, conditions of existence interact" (Csicsery-Ronay, Jr., 195). In some ways the kaiju do represent a version of this grotesque identity, but "seem to have an ontological legitimacy that Western sf does not supply" (196). They are impacted by the world of radiation, environmental destruction, genetic engineering, and so on but carry with them a density *which suggests they belong to the same world we inhabit.*

Kaiju came to be not intrusions from another realm, but symptoms of the unbalanced world. In this they share a lot in common with the sensibility of what has been called Weird Fiction, broadly represented by the work of H.P. Lovecraft or a contemporary like China Mieville. The transformations of the Japanese folkloric traditions in the middle of the twentieth century into the kaiju of cinema constitutes a similar move to the development of Weird Fiction in Europe and North America. Whereas the Weird was, in the European context, a kind of "revolutionary teratology" which broke from traditional imagery of werewolves, vampires, ghosts, and so forth, in the Japanese context *a science fictionalization*—even within more fantasy-driven narratives—of the folkloric beings formed the basis for the construction of a Weird sensibility. As many have pointed out, Lovecraftian tentacles represented a new kind of monstrosity within the European context but simply recalled a long history within Japanese fantasy.

In China Mieville's essay on Weird Fiction in *The Routledge Companion to Science Fiction*, he notes that the ostensible grandfather of the Weird, H.P. Lovecraft, produced works which effected "...a surrender to the ineluctability of the Weird, again implying no irruption of strangeness into a status quo, but a Weird Universe" (512). This necessitates a "focus on awe, and its undermining of the quotidian ... obsession with numinosity under the everyday is at the heart of Weird Fiction" (510). He situates the emergence of the Weird as a dialectical unfolding from the Gothic tradition, as much an heir as a break from it and its "Hauntalogical" sensibility.

In essence, the Weird represents a sensibility which uncovers the startling fact that the world itself is already bizarre, rather than a kind of running realist narrative periodically punctuated by fantastic energies. In his study of contemporary forms of cultural monstrosity *Monsters of the Market: Zombies, Vampires, and Global Capitalism* David McNally identifies the unique features of capitalist culture as the source of this everyday Weird:

> Instead, the very insidiousness of the capitalist grotesque has to do with its invisibility with, in other words, the ways in which monstrosity has become normalized and naturalized via its colonization of the essential fabric of everyday-life, beginning with the very texture of corporeal experience in the modern world. What is most striking about capitalist monstrosity, in other words, is its elusive everydayness, its apparently seamless integration into the banal and mundane rhythms of quotidian existence [2].

Of course, kaiju in the form of giant monsters do not appear in Japanese folklore and are the products of capitalist modernity. And yet, many of the narratives, from *Gojira* (1954) to *Varan* (1958) to *Mothra* (1961) provide a link between this pre–Meiji sensibility and the new world. Most of the monsters in these early films are worshipped and revered by islanders and rural dwellers left behind by the vast changes of capitalist industrialization. Rather than representing hauntings of the new world by the old, kaiju came to be modernizations of old sensibilities run rampant. They grew to gargantuan sizes and enjoyed enormous destructive powers in order to concretized the sense that the old world had been thrown into a state of disarray.

Eventually, the genre would fall victim to the constraints and needs of the Japanese cultural industry. Somber, critical reflections on current events would give way to super heroizations, young child friendly narratives, and a generalized taming of the creatures. One can see this sharp contrast, for instance, in the shift from a film like *Gojira* (1954) with its somber, haunting atmosphere and the upbeat and colorful *Son of Godzilla* (1967) which exuded a tone absent melancholy and deep social critique. This culminated in the passage from a vibrant film sequence led by Toho to an increasingly underfunded series of films and weekly TV shows such as *Ultraman* (1966). Nonetheless, before the closure of this crucial sequence running from 1954 to the mid–1960s, *Ultra Q* (1966) was developed by Tsuburaya Productions and quickly became the critical heart of what was becoming a decidedly uncritical genre.

What made *Ultra Q* (1966) such a seminal product was the ways in which it congealed and radicalized the best tropes of the genre up until that point. The show featured a rag tag team of investigators, scientists, and photographers who responded to new developments of strange creatures throughout Japan. These narratives took on somber, comedic, and adventurous tones all set within a world not unlike that of *The Twilight Zone* or *The Outer Limits*. The episodes expressed the full range of humanity's emotional relationship to a brave new world marked by ecological chaos and periodic threats of total annihilation within the context of the Cold War. Children found themselves transformed into the coin-spitting, clam-headed Kanegon and the mechanical ghoul-meets-foliage Garamon, pushing the limits of what remained of naturalistic kaiju design.

Indeed one can see in the passage of Akira Watanabe's naturalistic design work in the early Toho series to the more surrealistic design of Tohl Narita another dialectical in-folding, as kaiju began to become representative of their essence as strange beings rather than allusions to the products of evolution. Narita's design work departed from the template of dinosaurs and living animals into something more interpretive, not unlike the passage in art from realistic representations of actual things to the abstractions of modernism. This passage can be said to symbolize something like the new normality, as the kaiju cease to reference the old world and come into their own as embodiments of the new.

The Genre After 1966

In philosopher Alain Badiou's philosophical opus *Being and Event* he sets out a schema for understanding artistic movements as interruptions of the status quo—an event—which produce what he calls truth-events. In this system, artistic work continues in a regular arithmetic progression until it is interrupted by a qualitatively new artistic activity. This eruption of the new eventually runs its course, and subsequent artistic work takes a stance vis-à-vis this eruption of a truth-event. For our purpose, the two important responses to what we can call the truth-event of kaiju as ciphers for the sensibility of unbalance are those responses which are *faithful* and those which stand in *denial*.

A faithful stance would involve the creation of new artwork within the kaiju genre that creatively engages with the critical edge of such films as *Gojira* (1954). This says nothing for profitability, marketability, or enjoyability. These are markers for success for this genre inasmuch as it successfully acclimates to the commodity form. For the purpose of being faithful to an artistic truth-event, or eruption, these are at best secondary concerns to the purpose of making good artwork. Exemplars of this trend include films such as *Godzilla vs Hedorah* (1971), *Godzilla vs Biollante* (1989), or the 90s Gamera trilogy. Each of these films problematizes humanity's relationship to nature and sets these thematics at the heart of the narrative itself. Hedorah is literally a pollution monster, and both Biollante and Gamera are genetically modified organisms (GMOs) with their own purpose for being quite separate from the needs and desires of humanity.

On the other hand, there are those projects that abjure this critical edge and proclaim that the only essential components of the genre are monster action and city destruction. This approach is conducive to questions of profitability, marketability, and enjoyability first to such a degree that questions of artistic excellence are met with indifference or outright hostility. Among general audiences and fans, one could say that this sense of what makes a kaiju film is hegemonic—it holds sway as the "common sense" position on these films. They are immediately rejected as works of art and are instead looked to as pieces of distraction and shallow entertainment. Examples of such films include *Godzilla vs. SpaceGodzilla* (1994), *Godzilla: Final Wars* (2004), or *Monster X Attacks the G8 Summit* (2008).

Art with a critical edge afflicts its audience. It challenges them to see the world in unique ways, and it does so in a way that is captivating. It does not lead one to "escape" reality, rather it warps that reality and presents it in a new configuration, more meaningful than immediate perceptions can afford. This is why millions of ordinary people in Japan found *Gojira* (1954) so moving, whereas a similar cross section of the population did not, for better or worse, engage in a campaign of active politicization in order to come to terms with the legacy of World War II. The catharsis experienced by those theatergoers can never be replicated, as it was a unique historical moment with a unique and new artistic object in play. Instances in which works of the genre directly engage with this truth of kaiju as symbols of our experience of living with a metabolic rift in our societies take the genre seriously as a place for artistic activity.

Of course this does not mean that those with an eye for artistic excellence reject the commodity form of the art work. Further, it can be difficult to condemn an entire work within the genre to be faithful or in a state of denial, with some exceptions. Usually the actually existing artistic products are mixed in their outcome, and all of them are compelled to compete with other films as commodities for market share, otherwise the films cannot secure funding, staff, or distribution. Nonetheless we can with confidence argue that there are those threads in the genre that attempt to wrestle with its critical legacy after its initial movement from 1954 to 1966 and those which wish to reduce the genre to mindless escapism.

Let us take the aforementioned examples as a starting point. In each case of those that remain faithful to kaiju as ciphers for unbalance, it is important to note that they do not directly emulate what came before. This is to say, what makes the critical edge of *Godzilla vs. Biollante* (1989) work is not a rehashing of the exact nuclear themes of *Gojira* (1954), rather it is the way in which that sensibility is replicated with brand new content. The overarching question of humanity's relationship to nature is not explored through questions of nuclear war, but rather through the interrogation of the emerging biotechnology industry and its production of genetically modified organisms (GMOs).

The question of humanity's power over nature is thus explored through a timely social issue, the use of genetic engineering to modify life itself. Throughout the film, the geopolitical ramifications of this new technology are explored, and a new monstrosity born of the genetic modification of Godzilla, human, and plant cells is utilized to explore these themes. A similar move is accomplished in *Godzilla vs. Hedorah* (1971), as a monster made entirely of pollutants emerges as a biting commentary on the state of Japan's environmental situation in the 1960s and 1970s before major reforms were made.

On the other hand, we can look at another movie that acts as a sort of parody of the series to see the nadir of the genre. *Monster X Attacks the G8 Summit* (2008) carries with it the inherent potential for making strong socio-ecological commentary. Made on the eve of the 34th G8 Summit in Japan, the film was perfectly placed to make strong statements about the responsibility of the world's most extreme polluters to alter their course in order to begin the process of healing the rift between human civilization and the natural world. Instead, the film was a case study in ridiculous stereotypes and pointless (and repetitive) monster action. It could have retained its satirical and comedic structure while employing some of this critical commentary, but instead it shied away from any attempt at making a statement—even a subtle one.

Of course art should not be reduced to political propaganda. A film with the name of a political group like the G8 within its title ought to be suspect in this regard from the outset, and perhaps director Minoru Kawasaki thought it best to steer clear of any accusations of being "preachy." Indeed it has become something of a trope of kaiju films to have characters say something along the lines of, "If we don't start acting more ethically, a new monster will appear" after the climactic final confrontation. This trope emerged after Dr. Yamane (played by Takashi Shimura) made a similar pronouncement in the final moments of *Gojira* (1954) in a manner that was integrated into the plot in a far more successful way than became common in later years. Nonetheless, the existence of poorly executed moments of critical commentary does not imply that any and every attempt at doing so is inherently problematic, particularly with such stunning examples to the contrary.

The Cultural Cipher in Action

Beyond the films themselves, kaiju have become ciphers for the sensibility of unbalance in popular media. This takes the form of many different references to the genre in everything from movies to Sunday morning cartoons. These references tend to take two forms, however, one direct and one indirect. Direct references are those which simply refer to the popularity of the films for comedic or other purposes within the particular work in question. These tend to ignore any critical commentary and often even directly contradict the notion of the genre as a site of artistic activity. Indirect references are those which use the imagery of kaiju to convey the breakdown of order, which is to say a metabolic rift in the social order.

Examples of the direct kind of reference abound in media produced in the 1980s and 1990s when the early kaiju films were widely viewed by a large swath of the consumer market. For instance, *One Crazy Summer* (1986) features a scene in which a character wearing a Godzilla knock-off costume runs amok at a party after having a cigar thrown into the suit. The smoking Godzilla suit attack is intended for comedic effect and relies on audience's familiarity with the genre as a place of comedy and escapism. A similar scene occurs in an episode of *Arrested Development* titled "Mr. F," in which a series of unfortunate incidents leads a character in a mole monster costume to destroy a model city in front of Japanese investors. There is nothing inherently

72   Giant Creatures in Our World

critical about this incident in the show, it is simply a moment of levity and humor.

Indeed, the popularity of kaiju among audiences was directly exploited in Nike's 1992 marketing campaign "Godzilla vs. Charles Barkley." Commercials and even a comic book tie-in were employed to market shoes with the implicit message that those who wore them could be like Charles Barkley, a larger than life figure in the world of sports who could (metaphorically, at least) tackle gargantuan opponents without much effort. *The Simpsons* featured many iconic kaiju in the final moments of the episode "Three Minutes Over Tokyo" without any serious socio-ecological commentary, an all the more surprising omission for a show with a continuously running theme concerning environmental pollution brought on by the nefarious actions of the wealthy Mr. Burns, owner of the Springfield nuclear power plant.

This attitude is perhaps exemplified most directly by a Bloom County cartoon which features the following dialogue:

> MILO (on phone): Hello, Penrod. Oh … yes, indeed I did see *Dune* last week … what? How'd I like it? Well, I found it a quasi-religious allegory with fascist undertones…. The "Harkonnen" was clearly a Romanesque metaphor for centralized oppression and Atreides merely a messianic redeemer … on the whole, an eclectic cinematic experience, I would say.
> OPUS (to Milo): I, myself, saw *Godzilla vs. the Smog Monster* just yesterday. Uh…. Godzilla was clearly a Romanesque metaphor for something and Tokyo was stepped on a great deal…
> MILO (on phone): A moment Penrod…. A peon is in our midst.
> OPUS (to Milo): … on the whole, an electric, veg-o-matic experience, I would say [Breathed, "Bloom County"].

This exchange exemplifies popular attitudes to the genre which dismiss it as "low art." The juxtaposition of *Godzilla vs. the Smog Monster* (1971)—the American release title of *Godzilla vs. Hedorah*—and the theatrical version of *Dune* (1984) is important here. Frank Herbert's 1965 novel of the same name is widely considered to be an exemplar in the field of literary science fiction, which is set against pulp traditions which lack critical commentary or any sense of artistic excellence. The avant-garde cinematic techniques of director Yoshimitsu Banno's *Godzilla vs. Hedorah* (1971) and his critical commentary on Japan's worsening environmental crisis are ignored entirely as the film is held up as an exemplar of pulpy "veg-o-matic" escapism that can only be enjoyed by "peons," an offensive term laced with elitist assumptions. That something like *Godzilla vs. Hedorah* (1971) could ever be compared to *Dune* (1984) is considered laughable.

There are other references which militate against this attitude, and they are what concern us here as examples of kaiju as cultural ciphers. These references indicate that audiences are capable of immediately reading complex socio-ecological commentary when presented with kaiju imagery in film, television, comics, and more.

A prominent example of this which ties directly into our ecology-centric analysis is the popular scientific metaphor of the "Godzilla El Nino." NASA Climatologist Bill Patzert coined the term "Godzilla El Nino" in a *San Jose Mercury News* interview on May 8, 2015 (Melton, Truthdig.com). Patzert used the term "Godzilla" to separate the current El Nino weather system from the one that emerged in the 1990s, which is theorized to be a product of global warming. The vast majority of the warming experienced in the Earth System is absorbed by the oceans, making extreme weather events more frequent and intense. Patzert used "Godzilla" as a cipher to explain the severity and scale of the new El Nino to a non-specialist audience. The complex interplay of anthropogenic global warming and references to gargantuan scale are immediately intelligible to those who hear this information. Once "Godzilla" is coupled with "El Nino," itself a popularly understood consequence of civilization's metabolic rift with nature, audiences needed no further explanation.

Another prominent example concerns political cartoons that reference global warming, the Fukushima disaster, and other calamities while utilizing the imagery of kaiju. Perhaps the most prominent use of kaiju imagery in political cartoons came after the triple crisis of earthquake, tsunami, and Fukushima nuclear disaster that occurred in Japan in the spring of 2011. According to Japan's National Police Agency, 15,891 people died in this catastrophe and over 2,500 remain missing. Over 100,000 people were rendered homeless as a consequence of the devastation and the nuclear crisis. The damage was spread across a wide geographic area. The communities around the Fukushima nuclear power plant remain abandoned, populated by overgrown structures and robotic cars that document the no-go zone. Scandals continue to plague the Japanese government and the TEPCO corporation over the disposal of nuclear waste, and recently former Prime Minister Junichiro Koizumi has accused Prime Minister Shinzo Abe of lying about the situation.

Japanese prosecutors indicted 3 former TEPCO executives in February of 2016 for criminal negligence in the matter (New York Times). A political cartoon that came out in this period depicts a Godzilla-like kaiju with the TEPCO insignia on its neck urinating radioactive waste off of a beach with a sign that says Fukushima. Political cartoons of course rely on cultural ciphers to communicate complex ideas in an immediate and non-verbal manner, so the Godzilla imagery here is striking.

Other examples of kaiju imagery from the Fukushima crisis depicting nuclear waste clean up crews wiping down the open maw of Godzilla with the words "Fukushima" written on the monster as squiggles with atomic symbols burst from its mouth (Benson, "Fukushima—The New Godzilla 2.0"). This illustrates the dramatic and dangerous crisis of clean-up work engaged in by hundreds of workers following the reactor crises. Another shows a kaiju rising from Japan with the words "nuclear plant" written on it, blasting radioactive waste from its mouth onto the Pacific Ocean. During the crisis there were widespread fears of a far more cataclysmic meltdown than Chernobyl, and though the situation was ultimately contained, there had even been discussions of evacuating Tokyo Metropolitan Area, the world's largest urban agglomeration economy.

Similar imagery has been further employed in political cartoons that critique the fossil fuel industry. This cartoon depicts a kaiju with coal fired power plants on its back emitting greenhouse gases, with an elephant in a suit symbolizing the Republican Party in Congress's defense of the industry against opposition from environmentalists (Sack, "Scaling Down on Coal"). The spikes of the monster are titled "outdated coal plants," but the monster itself has written on it "climate change."

Once again, the imagery of kaiju as ciphers for socio-ecological crisis is employed because audiences need no further explanation to understand this association. A similar cartoon portrays Godzilla lying on his back, dead, next to several smokestacks that read "Coal Fired Power Plants." An observer notes to another, "Godzilla choked to death…" the implication being that even a force as destructive and powerful as Godzilla cannot survive the effects of using coal as a major source of energy production. Yet another cartoon shows a Godzilla-like kaiju clutching a person in its hand while wading through a flooded and burning city (Luckovich, "Choked to Death"). Written on the kaiju's back are the words "Climate Change," and the person is saying to the monster, "I still need more proof that you exist." This is aimed to pillory climate change skeptics who deny the scientific consensus around anthropogenic climate change with the implication being that they are ignoring major crises like Superstorm Sandy even when they have immediate, visible, and devastating consequences.

What each of these examples show us is that kaiju can be used as immediate symbolic representations of unbalance and broad socio-ecological crises. They act as indirect metaphors of these broader crises—Fukushima, global warming—in sharp contrast to direct references to the films themselves via comic relief in films, TV, and other media. The potential inherent in these symbols goes far beyond self-reference, they can be powerful symbols for those seeking to engage in systemic social change in order to avert further ecological disaster.

Rebirth of the Genre

Recent years have seen a return of kaiju to the big screen. After the success of *Cloverfield* (2008) made kaiju films viable for Hollywood, a new sequence of films launched with *Pacific Rim* (2013), *Godzilla* (2014), and *Shin Godzilla* (2016). In each of these cases the imagery of kaiju have seamlessly blended with that of recent global catastrophes from 9/11, to massive floods, and of course the Fukushima crisis itself. One of the first scenes of *Cloverfield* (2008) directly recalls imagery from 9/11, and skyscrapers tumble and civilians flee only to be consumed by billowing ash and dust. The inability of the world's governments to solve the problem of the kaiju invasion in *Pacific Rim* (2013) recalls the stunning lack of action world governments have taken to address climate change decades after the United Nations Convention on Climate Change was agreed to. The flooding of Honolulu upon Godzilla's arrival in *Godzilla* (2014) film alongside the overgrown ruins of the fictional city of Janjira recall the stark imagery of Japan's 2011 disasters. And *Shin Godzilla* (2016) directly addresses geopolitical concerns, the impact of ecological malfeasance carried out by government bureaucracies, and constructs a nightmare version of the titular monster that cannot but recall the nuclear zombie imagery of the original film.

Max Borenstein, the major screenwriter for *Godzilla* (2014), painted director Gareth Edward's film as, "…something off the beaten path … it felt, after my initial conversation with Gareth and the studio, that it was a cautionary tale about man tampering with nature" (Cotta 21). "It was not so much a monster movie as a disaster movie," Borenstein claimed (21). "We were also resonant with 9/11. Our idea was, how do you make this movie tap into some of these visceral feelings that we've all had about being powerless, to try to use a monster movie to get at deeper emotions?" (21). Though the film does not directly address the specific ecological crisis of global warming, it utilizes its imagery as well as other media spectacles of disaster to communicate a sense of powerlessness in the face of the overwhelming strength of nature.

This return of kaiju to the big screen more than half a century since their great boom in cinema signifies something more than the ambition of Legendary Pictures (the studio behind *Pacific Rim* and *Godzilla*, as well as the upcoming *Kong: Skull Island*) to make profits by resurrecting these old properties. It signifies that this imagery has, in the age of mega disasters, climate chaos, and gargantuan violence, resonated with audiences once more. We are in a brave new world in which superstorms, record floods, stunning droughts, record-breaking heat, and profound social instability have become the norm. These ciphers speak to us as "monstrous forms of everyday-life in a capitalist world-system" (McNally 2). The kaiju genre, like all fantastic genres "can occasionally carry a disruptively critical charge, offering a kind of grotesque realism that 'mimics the absurdity of capitalist modernity' the better to expose it" (McNally 7).

To understand contemporary popular culture as a ground of significance, communication, popular lore, and so on, we must understand the forms of the monstrous which are resonant today. Recent decades have seen the rise of zombies and vampires become the central forms of monstrosity, dominating media markets and public consciousness. It is too early to tell if kaiju will supplant these and form a new standard of monstrosity in popular consciousness, but one can say with confidence that their status as ciphers of unbalance—that peculiar imagination of our relationship to our metabolic rift with nature—has been confirmed by the genre's resurgence.

Works Cited

Angus, Ian. *Facing the Anthropocene: Fossil Capitalism and the Crisis of the Earth System.* New York: Monthly Review Press, 2016. Print.
Badiou, Alain. *Being and Event.* New York: Continuum, 2006. Print.
Benson, Steven. "Fukushima—The New Godzilla 2.0" http://www.freeduh.com/2011/ 03/ 31/fukushima-the-new-godzilla-2-0/ 31 Mar. 2011. Accessed 15 Nov. 2016.
Bould, Mark. Ed. *The Routledge Companion to Science Fiction.* CITY: Routledge, 2009. Print.
Breathed, Berkeley. "Bloom County." http://www.gocomics.com/bloomcounty/2013/02/26. 26 Feb. 2013. Accessed 15 November 2016.
Cotta, Mark. *Godzilla: The Art of Destruction.* San Rafael: Insight Editions, 2014. Print.
Csicsery-Ronay, Jr. *The Seven Beauties of Science Fiction.* Middletown: Wesleyan University Press, 2008. Print.
Jameson, Fredric. *The Political Unconscious: Narrative as a Socially Symbolic Act.* New York: Cornell University Press, 1981. Print.
Luckovich, Mike. "Choked to Death." *Atlanta Journal Constitution.* June 3, 2014. Accessed 15 November 2016.
Marx, Karl. *Grundrisse. Karl Marx: Selected Writings,* edited by David McLellan, Oxford University Press, 2000, 379–423. Print.
McNally, David. *Monsters of the Market: Zombies, Vampires, and Global Capitalism.* Chicago: Haymarket Books, 2011. Print.
Melton, Bruce. "Godzilla Nino and the Blob: How Weather Cycles and Ocean Temperatures Mask Global Warming." Truthout.org, 4 Oct. 2015, http://www.truthout.org/news/ item/33078-godzilla-nino-and-the-blob-how-weather-cycles-and-ocean-temperatures-mask-global-warming. Accessed 15 Nov. 2016.
Newitz, Annalee. *Pretend We're Dead: Capitalist Monsters in American Pop Culture.* Stanford: Duke University Press, 2006. Print.
Ragone, August. *Eiji Tsuburaya: Master of Monsters.* CITY: Chronicle Books, 2007. Print.
Rieder, John. *Colonialism and the Emergence of Science Fiction.* Middletown: Wesleyan University Press, 2008. Print.
Sack, Steve. "Scaling Down on Coal." *The Star Tribune.* June 4, 2014. Accessed 15 November, 2016.
Short, Jase. "The Theory and Appeal of Giant Monsters." Red Wedge Magazine, 14 Oct. 2014. Accessed 15 Nov. 2016.
Soble, Jonathan. "Japan Indicts 3 Former Executives Over Fukushima Nuclear Disaster." *New York Times,* http://www.nytimes.com/2016/03/01/world/asia/japan-indicts-3-former-executives-over-fukushima-nuclear-disaster.html?_r=0 29 Feb. 2016. Accessed 15 Nov. 2016.

Archetypes at War
Kaiju as Cult Icons in Pacific Rim

Nicholas Bollinger

On the surface, it appears that *Pacific Rim* (2013) is little more than a blockbuster that pits Transformer-like robots against monsters in assorted action sequences that are magnified to an epic scale while a flimsy human-based narrative holds it all together. And while there absolutely are moments of this movie with pure spectacle that prompts my inner second-grader to positively scream with excitement, it takes only minimal digging to unearth a bevy of material that can similarly make film scholars squeal with delight. The basic premise of the movie, written by Travis Beacham and Guillermo del Toro and directed by del Toro, is that *kaiju* are emerging from an interdimensional breach at the bottom of the Pacific Ocean and attacking humanity. In an effort to hold them at bay, an international resistance movement led by Marshall Stacker Pentecost (Idris Elba) constructs monstrous *jaegers*, which are two-pilot technological behemoths that are able to withstand the foe in hand-to-hand combat. The bulk of the movie's plot is concerned with an attempt to destroy the breach and thereby prevent any further kaiju from attacking, a plan which, after much tribulation, finally succeeds.

A few things are immediately evident about *Pacific Rim*. First of all, it is overflowing with allusions to other movies, constantly paying homage to these other texts by directly lifting names and phrases, or even by simply imitating standardized scenes and situations, all of which I will consider in detail. Another apparent oddity is that there are few, if any, individualized characters in the film, as most are reduced to common stereotypes of their nationality, gender, or narrative role. A final salient detail is that any quarrel between human characters seems unbelievably petty in comparison to humanity's struggle against the terrifying kaiju. When taken together, these elements unite to create a movie that is overwhelmingly concerned, first and foremost, with its kaiju. All such characteristics of *Pacific Rim* are emblematic of a movie with a unique appeal—that of a cult film. In this essay, I will attempt to explicate many textual qualities that are symptomatic of cult cinema and defend how *Pacific Rim* is a model of movies with that distinction. And at the center of this unique film, reaping the rewards of the material surrounding them, the kaiju become icons of cultness.

Pacific Rim's *Cultish Intertextuality*

Per Umberto Eco's assertion that a cult movie "is not *one* movie. It is 'movies'" *Pacific Rim*, as a movie composed of elements excerpted from countless other movies, supremely exemplifies cultness (74). The sheer number of references to other movies it contains, both specific, as in the case of alluding to a character from *Aliens* (1986) through Newton Geiszler's preference of being called "Newt," and general, such as with the destruction of the Golden Gate Bridge during the first kaiju attack, a fate the bridge has suffered in innumerable other action movies, is staggering, but this alone does not expound *Pacific Rim*'s cult appeal. As Eco describes it, a movie is imbued with cult universality if one is able "to break, dislocate, unhinge it so that one can remember only parts of it, irrespective of their original relationship with the whole" (68), a quality that comes from the narrative being constructed of intertextual frames, which Eco identifies as "stereotyped situations derived from preceding textual traditions and recorded by our encyclopedia" (69). The cult movie then becomes a conversation between archetypal characters and narrative situations, a conversation that *Pacific Rim* engages with to the umpteenth degree. Throughout the movie, characters who are reincarnations of countless predecessors encounter situations that have been enacted in so many movies, prompting a sense of déjà vu that lasts the entire runtime.

From the first scene, *Pacific Rim* immediately signals that it will be full of self-aware intertextuality. Following an opening monologue and montage, the first dialogue in the movie is a conversation that ends with Yancy Becket telling his younger brother, the eventual hero Raleigh, "Hey kid, don't get cocky," a direct line said by Han Solo to Luke Skywalker in *Star Wars* (1977). This clear nod to an iconic and oft-quoted movie informs the state of mind with which one may watch *Pacific Rim*; additionally, since this reference occurs early, it alerts the viewer to be aware of other movies that may be invoked and ready to understand the significance of such references. The parallel drawn between Raleigh and Luke also efficiently establishes the frame of Raleigh's character, as he bears a striking resemblance to Luke; both are young and headstrong until the deaths of family members, Yancy for Raleigh, his aunt and uncle for Luke, force them to mature quickly in a story that culminates in them ultimately saving the day by piloting missions that destroy an enemy base with a massive explosion.

As this opening sequence continues, it becomes increasingly clear that virtually all of the material is adapted from the cinematic lexicon of pop culture; much of the dialogue even consists of painfully clichéd lines like "A man's gotta do what a man's gotta do," which Tendo Choi says to the Becket brothers. The highlight of *Pacific Rim*'s opening is the battle between the Beckets' jaeger, Gipsy Danger, and a kaiju called Knifehead while the lives of crew members on a fishing boat hang in the balance. With the depiction of a fishing boat struggling to withstand a kaiju attack, *Pacific Rim* recalls a quintessential convention of classic kaiju cinema that can be traced to the opening of the original *Godzilla* (1954). This is one of the foremost frames of kaiju films, as it is rooted in the infamous Lucky Dragon incident of 1954, in which a Japanese vessel was contaminated by nuclear fallout from a hydrogen bomb test; however, *Pacific Rim* revisions the archetypal situation that traditionally sees the crew of the boat perish as a harbinger of the destruction the kaiju will soon bring to the mainland. In this case, the Becket brothers save the boat, although Yancy is killed and Raleigh barely makes it back to shore alive. It is only once this initial action sequence ends that the title appears on screen, by which point the movie's pattern of cult intertextuality has already been fully established; the remainder of the film is comprised of ubiquitous aphorisms and frames that have been self-awarely revisioned in a postmodern update of cinematic traditions.

The presence of such frames is a constant throughout *Pacific Rim*, and I will address many of them shortly, but it is first necessary to elucidate the distinction between "frames," as defined by Eco, and more transient references to prior movies, such as the quotation of a line from *Star Wars* cited above. Both are instances of the intertextuality that is characteristic of cultness, but while a frame is an easily recognizable narrative situation or stock character that repeatedly appears, other references invoke a single specific source. For example, the fishing boat facing destruction from a kaiju in *Pacific Rim* is a replication of similar scenes that open many other kaiju films, most notably *Godzilla* and *The Return of Godzilla* (1984). This replication imbues the narrative situation with associations that declare the genre of the movie and therefore also set up expectations of a pattern for the plot to follow; because this scene is immediately recognizable as the latest spawn of a cinematic genealogy, it can be identified as a frame and is therefore expected to follow the model of its forebearers. Of course, as has already been discussed, *Pacific Rim* rejects the history of this particular frame and gives it a different significance than what tradition would dictate, a modification that is only possible to discern because of the commonly expected formula the frame connotes.

Conversely, references to specific films, not being founded upon histories of implementation and consequently not beholden to standardized patterns, can be employed to serve more specific functions. Unlike a frame, which sets up an expectation of how the narrative will proceed, this type of Easter egg reference is a momentary signpost that communicates a point of interest to the discerning viewer. In the case of the *Star Wars* quote in *Pacific Rim*'s first conversation, the reference signals the presence of Raleigh's character frame; having served this purpose, the quotation no longer carries any weight and the frame assumes authority as the scene continues. An exhaustive account of all the intertextual Easter eggs throughout *Pacific Rim* would take up an irresponsible amount of paper for relatively little purpose, but there are several that merit recognition for the legacies they honor.

One of the most noteworthy of such Easter eggs can be found in how kaiju are categorized in *Pacific Rim*; they are ranked via a system called the Serizawa Scale, an explicit reference to Daisuke Serizawa, the scientist whose Oxygen Destroyer defeated the most legendary of kaiju, Godzilla, in his seminal appearance. To pay homage to a film that played a significant role in founding cinematic incarnations of kaiju is a clear acknowledgment of *Pacific Rim*'s ancestry. Ironically, the subsequent major kaiju film produced in Hollywood, Gareth Edwards' *Godzilla* (2014) paid tribute to the same history, as Ken Watanabe's character in is named Dr. Ishiro Serizawa, a name that combines those of the 1954 *Godzilla*'s scientist character with that of its director, Ishiro Honda. Another specific movie invoked by *Pacific Rim* is Ridley Scott's *Blade Runner* (1982), a bona fide cult film in its own right, which features a manufacturer of replicant eyeballs named Hannibal Chew who is tortured into giving up information and likely killed off screen. In *Pacific Rim*, Ron Perlman's character, who operates the Hong Kong black market of kaiju body parts, goes by the self-created moniker Hannibal Chau: "I took it from my favorite historical character and my second favorite Szechuan restaurant in Brooklyn." Neither of these characters factor significantly in the plots of their respective films; however, both the characters' nearly identical names and the similarity of their occupations merely pays homage to an influential predecessor. If nothing else, it is clear that the particular strategy of using a name to reference a specific movie is a favorite of del Toro's, given how often this practice occurs throughout *Pacific Rim*.

These Easter egg citations are fun inclusions that are rewarding to hunt for; they certainly contribute to making *Pacific Rim* not a single movie as much as it is an embodiment of lineages that are manifest across movies, to paraphrase Eco, but their ephemeral nature ultimately produces less cult appeal than the intertextual frames that are common throughout the film. One frame that has an enduring place in pop culture, especially in disaster movies where humanity is facing extinction, is the motivational speech that declares how humankind will fight to the end no matter how bleak the situation appears, rallying the troops and providing the inspiration necessary to win the day. Nowhere is this frame implemented with more vitality than in Roland Emmerich's *Independence Day* (1996), when the President of the United States, portrayed by Bill Pullman, gives a speech that is cringe worthy in its celebration and glorification of American imperialism: "The 4th of July will no longer be known as an American holiday ... today we celebrate our Independence Day!" *Pacific Rim* utilizes this frame at a moment that is narratively almost identical, just before the jaegers begin their final assault on the breach. The speech is delivered by Marshall Stacker Pentecost and builds to a climax when he exclaims, "Today, we are cancelling the apocalypse!" Just as the beginning of the movie features the revisioning of a frame with the face-off between a kaiju and a fishing vessel interrupted by a jaeger, Pentecost's speech is a reworking of how this frame is traditionally presented. As exemplified by *Independence Day,* such a narrative situation is commonly inflected with the politics that govern whatever ideology is being propagated; interestingly, *Pacific Rim* is noticeably devoid of political inclinations. While I will discuss in greater detail later the ways in which *Pacific Rim* is fervently post-political in its presentation of international relations, the most salient aspect of this scene at the moment is how it reframes a convention that historically preaches a specific ideology into one that evenly applies to all who are fighting the kaiju. By revisioning this frame, *Pacific Rim* continues to facilitate its dialogue between paradigms that have consistently appeared throughout movies.

The final moments of the film, with Raleigh and Mako Mori floating in the Pacific Ocean while awaiting rescue, bear a striking resemblance to yet another cinematic tradition with an indelible legacy: the conclusions of James Bond films. It hardly needs to be stated that the superspy ends practically every adventure in the embrace of one of the iconic Bond girls, and it can be almost taken for granted that the final shots of the movie will see the pair in the process of consummating their physical relationship. Additionally, more often than not, Bond and his partner are awaiting rescue while occupying themselves with the pleasures of each other's company; in *Goldfinger* (1964), Bond even hides himself and his companion, Pussy Galore, with a parachute while telling her, "This is no time to be rescued." The presence of water also frequently recurs in these scenarios, as every canonical Bond film in which Sean Connery starred, six movies over nine years, ends either in a boat, on an island, or, in the case of *Thunderball* (1965), suspended over the ocean while attached to a cable that is hanging from a plane. The number of overlapping elements between the ending of *Pacific Rim* and a conventional Bond finale is uncanny, but it is again in the departure from formula that the scene's significance can be found.

Specifically, the fact that Raleigh and Mako are not physically engaging in sex demonstrates how the focus of the scene is located elsewhere from where it would be in a Bond movie, since the entire 007 series is constructed around a fetishization of the loins, from Bond's obsession with his phallic gun to the unsubtly named female characters, including Plenty O'Toole in *Diamonds are Forever* (1971) and Sylvia Trench in *Dr. No* (1962). This franchise's traditional ending fulfills the urge to see two over-sexualized characters engage in the activity that has been built throughout the entire film. *Pacific Rim*, on the other hand, relocates its fetishization to the minds of its characters, and it similarly develops this fixation over the course of its runtime. The source of this fetishization of the mind is in the jaeger technology, as the copilots control the technological marvel by uniting the power of their minds in a process identified as "drifting" or as a "neural handshake," an amusingly formal label for an intimate operation. Ample time throughout the movie is spent exploring the significance of entering into a drift; Raleigh was drifting with his brother, Yancy, when he died, an event that proves to have ramifications for Raleigh's psyche, he learns why Stacker Pentecost is a father figure to Mako while in a drift, and Newton Geiszler even drifts with a kaiju brain to learn valuable information about how the kaiju travel through the breach. In much the same way that each James Bond movie is buildup to the physical union between Bond and his newest conquest, *Pacific Rim* emphasizes the importance of drifting so the viewer can understand the intimacy connoted by Raleigh's drift with Mako as they copilot their jaeger. At the film's conclusion, when the pair is floating in the ocean and awaiting rescue, the romance between them is undeniable, even though there is no traditional physical consummation, or even a kiss. Instead, they press their foreheads together in an act that clearly demonstrates the relocation of the romantic fetish, also making the "neural handshake" explicit. Even in this stereotyped scene that elicits images of so many Bond movies, *Pacific Rim* revisions the frame and defies expectation.

The intertextual frames that can be found throughout *Pacific Rim* are not limited to the individual scenes that constitute the film's structure, but also include many of the characters who populate the story. Amidst a movie full of characters defined by archetypes, the scientist characters of Dr. Newton Geiszler (Charlie Day) and Dr. Hermann Gottlieb (Burn Gorman) stand out as a pair who represent binary oppositions of a stereotypical conflict; however, in keeping with the film's treatment of its frames, the power dynamic of this conflict is reversed, privileging an archetype that would typically be expected to have little to contribute. Gottlieb is in every way a stereotypical scientist, described by del Toro as a "tweed-wearing, English, phlegmatic introvert that never leaves the lab" ("Guillermo del Toro On 'Pacific Rim'"), exactly the type of academic representative one would expect to hold answers to all scientific questions and the key to humanity's survival. On the other end of the spectrum, Geiszler is a much more passionate and excitable man who is obviously obsessed with kaiju and prone to more outlandish theories; tellingly, he is frequently described by Gottlieb as a "kaiju groupie." It is easy to recognize Geiszler as emblematic of certain strains of fan culture, particularly through the kaiju tattoos that adorn his body, his insensitivity when talking about his admiration for kaiju in front of jaeger pilots, and the genuine excitement he shows upon seeing Hannibal Chau's black market emporium of kaiju organs. As endearing as Geiszler is for his enthusiasm and disdain for the traditional power structure of his discipline, however, his character is also slightly marred by his arrogance, as he spurns Gottlieb's advice and embarks on a dangerous drift with a kaiju brain solo because if it works, he will, in his own words, "be a rock star." Fortunately, the experiment is successful and it leads to a moment of begrudging respect, as Gottlieb assists him with a later drift that provides the critical information about kaiju needed in order to close the breach and stop further kaiju from invading. Of course, Gottlieb's lab-based research about the frequency of kaiju attacks is also proved to be correct, but it is ultimately irrelevant, as Geiszler's contribution provided the critical key to saving humanity. The celebration of fan culture over academia is a striking reversal of the script that would be expected of these archetypes, archetypes that Geiszler and Gottlieb fit so perfectly, they border on caricature.

Inevitably, the frames that are the most vital to *Pacific Rim*, the frames that most capitalize upon the viewer's encyclopedic knowledge of iconic pop culture figures, are those of the kaiju and the jaegers themselves. These archetypes are so critical to the movie that the very first visual to appear after the obligatory studio logos is the terms, kaiju and jaeger, their definitions, "giant beast" and "hunter," respectively, and languages of origin, Japanese and German, although little of this information seems necessary since it can easily be surmised by the time the opening montage has concluded. As the movie proceeds, the broad categories of kaiju and jaeger each gain many entries, and it is worthwhile to consider how each of these is identified, especially because many are barely identified at all. Each kaiju and jaeger is given a name, but most of these, especially those of the kaiju, are seldom used again. In fact, the Newton Geiszler, as the kaiju groupie, appears to be practically the only character who cares enough to distinguish between kaiju in order to be familiar with all of their names. As a result of their primarily categorical identification, the monsters become interchangeable; if most of the characters fighting the kaiju don't care to differentiate between them, why should the viewer? This apathy stands in stark contrast to the history of cinematic kaiju, which have virtually always been memorably named (e.g., King Kong, Godzilla, Mothra, etc.) so that the spectator can recognize and form an emotional attachment to them, as well as so sequels starring the same kaiju can be produced. Disregarding the names of kaiju in *Pacific Rim* declares that they are not to be the target of any emotional connection from the viewer.

The jaegers pose a similar conundrum, since they are likewise referred to categorically. Admittedly, the jaegers have more distinguishable qualities than the kaiju, but even so, it is only Gipsy Danger and Striker Eureka that present enough identity to be individually significant; other jaegers like Crimson Typhoon, which has three arms and is therefore uniquely piloted by triplets, may be noteworthy for such distinctive traits, but lack sufficient development of their pilots or battle history to foster any viewer attachment. In truth, I would contend, there is precious little difference between the jaegers and the kaiju, and it is arguably valid to identify the jaegers also as kaiju that happen to require a pilot. It is even difficult to ascertain whether the kaiju or jaegers cause more damage to Hong Kong during one of the movie's most intense battles. If the moralities of these monstrosities were to be reversed and it was jaegers invading while kaiju defended humanity, the situation would have ample precedent in kaiju cinema, dating back to *Godzilla vs. Mechagodzilla* (1974). Additionally, the distinction between kaiju and jaegers is further compromised by the relatively little amount of information the viewer has about the attributes of either. During the battle in Hong Kong, both a kaiju and Gipsy Danger spontaneously reveal abilities that completely turn the tide of the duel; the kaiju emits an electromagnetic pulse that incapacitates all digital technology and then sprouts wings so it can move the fight to the sky while Gipsy Danger waits until the last possible moment to whip out a sword function that slices through the kaiju with apparent ease. The viewer clearly has little motive to find sentiment in any particular jaeger, and indeed, it scarcely registers an emotional blip that all the jaegers have been destroyed by the end of the movie. It seems that the specific site of emotional resonance in *Pacific Rim* is in the conflict between kaiju and jaegers, in the spectacle of these two archetypal giants engaging in a brawl where they can utilize every weapon in their arsenals in the most outrageous fashion. The action scenes throughout the movie are thus appropriately lovingly crafted to give fans of these iconic figures as much pageantry to bask in as possible.

Alternative Strains of Cult Appeal

Amidst such thick intertextuality, it is easy to get wrapped up in the constant references to pop culture phenomena, but to do so would be to the exclusion of other cultish elements in *Pacific Rim*. In their introduction to *The Cult Film Reader*, Ernest Mathijs and Xavier Mendik outline many textual qualities that frequently recur in movies that have attained cult status. Included amongst these are the idea of "badness," or, as they describe it, "those films being valued for their 'ineptness' or poor cinematic achievement, often placing them in some kind of opposition to the 'norm' or mainstream in that they attain a status of 'otherness'" (2). Similarly, cult movies often transgress the boundaries of good and bad taste, and, according to Mathijs and Mendik, "a common way of achieving this is through the challenging of one or more 'conventions' of filmmaking, which may include stylistic, moral or political qualities" (2). Most films exemplifying these characteristics exist strictly on the periphery of mainstream society, but one strategy for imbuing a movie with badness and transgression without being exiled to the margins is to make it excessively campy; as jazz musician George Melly remarked and quoted by Andrew Ross, "camp was 'central to almost every difficult transitional moment in the evolution of pop culture" and "it brought vulgarity back into popular culture'" (54). The specific implementation of camp can take a variety of forms, and many examples are described by Susan Sontag in her seminal essay "Notes on 'camp,'" but the consistent quality of these instances is that "the way of Camp, is not in terms of beauty, but in terms of the degree of artifice, of stylization" (43). She continues on to defend the notion of camp in artificiality, writing, "Nothing in nature can be campy" and that "it is the love of the exaggerated, the 'off'" (44). Through the amplification and distortion of that which is natural to the extent that it becomes wholly artificial, a work becomes campy, thereby embodying a level of badness and transgression that has come to be associated with cult cinema, and these are conditions at which *Pacific Rim* excels.

The campiness of *Pacific Rim* permeates all aspects of its cinematic language, from the action to the dialogue and the acting. In fact, the camp of each facet of the movie is dependent on the others being similarly stylized, and it is in the sharing of this quality that the film's camp manages to hide in plain sight. One need only to look at the central action sequence, when two kaiju attack Hong Kong, to see abundant campy moments, and these are the moments for which the scene is most memorable. For instance, as Gipsy Danger and a kaiju fight in the middle of the city, there is a shot that follows Gipsy's fist as is wildly swings and misses a punch, smashing through an office building in the process; at the moment it is fully extended, the massive fist taps a Newton's cradle on a desk that seems undisturbed amidst the sweeping destruction, gently starting the swinging of the cradle's balls to demonstrate conservation of momentum and energy before the next shot follows the fist back out of the building, demolishing even more of it. This instant of levity is situated at an apex of artificiality, and the pleasure that can be derived from its absurdity is due to its campy nature. Comparably, the same sequence also features a moment in which Gipsy storms through the city dragging an ocean liner that it proceeds to use as a bat with which it pummels the kaiju, an incomprehensibly stylized, but also undeniably entertaining and gratifying moment of camp.

Despite such overwhelming camp in the action, it does not feel out of place in the film because the interpersonal moments are likewise imbued with the same brand of artifice. Characters routinely spout lines that are already wincingly clichéd in writing, but are made even more so by their forced delivery. Charlie Hunnam as Raleigh is especially culpable in this regard, such as when he lectures Mako Mori on the stresses of fighting kaiju, telling her, "One day, when you're a pilot, you're gonna see that in combat you make decisions and you have to live with the consequences. That's what I'm trying to do." Hunnam utters this and all of his other lines in a uniform monotone, a delivery that is so painfully earnest it would be impossible to take seriously in any other context, yet it is so in keeping with the style of this entire movie that it is perfectly natural to its setting. Extreme levels of camp are so pervasive throughout all elements of the movie that they fail to stand out as individually campy, but rather build on each other to create a homogeneous aesthetic that is truly so bad that it becomes amazing.

A final textual quality of cult films that *Pacific Rim* epitomizes is the evocation of nostalgia. Mathijs and Mendik write about how cult films are frequently recognized for "their ability to trigger a sense of nostalgia, a yearning for an idealized past," a feeling that can be set off by the literal representation of a past time or place, but "most likely it is an emotional impression" (3). *Pacific Rim* uses technology as the site for its nostalgia, specifically the technology that is used to create motion pictures. At the beginning of the attack on Hong Kong, a kaiju emits an electromagnetic pulse that disables all digital technology, sending the control room into a frenzy because all the jaegers are digital, at which point Raleigh boldly steps up and proclaims "Not all of them, Marshal. Gipsy's analog, nuclear." The notion of equating analog and nuclear technology is ludicrous, but Raleigh's disdain for the digital and the supremacy of a technology that is supposedly analog strikes a chord with the contemporary moment of cinema. The entire filmmaking industry, and indeed much of the world, is in the midst of a shift from being analog to digitally-based on the levels of both production and consumption. When Gipsy Danger steps in and wins the battle using nuclear technology that is supposedly analog, the relevance to and implications for *Pacific Rim*'s medium are obvious, and the victory of a system that is becoming increasingly outdated professes a severe amount of nostalgia. In a corresponding moment of the film's opening montage, while Raleigh narrates the development of jaegers, there are images of early jaeger tests shown concurrently; several of these shots depict an early jaeger test pilot who dies as the test fails, images that are shot in grainy black and white photography. Such image quality, taken in conjunction with the scientific nature of the scene, recalls B-level science-fiction movies of the 1950s, an era that, not coincidentally, produced many seminal kaiju films. With a few quick shots, *Pacific Rim* demonstrates acute self-awareness of its genre and the history of its medium, creating intense nostalgia for its predecessors and contributing to its all-around exemplification of cultness.

Pacific Rim *as a "Post-" Movie*

Through a variety of means, *Pacific Rim* encompasses a well-rounded array of cultish textual qualities, from its onslaught of intertextuality to the campiness that makes it nigh impossible to take seriously and the longing for idealized technologies that have either been phased out of usage or are verging on extinction. Every element of its cultness is founded upon an engagement with pop culture that is frequently dependent on the kaiju themselves, either directly or tangentially. In order for the kaiju to assume this role of authority in guiding the viewer's experience of the movie, many other aspects of the film function to tone down or eliminate the possibility of focusing on anything else. This unique necessity is fulfilled by creating a world that is post-human conflict. Many individual components of social and political realities are addressed with the goal of realizing such a vision, all to allow the kaiju to reign supreme over the characters' and viewer's consciousness.

Because *Pacific Rim* is a movie that extensively revisions a multitude of histories and legacies that preceded it, the ideologies of its precursors must first be considered in order to examine how *Pacific Rim* departs from them. The primary influence that it is directly spun-off from is obviously kaiju cinema, a category of movies with ancestry that includes the films of King Kong, Godzilla and his entire franchise, and hosts of other similar monsters. Jason Barr defines kaiju cinema as a veritable genre, defending it as a type of movie that "presents Sontag's worldwide anxieties to audiences but often without seeking to comfort or reassure the audience ... the primary theme is not only the acknowledgment of worldwide anxieties but also the underlying realism that allows those anxieties to fester" (12). I argue that *Pacific Rim* is not concerned with presenting any such realism that gives rise to universal concerns and therefore, however counterintuitively, it does not fulfill these essential criteria of the genre. Fortunately, Barr's definition allows for this possibility, as he continues on to clarify that "all films with kaiju may not be a part of the kaiju genre" (13). *Pacific Rim* chooses to honor the creatures whose nominal identification is lent to a cinematic genre without paying attention to the associated anxieties that are at the heart of the classification. Rather, it goes to great lengths to obscure any of the potential conflicts that might give rise to such anxieties, allowing the kaiju themselves to become the focus.

A common theme central to films of the kaiju genre is the political realities that would face the world in the event of such a calamity. As Barr points out, an avenue to understanding this thesis of many such movies is "to examine the oft-forgotten *people* in kaiju films, those who do represent nations, and to discuss emerging trends in international relationships," a methodology that is possible because "kaiju films are ... snapshots of the frequently tenuous and sometimes roiling relationships among various cultures and nations" (69–70). In perfect opposition to this point, *Pacific Rim* erases any potential human conflict almost immediately; in the opening narration, Raleigh informs the viewer how "the world came together, pooling its resources and throwing aside old rivalries for the sake of the greater good." And as the movie develops, it is a striking international group of individuals who comprise the central cast: the jaeger teams consist of American, Japanese, Australian, Russian, and Chinese pilots, and they are overseen by a British officer and a Peruvian operational manager. Stacker Pentecost even faces a totally international board early in the movie when he is informed that the jaeger program is being shut down. It is also noteworthy that this totally fictionalized international cooperation garners little attention throughout the movie; once the thoroughly post-political landscape has been introduced it is permanently taken for granted. Establishing a world that has overcome political difference allows for a more focused approach to the true conflict of the movie, that of the kaiju versus a united humankind.

Another frequently recurring conflict in the kaiju genre that *Pacific Rim* expertly brushes aside is between imperial and colonial powers. Barr situates the rise of the kaiju genre in conjunction with the end of World War II, and thus the downfall of many colonial empires; the generic story of a kaiju movie, therefore, "can be seen less as an example of repeated or regurgitated plots and more of a sort of global fascination with the seemingly unending roll call of new independent countries entering the global community" (76). In one efficient scene, *Pacific Rim* not only confirms the non-existence of this conflict between countries and cultures, but also relocates the anxiety of colonialism onto the war between humanity and kaiju. After drifting with a kaiju brain, Newton Geiszler realizes that kaiju have been invading Earth as colonists, intending to exterminate people so they can overtake the planet. Additionally, it is revealed that the conditions on Earth are perfect for such an attack, since pollution and greenhouse gases, as Geiszler puts it, "practically terraformed it for them." The shifting of imperial power to the kaiju may be a tactic to alleviate the postcolonial guilt felt by many imperial countries, but it again functions to unite humanity in the story of *Pacific Rim*, just as the blame for the pollution that enables kaiju to thrive is spread worldwide, making all peoples equally culpable and simultaneously equally responsible for contributing to the resistance effort. Yet again, the focus of attention and the site of antagonism is not between groups of humans, but rests squarely on the kaiju.

Interestingly, the ways in which *Pacific Rim* unites humanity are not limited to the text of the film itself, but also extend to its reception. An article by Aja Romano of The Daily Dot published in August of 2013, a month after *Pacific Rim*'s release, evaluates the movie using the Bechdel Test, a tool to determine the quality of a movie's female representation by identifying conversations between female characters about topics other than men, with disappointing results: "despite the general cultural awareness that has garnered the film praise, it falls dismally flat on the subject of women" (Romano). Romano, however, considers the praise that the film's only significant female character, Mako Mori, has received, providing an account of how fans have gone as far as to coin a Bechdel alternative called the Mako Mori Test, which, as explained by a Tumblr user Romano cites, "is passed if the movie has: (a) at least one female character; (b) who gets her own narrative arc; (c) that is not about supporting a man's story." This conclusion of praise for the movie's depiction of women is certainly debatable, as it does utterly fail the Bechdel Test, but the innovation of an alternative method of evaluation founded upon Mako is, at the very least, indicative of the variety of ways *Pacific Rim* has been read by scholars and fans alike. The way the fan community has reacted to this movie and its gender representations may even instill the film with a degree of post-sexism to complement its explicit post-political and postcolonial ideologies. All told, it is abundantly clear how the plot of *Pacific Rim* is a significant departure from any strain of the kaiju genre, leaving the kaiju themselves as the only remnant of a connection to previous kaiju films, an homage that the movie repeatedly reinforces.

When the multiple iterations of a post-human conflict ideology in *Pacific Rim* are considered in tandem with its multitude of cultish qualities, it becomes clear that in order to fully understand and appreciate the quantity of operations that are occurring, the viewer must be extraordinarily well-versed in popular culture. For the significance of this prerequisite, we must return to Umberto Eco, who identified such a characteristic as "postmodern"; he argues that what many cult classics may do unconsciously, "other movies will do with extreme intertextual awareness, assuming also that the addressee is equally aware of their purposes. These are 'postmodern' movies" (74). The recognition of such postmodernity is predicated on the existence of a vast quantity of popular cultural items that are known by the viewer and can be automatically spotted, recognized, and have their significance be therefore known intuitively. Lev Manovich, in one of his many writings on new media, theorizes such a bank of information in terms of computer science, in which "database is defined as a structured collection of data" (81). If we take *Pacific Rim*'s model viewer's infinite assemblage of pop culture knowledge as a database, then, following Manovich's logic, the movie's structure is identifiable as an algorithm comprised of standardized pieces of information, those being the multitudes of frames à la Eco. The theory Manovich outlines of how these concepts of database and algorithm interact seems to perfectly describe *Pacific*

Rim: "Algorithms and data structures have a symbiotic relationship. The more complex the data structure of a computer program, the simpler the algorithm needs to be" (84). Because the database of intertextual frames is so enormous, *Pacific Rim*'s narrative, the algorithm that is composed of these frames, is simple by necessity; instead of constructing a complex plot with characters who break from tradition in an unpredictable storyline, the movie uses the viewer's pre-existing database as a shorthand to direct attention away from superfluous elements and towards the main attraction: kaiju and jaegers awesomely destroying each other with reckless disregard for collateral damage for the viewer's sheer vicarious pleasure.

With a meticulously crafted story that is unencumbered by petty human conflict and structured by the relentless evocation of predetermined pieces of data, *Pacific Rim* is a model of post-ness; as I have enumerated, it displays features of being post-political, postcolonial, post-sexist, and above all, exceedingly postmodern. According to Eco, postmodernism and cultness are often interconnected, especially through their shared propensity for intertextuality. This intertextuality that Eco venerates need not be limited to the many references and intertextual frames that are present throughout *Pacific Rim* and were discussed earlier, but can more comprehensively apply to all the discourses that surround the film and with which it engages. When understood in this more inclusive sense, *Pacific Rim* becomes a model of postmodernity, and its central figures, the kaiju and jaegers, become emblematic of postmodernism, and therefore also attain the status of cult icons.

Conclusion

One final question that needs to be pondered is this: Is *Pacific Rim* a cult movie? As absurd as it seems to ask this question now, it still has yet to be answered. The qualities of cultness that are evident throughout the film and were explored in this essay are certainly indications that it has a strong propensity to garner a cult following, but in truth, they can only be said to exemplify characteristics common to other films that have enjoyed such canonization over the years. For *Pacific Rim*, or any movie, to attain cult status requires time in order for a mass culture to develop around it, and it will ultimately be in the hands of the fans to collectively decide if such a following will evolve. As Mathijs and Mendik write about the process by which fans codify such a film, "cult cinema relies on continuous, intense participation and persistence, on the commitment of an active audience that celebrates films they see as standing out from the mainstream of 'normal and dull' cinema" (4). Now, as a blockbuster production that grossed over $400 million worldwide, per Box Office Mojo, and is spawning an equally high-profile sequel, *Pacific Rim* is unquestionably situated squarely in the mainstream, but, as I argued, it constantly subverts its place in this realm of conventional cinema by recycling countless elements from the encyclopedia of pop culture, often in a destabilized manner, with extreme stylization that is on the precipice of falling into parody. If one thing is for certain, it is that all the textual pieces for a bona fide cult classic are in place—thick intertextuality, levels of camp that border on transgressing any boundary of good taste, and rich nostalgia for the technology used to create the movies that inspired Guillermo del Toro to pay homage to kaiju; perhaps the fan support for the Mako Mori test is even an indication that the community is already beginning to rally in support. In the meantime, fingers are crossed that the sequel lives up to its predecessor's standard of a blockbuster that manages to combine breathtaking spectacle with enough academic intrigue to satisfy fanboys and scholars alike.

WORKS CITED

Anovich, Lev. "Database as Symbolic Form." *Convergence* 5.2 (1999): 80–99.
Barr, Jason. *The Kaiju Film: A Critical Study of Cinema's Biggest Monsters.* Jefferson, NC: McFarland, 2016. Print.
Eco, Umberto. "Casablanca: Cult Movies and Intertextual Collage." *The Cult Film Reader.* Ed. Ernest Mathijs and Xavier Mendik. New York: Open University Press, 2008. 67–75. Print.
Julian, Mark. "Guillermo Del Toro On 'Pacific Rim'" *YouTube.* YouTube, 29 June 2013. Web. 16 Sept. 2016.
Mathijs, Ernest, and Xavier Mendik. "Editorial Introduction: What is cult film?" *The Cult Film Reader.* Ed. Ernest Mathijs and Xavier Mendik. New York: Open University Press, 2008. 1–11. Print.
"Pacific Rim (2013)—Box Office Mojo." *Box Office Mojo.* The Internet Movie Database, 14 Nov. 2016. Web. 15 Nov. 2016.
Romano, Aja. "The Mako Mori Test: 'Pacific Rim' Inspires a Bechdel Test Alternative." *The Daily Dot.* N.p., 18 Aug. 2013. Web. 9 Sept. 2016.
Ross, Andrew. "Uses of camp." *The Cult Film Reader.* Ed. Ernest Mathijs and Xavier Mendik. New York: Open University Press, 2008. 53–66. Print.
Sontag, Susan. "Notes on 'camp.'" *The Cult Film Reader.* Ed. Ernest Mathijs and Xavier Mendik. New York: Open University Press, 2008. 41–52. Print.

"Was it me? Did I kill them?"
The Monsters and the Women in King Kong *(1933)*, Gojira *(1954)*, Monster Zero *(1965)*, Destroy All Monsters *(1968) and* Gamera III: Revenge of Iris *(1999)*

SIGMUND C. SHEN

> The void is the creatrix, the matrix. It is not mere hollowness and anarchy. But in women it has been identified with lovelessness, barrenness, sterility. We have been urged to fill our "emptiness" with children. We are not supposed to go down into the darkness of the core. Yet, if we can risk it, the something born of that nothing is the beginning of our truth.—Adrienne Rich, "Women and Honor: Some Notes on Lying"

When asked to comment about her work on Gareth Edwards's *Godzilla* (2014), Juliet Binoche joked dismissively that she played "the one real woman character [who was] dead in three minutes" (Eisenberg). This straightforward observation—framed by instigating, clickbait headlines like "Juliette Binoche Thinks Women Got Short-Changed in 'Godzilla'" (Yahoo!) and "Read Juliette Binoche's Blunt, Harsh Assessment Of Shooting Godzilla" (Cinemablend)—triggered predictable, multiply redundant cries of grief from anonymous commenters: "'I'm pretty sure she got paid well for that brief role. This is a joke' ... 'Why did she even take it to begin with?' ... 'Oh please; Godzilla is a popcorn monster flick, not a women's issues platform' ... 'Not everything is a damn feminist issue'"(qtd. in Eisenberg). Despite the insipidity of such posts, the confused young men of the #gamergate trend are obviously not the ones to blame for systemic, institutional sexism in mass media.[1] It is the male-dominated cultural apparatuses, movie studios like Legendary and Toho, that create the final product. Binoche's remark is as much a comment on the *daikaiju eiga* genre as a whole as it is on her particular character, a knowingly understated critique of a hoary tradition of roles for women that are stripped of both power and agency, relegated to sexualization and victimization.

Filmmakers have become more attentive to this imbalance in late 20th and early 21st century iterations of the genre: women have become scientists, soldiers, and rescuing "heroines" in the revamped Godzilla and Gamera series of the 1990s and 2000s, for example. Yet such instances of obvious social progress have also obfuscated a continuing strain of the genre: the way in which women's roles, through outlandish and elaborately constructed scenarios, continue to facilitate a kind of changing of the subject: the denial and displacement of patriarchal guilt. In giant monster cinema, this demonization has performed a historically specific function: quieting concerns about militarism and imperialism by stoking nationalist pride and fear.

This pattern manifests in interesting ways in five notable films of the genre. *King Kong* (1933) and *Gojira* (1954) are, of course, foundational texts, whose power endures partly because they impart both a poignant ambivalence to their eponymous anti-heroes, and a hint of guilt to their human characters. *Monster Zero* (1965) and *Destroy All Monsters* (1968) forged the template for the distinctive alien invasion plot which Toho adapted from H.G. Wells's *The War of the Worlds* and made emblematic of Japanese science fiction fantasy films during the heyday of Japanese cinema in the 1960s. And to this day *Gamera 3: Revenge of Iris* (1999) is one of the darkest and most visually striking films in the genre. Coming right after the critical disappointment of the first U.S. *Godzilla* remake in 1998, *Gamera 3* was given special scrutiny by fans as a potential standard bearer for the future of the genre— so much that its director, Shusuke Kanno, was subsequently hired by rival studio Toho to reinvigorate its own Godzilla series. All five films are worth seeing for many reasons, even for viewers and scholars who are not particularly interested in *daikaiju eiga*, but this is the first critical study of metaphors of misogyny common to all five, focusing on how each has adhered to the ideological needs of its respective historical and cultural context.

Adrienne Rich once remarked, "Women's honor [is defined as] virginity, chastity, fidelity to a husband." But during the social and political revolution that washed over Japan from 1854 to the economic bubble of the 1990s, from the Meiji Restoration through World War II to the Japanese government's own complicity with the U.S. government and nuclear industry in the postwar period, the destabilizing question, in both the apprehension and enforcement of women's roles, became, "fidelity" to whom—to which "husband?" Sexism in patriarchy is a broader topic—but this essay focuses on sexism in the jaws of two opposing patriarchies. In this triangle of dual interpellation, a woman was portrayed as always-already a double agent, equally scapegoated and "treasured" by antagonistic factions, and gaslighted by the realization that no matter which "loyalty" she chose, she was guilty of betrayal to both, and unable to conform to the social expectations of either dominant narrative. In this and other, more literal ways, the woman became one with the monsters.

A White Woman's Burden in King Kong

Although part of the tragedy of the original *King Kong* (1933) is felt in the heroine's terrified obliviousness to the beast's unrequited love, the suspicious implications of Ann Darrow's character are clarified in both remakes, when she risks her life trying to protect Kong from the military aircraft, effectively siding against her own species, and therefore, against all of civilization. But the counterweight to her monstrous menace, the equal danger she poses to Kong himself, extends beyond her conscious calculations to something that precedes her agency: the signification of her gender and race.

In a recent celebrity rape case in Japan, actor Yuta Takahata claimed he "'couldn't control' his desire after looking at" a hotel worker he had attacked. (Kikuchi). This rationale appears to rely upon a conveniently self-aggrandizing premise: that he "couldn't control" himself is meant to imply that he is too masculine to contain his overwhelming instincts and power. No monster in cinema history is depicted as more stereotypically "masculine" than King Kong, from his anthropomorphic heterosexual desire to his monstrous size and physical strength, and this is by design—the giant ape, the quintessential "noble savage," is an example of how white patriarchy projects its own primitive masculinity upon the criminalized black male. The fantasy of black men kidnapping and raping white women is regularly conjured anew when white male supremacy is challenged, going back at least as far as the antebellum period in the American south (Bouie). Indeed, it's no accident that the plot of Mary Shelley's *Frankenstein* (the eponymous monster of which was once invoked during a debate in England's House of Commons as a warning of the chaos that would descend if African slaves were freed too precipitously [Canning]) has its dramatic climax triggered by the panic over an imagined racial apocalypse: a premonition of the monster and his mate escaping into the American wilds to become Adam and Eve of a new tribe that could dilute and menace the hegemony of "the Old World."

The central metaphor of *King Kong* is so instantly recognizable that 76 years later it is treated as a joke in Tarantino's *Inglourious Basterds*, in which American spies in a German beer garden get their covers blown because the racist subtext of the movie is painfully obvious to everyone in the room except their oblivious selves; however, when *King Kong* was produced, the slavery era racist fantasy had shifted out of publicly expressed, mainstream American thought. Because it was not politically palatable, the guilt of its enjoyment and financial success had to be deflected away—not only from the male filmmakers, but also from the male audiences targeted by this homage to the "boys' adventure" romances of Jules Verne, Rider Haggard, and Edgar Rice Burroughs. And that's where Ann Darrow comes in. It is not just her beauty that is overpowering to Kong's uncontrollable sexuality—it is her *white* beauty. If, as Carl Denham says, King Kong is "something on the other side of that wall that no white man has ever seen," then the correlative is that the blonde Ann Darrow is "something" that no black man has ever seen either. The wooden altar just beyond that wall implies that Darrow is the next in a long history of female sacrifices to the monster—but if that's the case, where are all the others?

If he killed all of them, then why does he never harm Ann Darrow? What makes her so special? This is both Kong's redemption and his downfall: if only an attractive woman can bring out the rapist in the man, then only an attractive white woman can bring out the noble in the savage. The motive for the fantasy of racial rape and miscegenation is not simply guilt for white racism, as if the constantly feared sexual assault would simply be an eye-for-an-eye payback for slavery. King Kong's protectiveness and fetishism of Ann Darrow implies that black aggression exists prior to white greed, because black men, including those who have never even seen a white person before, simply cannot control their actions when a white woman is within grabbing distance. This both reifies white male standards of beauty as "natural" and vindicates white hegemony as an act of self-defense, because even if historic grievance did not exist, black men would still be an implicit, categorical threat. In the 1980s Hollywood comedy *Soul Man*, a conservative suburban mother fantasizes that the protagonist is a jungle warrior, who crouches and mutters, right before tearing her bodice, "All my life I have wanted one thing—white woman! And now, I am going to have one!" Thus Kong's worshipful treatment of Ann where he presumably killed all the other sacrifices suggests that slavery and other forms of white domination were justified to preserve the genetic purity of the white race. At the end, a reporter approaches Carl Denham, who pronounces, "'Twas beauty killed the beast," as if Ann's month hadn't already been bad enough. No it wasn't; it was him, his military, and his crew of hired pirate capitalists. Which is exactly why he must be given the last word, and tell the press, as the recorder of official history, that it was actually Darrow who killed Kong, and not Denham who was the real beast all along.

Emiko's Silence and Suffering in Gojira

In an article titled "Monster of Mourning, Ritual of Remembering: Ishiro Honda's *Gojira*," Dr. Serizawa's character and subplot are taken as allusions to Unit 731, the joint Japan–U.S. conspiracy to cover up inhumane human experimentation that had been conducted by the Japanese Imperial Army to advance its biological weapons project during World War II (Shen). Without recounting that thesis in full here, a clear allusion to this secret history is delivered by a scene that is not otherwise necessary to the narrative, where a reporter asks Serizawa about his alleged German ties and he flatly denies it. As a story, the film doesn't "need" an extra subplot about German scientists, which David Kalat points out "would be a considerable stretch unfounded in any other aspect of the film" (29). But this assessment, while logically sound, misses the point. There doesn't need to literally be a Nazi subplot, any more than there literally needs to be a "Hiroshima" subplot, allusions to both of which are all the more effective for not being spelled out.

Unit 731 was not just a betrayal of the old feudal traditions of Japanese battlefield honor (Barenblatt 101); its postwar history was also a betrayal of the martyred Japanese soldiers themselves, because what America got in return for helping to cover up this horrific history was the wealth of research data, cannibalistically harvested from America's own slaughtered soldiers and wartime allies. Guilt over this final betrayal of Japan, through complicity with the enemy its young fighters had sacrificed themselves to resist, can be traced back to its origins in the humiliating invasion of Commodore Perry in 1854 and the Japanese government's subsequent scramble to westernize during the Meiji Restoration. So how do you purge such guilt? One way is through Serizawa's fiancée Emiko. Although the use of human medical experimentation by Unit 731 was widely known in Japan, it was kept an "open secret" by self-censorship and the fear of retaliation both during and after the war (Shen). Like the Japanese doctors, scientists, and military personnel who were pressured to act as if they didn't know what was going on, Emiko is sworn to secrecy about Serizawa's chemical weapons research. By finally choosing to betray the trust of her groom-to-be, Emiko becomes a scapegoat for the westernization of gender roles during the Meiji Restoration.

In his retrospective review of *Gojira*, Roger Ebert admired the political resonance of the story but still believed it was a "bad movie": "When Dr. Serizawa demonstrates the Oxygen Destroyer to the fiancee of his son [sic], the superweapon is somewhat anticlimactic. He drops a pill into a tank of tropical fish, the tank lights up, he shouts "stand back!" the fiancee screams, and the fish go belly up." Although this may not be the most fair reading of the scene, part of the unintentional humor that Ebert gently hints at is due to an element he is too diplomatic to name: the sexist trope of the fragile heroine whose reaction to having her delicate sensibilities hurt is to fall into the arms of a stronger male. Her anguished scream and near-swoon illustrate the belief that women are too innocent and naïve to "handle the truth" about the male realm of scientific research and the waging of war, and, further, the accompanying conviction that any woman who is afforded a glimpse into this forbidden world must effectively be punished, as a warning to others. But Serizawa forces her to witness this painful demonstration anyway. It's an oddly touching, vulnerable gesture by Serizawa, as if he needs her to help carry the burden of his knowledge of both the terror of what he has made, and his refusal to end the destruction of his nation. Her fate as a mute fiancée who must loyally remain silent about the literally underground work of her groom-to-be may thus symbolize the self-censorship of Japanese citizens whose silence about Unit 731 was enforced by the threat of both state terror and public ostracization for disloyalty during the war.

Emiko's choice to remain complicit in Serizawa's secret leads to more death and suffering at Godzilla's invasion of Tokyo, and the pain of this guilt finally drives her to let out the truth. But it's not awkward enough that she does this: the person she tells is not, say, her father Yamane, but her lover Ogata, who has the ignominious distinction of being not only Emiko's illicit lover, but also the target of her own father's wrath for disagreeing with Yamane's desire to keep Godzilla alive. When Emiko and Ogata confront Serizawa, his violent lashing out at him (which results in Ogata's head wound, and Emiko immediate rushing to his side) plainly bespeaks the unspoken. Tormented as Serizawa has been by the burden of his secret research, it is his fiancée's betrayal of that secret to her true love, Ogata, that makes him realize, for the first time in his life, how alone he truly is. At least this knowledge makes his next decision easier; this should have been a triumphant moment for Emiko—it's both a declaration of her own sexual independence, and the moment when she proves her patriotism by sacrificing her personal relationship to save Japan. It certainly would have been seen this way by other women characters in the same story, such as the left-wing contingent at the Diet debate who insist "The truth is the truth! The truth must be made public!" This, however, is not their story, and the politics espoused here is not their politics.

For Emiko, the burden of the secret has been twofold. If she keeps it safe, she prolongs the suffering and destruction of her people. She embraces the role of the double agent for the sake of her fiancé's internationalist, humanitarian determination to stop another apocalyptic weapon from being unleashed upon the world. The guilt of this predicament is demonstrated when she, Masaji, Ogata, and Yamane witness Godzilla's next attack: all the men's eyes are fixed on the rampaging monster, while her eyes alone shift to the sides anxiously, as if its every step advances the exposure of her own secret. Her eventual exposure of the secret is likewise treacherous; in another moment of unspoken insight, her character's grasp of the full implications of her double bind is made clear. Serizawa's decision to burn his files is, after all, illogical and unnecessary—he had just made a point, not two minutes ago, that even if the notes are destroyed the secret will still be in his head, subject to extraction by torture at the hands of "politicians around the world." So when she breaks down in front of the fireplace and cries, and he tries to console her by, for the first time in the movie, smiling peacefully, it is because they both see clearly that which escapes Ogata: that Serizawa has resigned himself to the decision to put himself well beyond the power of any torturer.

Thus is Emiko repaid for her conscripted service as the keeper of the secret: the cruel realization, while kneeling before a hearthlike fire as if to mock her rejection of a socially sanctioned domestic future, that it is she, not the torturers, politicians, or even Godzilla itself, that is ultimately responsible for Serizawa's death. Ogata reports to Emiko Serizawa's final wish: "I hope you two will be happy. Farewell." Emiko bursts into wordless tears, and immediately the curtain descends on this family plot. It is effectively erased by an ideologically "safer," because more generic, horror movie theme, as Yamane brings the subject back to nuclear weapons. That crime is easier to speak of because the guilt for it lies squarely at the feet of U.S. government officials, but the westernization of Japan and consequent transformation of gender roles that allowed Emiko to save Japan by rejecting and betraying Serizawa is in some ways more painful and more deeply hidden.

Indeed, the punishment of Emiko Yamane is imagined to have lasted a lifetime. In *Godzilla vs. Destoroyah* (1995), we are reunited with Emiko to find that she has grown old in her father's house, because in the end, she never married. The director of the film, Takao Okawara, has stated unambiguously that "Emiko did not marry Ogata because she was so upset by the death of Dr. Serizawa" (Milner). Why is the woman the one effectively "punished" with guilt for the death of traditional gender roles? Why not Ogata, who pursued Emiko knowing she was promised to someone else? Why not Yamane, who arranged the marriage when she and Serizawa were just children?

"Yokai of the Showa Era"

Four years after the first Godzilla film, and thirteen years after Hiroshima, Japanese Prime Minister Kishi provoked massive demonstrations, strikes, and social unrest by signing a security treaty with the U.S., which was depicted as selling out Japan to western imperialists all over again in the name of a sham internationalism. For his betrayal, Kishi was dubbed the "Yokai of the Showa era" (136), a phrase which equated this arrogant politician with the troublemaking monsters of Japanese folklore. Six years after that, a more palatable side of this suspect internationalism began to be felt in the leadup to the 1964 Olympic Games. The national sentiment was beginning to turn away from militant patriotism and demonization of politicians, but bitterness over the war and colonial subjection was still expressed, this time in a safer form of hostility, directed at a more helpless target. As historian Yoshikuni Igarashi writes,

> The chastity of the Japanese—particularly female—body was of great concern, as it was during the time Japan waited for the arrival of American soldiers right after the defeat. In the midst of frenzied preparations for the Olympics, popular magazines expressed the fear of the corrupting influence of foreign (American and European) male sexual desire: naïve Japanese women might end up as victims [149].

Brothels were closed down, and high schools were bombed with moralistic pamphlets that effectively pre-supposed the sexual vulnerability of female students (149). At the same time, the U.S. was turned from enemy to paternalistic guardian; thus, Japan had lost two enemies from its cultural narrative: the U.S., and its own corrupt politicians. Make that three if you count Godzilla: during the 60's, the monster was changed from a destroyer of Japan to a superhero protecting Japan against alien Others who were even worse than himself. But as physicists know, patriarchy abhors a vacuum. In two Godzilla films from this period, *Monster Zero* and *Destroy All Monsters*, the antagonists are ostensibly Others from Outer Space, but they are really metaphors for women who must be disciplined at any cost.

This distrust of female sexuality/loyalty (recall how Rich says that women's "honor" is defined through sexual fidelity), and the scapegoating of them for the sake of international (interplanetary) harmony, is colorfully dramatized in *Monster Zero*. When an American astronaut, Glenn, who has become romantically involved with the spying alien female Namikawa, challenges the Controller of Planet X about the uniformity (which implies conformity) of the females of his planet, the alien knowingly insinuates that the astronaut's own colonial and sexual desire belie his accusations of sexism: "I should think that you Glenn, would agree that our girls are attractive." Glenn, bristling at the Controller's implication that his interest in Namikawa is only sexual, retorts "Beauty is more than skin deep. Beauty is also what's in the heart." He is essentially saying "She's not like that! What we have is not like that!" a plaintive protest to which the Controller simply replies, "Let's not argue the matter," dismissing the criteria for Namikawa's worth as a topic of debate unbecoming of alpha men.

Later, Namikawa comes clean about her spying, assuring Glenn that this time he can trust her. Taking her at her word, he tries to persuade her to flee her repressive society and join him on the more enlightened Earth, but instead she wants him to become one of her people and marry her:

> NAMIKAWA: True I was assigned to spy on you, but you've come to mean more to me than anything.
> GLENN: You've got to get out of this place and take off that getup of yours.
> NAMIKAWA: No. You have to become a citizen of our Planet X. So we can marry. That's the only way we can save you.

GLENN (pulling her close with contained anger): Look, Namikawa, we're not robots. What kind of peace would it be if we were controlled by machines? (She looks down in shame.) In defense of Earth we're gonna fight to the last man, baby.

From belittling her culturally appropriate attire, to manhandling her in an argument, to dismissing her culture's—and by implication, her own—ability to exercise true agency and free will, Glenn continues to play the role of the sexually "liberating" colonial occupier. The sexual politics at play—he the cultural superior, she the secretive, untrustworthy "bait"—is clearly reminiscent of familiar stories of American occupation forces in Japan and other Asian countries like South Vietnam and South Korea. When Namikawa asks him to marry her, the tone of the conversation anticipates the demure Trinh in *Good Morning Vietnam*, lecturing Robin Williams's character Cronauer about how a "lady" of her society is expected to behave. In that Hollywood story of wartime sexual politics, Williams's character's best insult is "You are in more dire need of a blowjob than any white man in history." The innately gendered duplicity of Trinh, the woman Cronauer courts when he's not making fun of her broken English, is revealed near the end of the movie when we find that her brother is a Vietcong operative.

Likewise, in *Monster Zero*, even Namikawa's last words, which of all her lines we would expect to be unequivocal, are ambiguous. She runs to Glenn and says "Don't go! They'll destroy you. I love you." While gazing into his eyes with a look of undivided attention, the camera pans down to show her reaching into his pocket. This final detail marks her, too, as a double agent whose untrustworthiness transcends male-defined notions of honor in war. Although this time her deception is aimed at the alien invaders, it still suggests that with her, even a declaration of love may be just another performance.

By the time we arrive, three years later, to *Destroy All Monsters*, the misogynist metaphor has become considerably more prominent. Now the Xians, men who enslaved their women, have been replaced by the Kilaaks, women who enslave human men, human women, and Earth monsters alike. Namikawa, the tragic slave who yearned to marry a human, is replaced by Kyoko, the human female who is most talkative, expressive, and assertive during the scenes when she is brainwashed by the troublemaking femaliens. While the Controller of Planet X was robotic and stoic, his eyes covered by a visor to conceal any emotion, Kyoko's alien leader, the Kilaak Queen, is seductively charming. In the scene of her introduction, she exhibits an uncanny combination of pacifying submissiveness and enlightening scientific reason, which Julia Kristeva terms "abjection":

> Abjection, on the other hand, is immoral, sinister, scheming, and shady: a terror that dissembles, a hatred that smiles, a passion that uses the body for barter instead of inflaming it, a debtor who sells you up, a friend who stabs you.... In the dark halls of

the museum that is now what remains of Auschwitz, I see a heap of children's shoes.... The abjection of Nazi crime reaches its apex when death, which, in any case, kills me, interferes with what, in my living universe, is supposed to save me from death: childhood, science, among other things [4].

When the queen appears, smiling, and highlighted by a slow "Spielberg close-up" as an eerie theremin plays, her first words are a disarming apology:

> QUEEN: I'm sorry to keep you waiting.
> DR. OTANI: Everyone, she's here to answer your questions.
> QUEEN: We are not here as your enemies. With everyone's cooperation, we can make the earth into a new and advanced civilization.

Katsuo retorts "What if the earth doesn't want to cooperate with you?" but is shaken by the perceived insolence of the enslaved Kyoko: "Katsuo, why don't you listen to what she's saying?" The male scientist Otani then vouches for the queen's authority, saying "I'm ready to accept her story as the truth because of her scientific ability." Ogata charges the Queen, his fingers at the level of her chest, and he is punished for this pointedly sexual aggression by an invisible electric field.

Katsuo and his men are attacked by more men who have also been mentally enslaved, and the Queen smiles silently as a mysterious smoke begins to fill the room. The mind control and the magician's tricks constitute a betrayal of masculine battlefield conduct through sabotage of the advantage to which Katsuo and his men feel entitled by virtue of their phallic weapons. (It's also a visual reference to the treacherous use of chemical weapons, outlawed by international agreements after World War I.) As the chaos of this scene unfolds, Kyoko is fixed at the center of the moving frame, staring dispassionately at her countrymen as she allows herself to be pulled backward while staring silently with the same flat affect. She eventually disappears into the smoke, and in a shot that may again recall Kristeva's disquieting abject, the Kilaak Queen smiles enigmatically again as she likewise retreats backwards into the smoke.

Later, this military rout is mirrored by a press meeting, unremarkably dominated by men, that is again sabotaged, this time not by the Kilaak Queen but by the now-uncanny Kyoko herself. In it, Japanese military officers and an older "distinguished" white male shake hands, but suddenly, Kyoko appears at center, in a red dress, descending the stairs like indifferent royalty:

> KYOKO (speaking in a loud voice to compel attention): I've come to speak to everyone here.
> KATSUO: You're wasting your time! We won't let them take over our minds!
> KYOKO (condescendingly glancing at Katsuo): You don't have to stay if you don't want to listen. (Looking around and smiling, as if fantasizing that she has supplanted the Kilaak Queen from the previous scene) I'm here to answer everyone's questions.

As Katsuo tries to hijack back her commandeered press conference, Kyoko seems annoyed and yearning for the safety of her public audience: "I came to speak to everyone. You should just shut up." Katsuo is outraged at her defiance of his authority, yelling "You!" and manhandling her while declaring "Don't try to struggle! I'm saving you from their control!" As he strong-arms her, the camera pans over the other men in their power suits, who are watching silently without intervening. Katsuo wrenches off her earrings and, as the men murmur around him, holds up for their scrutiny what is now revealed to be alien jewelry: "This is how they controlled her." Flash photography now signals that Katsuo has regained control over the press conference. Of course, the fact that the male Dr. Otani and Godzilla were controlled by the same technology is irrelevant—we are only *told* about them, but what we are *shown* is the attack on Kyoko's earrings. The tone of this conflict, and its appeal to the misogynist desire to gawk at an uppity female being served her comeuppance, would be completely different if, instead, Katsuo had ripped "earrings" out of the aging male Dr. Otani's body.[2]

When Kyoko collapses again, Katsuo finally tries to "help" her—by shouting and shaking her roughly. When Kyoko slowly awakens and sees Katsuo, her lips part alluringly and Katsuo grins. She almost swoons at the sight of her own blood, yet another indication that she's back to the "normal" behavior of her delicate gender. When a man asks her where the Kiraku base is, she looks bewildered, then perplexed, then clutches her ear in pain and says, in a traumatized voice, "I ... I ... don't know where!" As if to block out the intolerable memories of her fleeting enslavement—or liberation?—she tunnels into Katsuo's chest and, as the expression goes, there are no further questions. Her last line, and retreat from the interrogation, implies a rejection of conscious knowledge, which satisfies the misogynist narrative that women are too weak to confront the truth about their own actions and must hysterically repress their memories for their own sanity. Although the dominant men have not discovered the information they wanted, a gratifying consolation goal has been achieved: the physical and emotional surrender of Kyoko back to male control. When she was enslaved, she was the only character who disobeyed Katsuo, told him to shut up, told him to listen, and treated him dismissively. She also had exhibited a soldier's courage, interposing herself between him and Dr. Otani at the meeting with the Kilaak Queen, but all this threatening agency is lost when her spell is broken—now her weakness is shown in her tears, in her confused awakening from the bad dream, and in her refusal to face the deep repressions she has arrayed around her own memory.

If there is any doubt that *Destroy All Monsters* is an allegory for outright gender warfare, consider the over-the-top phallocentrism of the final assault on the Kilaak stronghold, and how this sequence is punctuated by the erotic reclamation of Kyoko. Like Princess Leia standing in the control room while the men fly out to assault the Death Star, Kyoko listens passively at Earth HQ while Katsuo and his men in the fly to the moon. The earthmen penetrate a crater with their rocket ship. The crater responds to this intrusion by heating up with emanations of flame. This heat triggers the men to swarm out of the rocket into a hidden chamber where they locate a globular mechanism that can only be described as an ovic symbol. The alpha male Katsuo barks orders at his subordinates, takes aim with his laser gun, and fires steadily on the object. For some reason, the "exertion" of using his weapon causes him to visibly perspire. Finally, the object is destroyed and the sequence ends with a shot of Kyoko, wordlessly sighing in postcoital contentment.

Looking at the ill-fated Kilaak Queen alongside these other two "monsters," Namikawa and Kyoko, we can see numerous ways that the disobedient, uncontrollable women are mistreated by the men. They are punished for forbidden sexual desire, and for collaboration with those who have been classified as enemies of human patriarchy. They are always-already assumed to be double agents, or they should be by any man who isn't hopelessly naïve. When women assert authority and power of their own, usually through deception, or otherwise subversive means such as embarrassingly public revelations, they speak as simple-minded children proudly defying adults, or in smug, unnerving parody of the honey sweet tones of a submissive female. When they make use of any form of resistance against men whatever, including verbal objections and even simple dispassionate questioning of male authority, they are met with incredulity, harsh words, sexual groping, physical violence, and even murder, all in the name of "saving" them from the influence of the enemy. Yes, the male enemy aliens are openly dangerous, but what female humans and female aliens share in common is that they are both far worse than being openly dangerous—they are, like a fast runner on first base keeping the pitcher in a state of nervously divided attention, *potentially treacherous.*

Melancholic femininity in Gamera 3: Revenge of Iris

The complicated gender trouble of *Gamera 3: Revenge of Iris* is easier to untangle if we bring two Freudian concepts to bear. The first is abreaction, whereby the sudden recollection of a childhood trauma—both of the event that occurred, and the deeply repressed emotions that were triggered by it long ago—allows a patient to finally overcome his own irrational emotions and behavior. The second is melancholia, whereby a patient cannot overcome his grief for the loss of a parent or parental figure. To cure this condition, what we would call clinical depression, the patient must be guided to abreaction, so he can realize that before the loss of the parent, he was angry at that parent. When the parent died, that anger had no place to go but inward. It gradually becomes repressed and then turned into guilt because of the childish unconscious belief that the patient's own anger must have magically played some role in the disappearance of parent. In this view, all death is abandonment and abandonment is tormenting proof that the patient must have done something to be unworthy of his parent's love.

The main human character of *Gamera 3: Revenge of Iris* is an only child named Ayana. During the last invasion of Japan by Gamera, she was told by her father to stay home while he rushed outside to retrieve her mother. Before he left, Ayana's father said to her, "Don't worry, it's not your fault." A few minutes later she watched as the collapsing buildings in Gamera's wake left her parents and her cat Iris killed. She is adopted by a foster family, but doesn't get along well with them, and her rage against Gamera haunts her. One day, she finds an egg in a Shinto temple that hatches into a monster that becomes her pet and sole friend; she names the monster Iris. The monster grows exponentially larger and slaughters her foster family, then transforms into a giant monster and ravages the city of Kyoko. Ayana's anger at Gamera for causing the death of her family and cat lead her to enter into a psychic bond with Iris to make the monster even stronger and empower it to defeat Gamera.

At the final confrontation, Iris mortally wounds Gamera, and summons Ayana to a physical bond to complete their shared evolution, but right before the "consummation" of this union, her foster brother cuts her cheek with an ancient Shinto sword. The attack by the boy breaks the psychic bond between Ayana and Iris. Now wide awake, she realizes that the monster is dangerous to herself and her foster brother, but the realization comes to late as the creature engulfs her into a womblike chamber. While floating in a solution that evokes amniotic fluid, Ayana is revisited by her memory and realizes that her parents and cat were killed not by Gamera, but by another monster. Gamera was not attacking Japan, but trying, messily, to defend Japan against the other invader. She then realizes that her own rage at Gamera, including the transference of that anger upon her foster parents, also drove the monster to kill her foster parents. Essentially, none of her personal loss has been Gamera's fault, but some of it has been her own. By the end of this scene, she is drowning in melancholic guilt and regret inside Iris's "womb." She has experienced abreaction, purging herself of her rage, but it has seemingly come too late to undo the misguided actions caused by her own misplaced aggression.

Inevitably, genre conventions must be reasserted and Gamera must rescue her from Iris's womb. But before that happens, the implied message of the story—that Ayana blamed the wrong giant monster and caused even more death and destruction from her own emotionalism and moral confusion— carries a historical ideological dimension as well. After August 1945, Japan embraced its former wartime foe and became its staunch ally; this alliance was partially based on Japan's dependence on the U.S. for protection against China because MacArthur limited its legal right to have its own standing military. Thus the U.S., like Gamera, became a misunderstood hero, selling itself as the paternalistic authority that altruistically fights to protect Japan against invaders. If some of Japan's people suffer as a result of this protection, such as, say, Okinawan women raped near U.S. military bases, well, clearly that's the price one pays for security. In this dialectic, Iris, having come from an egg in a Shinto shrine, would then represent the animistic, nationalistic, pre–Meiji era, soul of Japan, which punishes Japan for selling out to the west and betraying its ancient ancestors. Thus, Ayana can be taken as an object lesson in the consequences of resisting geopolitical realities and nostalgically, irrationally remaining spellbound by the old folk traditions.

In his book *Bodies of Memory: Narratives of War in Postwar Japanese Culture, 1945–1970*, historian Yoshikuni Igarashi finds evidence in Japanese media narratives of the postwar period that the "relationship between the U.S. and Japan ... is highly sexualized. The drama casts the U.S. as a male and Hirohito and Japan as a docile female, who unconditionally accepts the U.S. desire for self-assurance" (29). Indeed, the first post-war photograph of MacArthur and Hirohito that was released to newspapers in both countries was jeered by Japanese press as a "wedding photo":

> MacArthur towers over the emperor in a relaxed position which his hand on his own buttocks. Meanwhile, the stiff figure of the emperor, dressed in formal wear, stands gazing straight into the camera.... The ministry of the interior banned the circulation of newspapers carrying the photo, finding the contrast between the two figures demeaning to the emperor. Yet [MacArthur] immediately intervened to enforce the freedom of the press and had the Japanese government lift its ban the very same day [31].

To build up our anticipation for the final conflict between Gamera and Iris, director Kaneko throws in a stylish flourish worthy of Sergio Leone: a panning tableau of, not two, but three "monsters," framed by fire and rain. First we are shown Gamera, then Iris, and finally Ayana herself, unhinged with rage like Stephen King's *Carrie* and the ghostly Sadako from Hideo Nakata's *Ringu*. The gender signifiers of this interlude even extend to sound design: Gamera emits a low growl, while the images of Iris and Ayana are accompanied by high-pitched, "shrill" tones. She is only "saved" from the role of the dangerous woman by two didactic punishments. The first of these is the physical attack of her foster brother's sword, which grazes her cheek pointedly as if to teach her a lesson without disfiguring her commodified beauty. The second thing is the psychological slap in the face of her abreaction, a humbling submersion in cold water which comes too late to save her from the torment of her own self-destructive melancholia. Reliving the massacre of her foster parents' household through Iris's eyes, she wonders, "Iris, was it you? Was it me? Did I kill them?" and then cries, "I'm falling! Somebody help me! Help me!" Of course, punishment is not enough—she must also be rescued and redeemed by forgiveness on the part of the paternalistic monster and gratitude on the part of herself. How else is she supposed to find redemption as a docile Japanese woman in a world dominated by U.S. hegemony?

Cinematic Monsters, Cyborgian Circuits

In the preceding two episodes of the *heisei* Gamera trilogy, the giant turtle is cast as a defender of Earth who is out to maintain the balance of Gaia's spiritual energies, whether from human activity or alien invasion. But in *Gamera 3: The Revenge of Iris*, the conflict doesn't seem so simple. What would have happened if he hadn't stopped the union of Ayana and Iris? Is Gamera, like *Godzilla* (2014), driven to prevent any new symbiosis or new form of life, and therefore, is he a conservative protector of the status quo? Despite her biomechanical design, Iris is the first monster of the trilogy to be associated with ancient Japanese folk belief. It seems significant that her "roar" is an unmistakable recording of whale song, more so considering that the movie was released one year after a highly publicized event in Japan that symbolized the growth of the anti-whaling movement: "The first whale watching in Japan was conducted in Bonin Islands in 1998 by a group called "Geisharen 鯨者連" which was formed by groups of domestic and international people including both domestic and international celebrities." (Whale Watch Advisor) This movement, controversial as it was, strongly evoked a nationalistic worship of nature associated with mythic Japan before the invasion of Commodore Perry and Western materialism:

> The Meiji era, 1868–1912, saw the introduction of power-driven vessels with guns designed after the Norwegian style of whaling. However, Japanese fishermen opposed this practice, as they believed it promoted indiscriminate killing of whales. The early Japanese viewed whales as deities of the sea as well as being useful for corralling fish. Many whaling villages built Whale Shrines, or Kujira Jinja, to worship the whales they hunted as gods…. A famous proverb in Japan says, "There's nothing to throw away from a whale except its voice" [Facts about Japan].

If Iris is associated, both through her cetacean roar and the Shinto shrine where her egg is first found, with Japanese nationalism, then Gamera's alignment with U.S. hegemony, like Godzilla's in the Toho films, seems clear. Following this logic suggests a repressed hope that the thwarted Ayana-Iris singularity could have represented a hybrid resistance to Western imperialism. At the end of *Monster Zero*, Glenn and Fuji are surprised to be assigned as "ambassadors" to Planet X, to start over and win a real peace. This utopian postscript is loudly silent about the fate of the real ambassador: the late Namikawa, who was the only being of the two species to sacrifice herself for love and at least dream of alien miscegenation. In the logic of all these stories, this dream is impossible. Ann Darrow can never save King Kong. Emiko was destined to never marry either Ogata or Serizawa. Kyoko's liberation is cut short when her boyfriend takes away earrings that were a gift from someone else. Namikawa is lost, and Ayana is "corrected" by rescue. Yet Ayana's abreaction may serve as a metaphor for the cathartic reconciliation with an unconscious utopian wish that is enabled through cinematic fantasy. Donna Haraway, in her essay on the liberatory energy of the cyborg's wish, writes

> Unlike the hopes of Frankenstein's monster, the cyborg does not expect its father to save it through a restoration of the garden; that is, through the fabrication of a heterosexual mate, through its completion in a finished whole, a city and cosmos. The cyborg does not dream of community on the model of the organic family, this time without the oedipal project. The cyborg would not recognize the Garden of Eden; it is not made of mud and cannot dream of returning to dust. Perhaps that is why I want to see if cyborgs can subvert the apocalypse of returning to nuclear dust in the manic compulsion to name the Enemy.

In the films we have examined, the women and the monsters are sacrificed for the perpetuation of Western, materialistic, imperialist, masculinist hegemony. But at the same time, the *frisson* of their resistance, symbolized by both the spectacularly satisfying rampages of the daikaiju themselves, and the equally fulfilling disobedience of the women, may express a hope for the possibility of rebirth outside and after the cinematic dream: a world that's big enough for life among monsters and women.

Notes

1. #Gamergate was a hashtag trend uniting social media users who were unhappy with what they perceived as undue "political correctness" in video game culture and other American geek culture realms traditionally dominated by men. Beneath the banner of this hashtag, users targeted feminists in the gaming industry for harassment and threats of violence. For more information, see: Hathaway, Jay. "What Is Gamergate, and Why? An Explainer for Non-Geeks." *Gawker*. October 10, 2014. Web. November 16, 2016.

2. Much has been written of feminine jewelry as a marker of male ownership (see, for example, Rebecca Ross Russell's self-published study *Gender and Jewelry: A Feminist Analysis*). The contestation of jewelry as a reassertion of that ownership is enacted in a 1987 song by Prince named "Bob George": "Who bought you that diamond ring? Yeah right! Since when'd you have a job? You seeing that rich motherfucker again!"

Works Cited

Barenblatt, Daniel. *A Plague upon Humanity: The Hidden History of Japan's Biological Warfare Program*. Harper, 2005. Print.
Bouie, Jamelle. "The Deadly History of 'They're Raping Our Women.'" *Slate*. June 18, 2015. Web. December 2, 2016.
Buruma, Ian. *The Wages of Guilt: Memories of War in Germany and Japan*. Phoenix, 2002. Print.

Canning, George. "Papers in Explanation of the Measures Adopted by His Majesty's Government, for the Amelioration of the Condition of the Slave Population in His Majesty's Dominions in the West Indies" Debate in the House of Commons. March 16, 1824. (London: John Murray, 1824), 21–22. Print.
Destroy All Monsters, Directed by Ishiro Honda, Toho, 1968.
Ebert, Roger. "Godzilla." Reviews. RogerEbert.com. July 2, 2004. Web. November 28, 2016.
Eisenberg, Eric. "Read Juliette Binoche's Blunt, Harsh Assessment Of Shooting Godzilla." *Cinemablend*. 2014. Web. October 4, 2016.
Erb, Cynthia. *Tracking King Kong: A Hollywood Icon in World Culture*. Wayne State University Press, 1998. Print.
Facts about Japan. "History of Japanese Whaling." Facts-about-Japan.com. 2016. Web. November 28, 2016.
Figal, Gerald. *Civilization and Monsters: Spirits of Modernity in* Meiji *Japan*. Duke University Press, 1999. Print.
Freud, Sigmund. "Mourning and Melancholia." *The Standard Edition of the Complete Psychological Works of Sigmund Freud*. Vintage, 1999. Print.
Gamera 3: Revenge of Iris, Directed by Shusuke Kaneko, Daiei, 1999.
Godzilla vs. Destoroyah, Directed by Takao Okawara, Toho, 1995.
Gojira, Directed by Ishiro Honda, Toho, 1954.
Good Morning, Vietnam, Directed by Barry Levinson, Walt Disney Pictures, 1987.
Haraway, Donna. "A Cyborg Manifesto: Science, Technology, and Socialist-Feminism in the Late Twentieth Century." *Theorizing Feminism: Parallel Trends in the Humanities and Social Sciences*. Ed. Anne C. Hermann and Abigail J. Stewart. Boulder: Westview Press, 1994. 424–57. Print.
Igarashi, Yoshikuni. *Bodies of Memory: Narratives of War in Postwar Japanese Culture, 1945–1970*. Princeton University Press, 2000. Print.
Inglourious Basterds, Directed by Quentin Tarantino, Universal, 1999.
Kalat, David. *A Critical History and Filmography of Toho's Godzilla Series*, 2nd ed. McFarland, 2010. Print.
Kikuchi, Daisuke. "Actor Yuta Takahata arrested for alleged sexual assault of hotel staffer." August 24, 2016. *Japan Times*. Web. November 16, 2016.
King Kong, Directed by Merian C. Cooper and Ernest B. Schoedsack, Radio Pictures, 1933.
Kristeva, Julia. *Powers of Horror: An Essay on Abjection*. Leon S. Roudiez, transl. Columbia University Press, 1982. Print.
Milner, David. "Takao Okawara Interview III." Yoshihiko Shibata, transl. December 1998. *Kaiju Conversations*. Web. November 28, 2016.
Monster Zero, Directed by Ishiro Honda, Toho, 1965.
Rich, Adrienne. "Women and Honor: Some Notes on Lying." *On Lies, Secrets, and Silence: Selected Prose*. Norton: 1979. January 4, 2005. Web.
Shen, Sigmund. "Monster of Mourning, Ritual of Remembering: Ishiro Honda's *Gojira*." *Reconstruction* Vol. 13, No. 3/4. 2013. Web. 1 Nov. 2016.
Soul Man, Directed by Steve Miner, New World Pictures, 1986.
Whale Watch Advisor. "Whale Watching." Web. September 1, 2016.

Soft Power
Narrative of Neutrality in King Kong Escapes and Frankenstein Conquers the World

FERNANDO GABRIEL PAGNONI BERNS
and EMILIANO AGUILAR

There are not many things that say "Japan" as the mighty figure of *Gojira* (Godzilla), the towering lizard that began stomping Tokyo in 1954. Like Hello Kitty, Godzilla quickly become a national icon, an image of "pop-nationalism" recognizable as a "made in Japan property" even if mostly saw as a cheesy figure for foreign audiences (Kushner 74). The man-within-a-rubber-monster-suit is a well-known trope in Japan and was adopted by other Asian nations including North Korea (Sang-ok Shin's *Pulgasari* in 1985). However, it seems that nobody does *kaiju* better than Japan. Creatures such as Godzilla and the flying turtle Gamera have fought a plethora of monsters through the years, all of them easily recognizable as Japanese; however, there were exceptions and some kaiju films used foreign monsters as their main menace. *Kingu Kongu tai Gojira* (*King Kong vs. Godzilla*, Ishiro Honda, 1962) was an effort to unite nationalistic issues of both Japan and United States to the point that it was rumored that two endings were filmed to protect the dignity of both national monsters (Kalat 48): in one, made for Japanese audiences, Godzilla wins, while in the other, made for American viewers, King Kong is the creature who ends the battle triumphant. While, in fact, this rumor was proven false, it nonetheless demonstrates the importance of safeguarding nationhood.

It seems, at first, that *King Kong vs. Godzilla* remains an oddity within kaiju film, the only example in which an American monster takes center stage in the Godzilla franchise. Two kaiju films, however, continued the idea of international monsters battling within Japanese terrain: *Kingu Kongu no Gyakushu* (*King Kong Escapes*, Ishiro Honda, 1967) revolves around King Kong brought in by evil Doctor Who (Hideyo Amamoto) to dig for the highly radioactive Element X at the North Pole when the robot Mechani-Kong is unable to do the task. *Furankenshutain tai Chitei Kaiju Baragon* (*Frankenstein Conquers the World*, Ishiro Honda, 1965) tells about Frankenstein's heart, taken by Nazis from a lab in Europe and kept in a Japanese lab, where it gets exposed to the radiation of the bombing of Hiroshima. The heart is eaten by a young boy who survived the destruction of Hiroshima. He starts to grow at a rapid pace until resembling a giant, Americanized version of Frankenstein's monster.

In both films, the monsters are American, thus Toho was obliged to engage with Japan's relationship with the U.S.; also, they are transnational affairs in nature (one of them a co-production). As a result, it is interesting to investigate where Japan fits within this "monster-land." In this regard, it should be kept in mind that kaiju is all things hybrid: a fusion of cultures, styles, genres and identities, accelerated in part by the developments in media circulation, without eliminating Japan's particular traditional values and aesthetics.

We will argue that following the process of national identity built upon a narrative of neutrality, victimization, and historical amnesia (Flores 91), the films mostly use Japan and Japanese as neutral observers, victims/toys of transnational business. In this sense, these films works as forms of "soft power" (which rests centrally upon state's diplomacy, general culture and popular culture circulation), i.e., transnational pop cultural artifacts which, in one hand, cope intellectually with national decline (Leheni 212) and in the other, were a way for establishing national identity in the global order in the postwar era. Soft power is an analytical tool increasingly used in relation with popular culture (Press-Barnathan 29) since the latter is a perfect mechanism to channel social anxieties regarding nationhood. Through this framework, we will make a close reading of two overlooked Honda's films to point the ways in which transnational popular culture meets national constructions of identity.

Americanization, Popular Culture and Soft Power

Americanization is a specific process of Westernization, through thought and action, in which U.S. culture and values have a decisive influence on the culture of another country; undoubtedly reflecting U.S. success in the military, economic, cultural and diplomatic spheres. This influence is to such a degree that the Americanized countries assimilate the American culture as their own, producing a sort of hybridization or overlapping of national interests. Some of the main elements that make up this cultural influence are the media (including cinema) and large multinational companies (representatives of late capitalism that exploded with the phenomenon of globalization). Such circulation of images and discourses, along with the Marshall Plan propaganda, promoted "politics of productivity," asserting that these images of the "American way of life" reflected "the demand side of the economic and social transformation, speeding and channeling the changes in mentality and behaviour" towards an Americanized "era of high mass consumption" (Zeitlin 7).

After the military occupation of Japan by U.S. after World War II, political and material circumstances dramatically (almost traumatically) changed. Japan was stripped of its former colonies and colonial holdings, including Korea, Taiwan, Palau, and the Pacific islands; through the occupation, monarchy was abolished and a democratic government was forcefully installed by the American occupation. The military occupation forced a modernization on a country still largely feudal, with the emperor at the center, now dethroned in favor of democratic values. If an economic success to the point that it can be called a "miracle," all these societal, economic, political, and cultural changes had a profound social effect on Japan's sense of nationhood and identity, causing anxieties around the demise of traditional religion and the political system (Forsberg). The trauma of defeat left scars on Japan's national psyche which have never fully gone away, and many horror films from the 1950s onwards would "signal metonymically the continuing impact of the Second World War on Japan" (Balmain 22).

We can find two kinds of powers here: First, the deployment of what some call "hard power" in the form of coercive occupation of a national territory by direct military and economic intervention (Chong 5). On the other hand, there is another form of domination constituted through the dynamics of "soft power," which rested more on cultural factors such as symbolic values or institutions and can be conceptualized "as the ability to produce outcomes through attraction instead of coercion" (Chong 2). This form of cooptive power may be channeled via popular culture and social and cultural discourses, resulting in an occupied nation defining its own national interests in ways consistent with those of the occupying country. In the case of the American occupation of Japan, Western values of democratic freedom and individual expression were imposed through the cooption of Japanese cinema.

One of the most popular forms of soft power is through diplomatic interventions and specific foreign policy prescriptions. The other one, already mentioned and of particular interest for this essay, is via popular culture or the ability to co-opt others through the attractiveness of images and discourses transmitted via media: "The jousting of ideological discourse in an intensely globally mediated public space—manifested by 24-hour press, television and Internet—necessarily introduces considerations of soft power" (Chong 22). How can popular culture defend or project national political and cultural sense of belonging and identity using soft power to articulate their particular existence in the information space opened up by a world gone global after World War II?

Basically, American ideals were imposed upon Japan through military intervention and the material occupation of the land. Within this coercion in which Japanese studies and directors were obliged to comply with American dictates, there was a form of soft power running parallel to the hard forms. Soft power is just as valuable as hard power to boost cohesive images of nationhood because it could reflects identity's sensitivities. Soon, Coca-Cola and other American brands were everyday items and well-known names within Japanese culture, slowly replacing a national sense of Japanese identity for a naturalization of American way of life.

Of course, the circulation and reading of products of popular culture is not univocal. As has been stated, popular culture is integral to the dissemination of hegemonic thinking. In traditional readings, it was common to distinguish between highbrow culture, including literature, and popular culture, including mass entertainment. Popular cultural products have the benefit of eliciting and renewing the readings through history; this is not to deny that popular culture is often a resource that produces soft power, but "the effectiveness of any power resource depends on the context" (Nye, Jr. 12). In this sense, popular culture is "more likely to attract people and produce soft power in the sense of preferred outcomes in situations where cultures are somewhat similar rather than widely dissimilar" (Nye, Jr. 14–5). If true that all power depends on context, "soft power depends more than hard power upon the existence of willing interpreters and receivers" (Nye, Jr. 15).

Soft power manifests itself most clearly in *King Kong vs. Godzilla*. After all, Godzilla is globally known as the "king of the monsters." When facing Kong, Godzilla reassures his own global status as a giant monster while Kong reminds audiences that he was there first, since he was the first giant monster to occupy the big screen to scare audiences worldwide. Neither monster nor the battle is totally implausible for audiences habituated to kaiju. There is more feedback between American and Japanese cultures than just two big creatures; we must keep in mind that the American 1950s was the decade for antonomasia for filmic giant monsters, stomping many cities and citizens to bits. Before *Gojira* (Ishiro Honda, 1954) there was *The Beast from 20.000 Fathoms* (Eugene Lourie, 1953), another giant dinosaur awakened by an Arctic atomic test. Scholars reaffirm the idea that *Gojira* is merely an imitation of Lourie's film (Shapiro 273; Ryfle 19). Thus, it is possible to claim there would be no Godzilla if not for these American monsters, even if the King of Monsters is a creation imbedded in Japanese culture. The circulation of giant monsters, with their characteristics and tropes, is highly mobile and global rather than unidirectional; thus, amidst this battle of international giant creatures, critics can trace values and objectives supporting forms of soft power. What remains to be interpreted is how the politics of soft power inform the action within these films, and what place both America and Japan occupy within this scheme. In other words, which image of nationhood do these films promote and legitimize?

For almost any Japanese kaiju film, there is an Americanized version, as American production companies bought many kaiju films only to recut and dub them with the order of scenes changed before showing them to American audiences (Guthrie-Shimizu 59). The influence of America upon Japan and Godzilla was so strong that the giant lizard itself was transformed into a juvenile narrative in the late 1960s in Japan. The feedback was far from unidirectional; instead, it was a back and forth negotiation between the two nations. In parallel, the power plays between Japan and America taking place within the films also were far from been fixed. Rather, the films support shifting point of views and categories of evilness and monstrosity. Still, the image of Japan as a mute witness to American proceedings prevails, legitimating a construction of neutrality and stoicism framing the Japanese characters. We will point out the conflicting ways in which Japan depicts itself and America within these monsters/nationalities mash-ups. If popular culture is a medium through which people around the world constantly reorganize their individual and collective identities, then, how Japan formulates nationhood within these examples of international kaiju?

Victimization, Evilness and Japanese Passivity

King Kong Escapes (an U.S.–Japanese co-production) establishes its transnational nature since the first scene. Three scientific researchers, aboard a submarine, travel around the world on a mission led by America. Two of the investigators, Commander Carl Nelson (Rhodes Reason) and Susan Watson (Linda Miller) are Americans while the other, Jiro Nomura (Akira Takarada) is Japanese. Within the submarine, both men share duties, but it is actually Nelson who gives the orders and makes the most important decisions. When the submarine malfunctions, it is Nelson who commands the vessel to surface. It is he who explains that the mission cannot go to Kong's island since time cannot be wasted and it is he who decides to visit—what else?—Kong's island when there is time to spend while the submarine is under repair. Also, Nelson can translate ancient languages (those that the natives on Kong's island speak), demonstrating that American men of science are well prepared. Nomura goes through the film mostly nodding to what Nelson says. It is interesting to note that when the submarine crashes with the bottom of the sea after some malfunctioning, Nelson remains unscratched while Nomura is hurt; this contrast suggests that Japanese may not be up to the task.

The film has two main villains plus a robotic giant ape. Doctor Who is an international terrorist who rents his services and intelligence on robotics to those who can pay for them. His new client is evil Madame Piranha (Mie Hama), an Asian woman who has bought Mechani-Kong, a mechanized/robotized replica of King Kong. The giant robot has been built so it can extract highly radioactive material from the depths of Earth.

Under the frame of a kaiju film, *King Kong Escapes* is indebted to another product of popular culture: The James Bond spy formula (so popular in the 1960s), an ideal narrative to speak about transnational inscriptions. There are gadgets (microphones passing for lipsticks), transnational treason, global affairs, and a campy villain. Doctor Who clearly refers to the main villain of *Dr. No* (Terence Young, 1962), James Bond's first venture into film. Doctor Who also displays all the camp traits associated with Bond's villains: colorful outfits (in this case, a silver-lined long cape), a propensity to long, evil speeches and, of course, a name that only Bond's villains can use. Also, he does not respond to any nation but to his own interests.

Frankenstein Conquers the World is also an international affair. The references to Victor Frankenstein links the story to Mary Shelley and, by extension, to Great Britain and their national monster: the creature made with dead parts and reanimated by a mad doctor who believes himself above God. But there is more. The creature, as is seen in the film, is depicted as wearing all of the tropes heavily associated with the American production. The monster of *Frankenstein Conquers the World* has the Neanderthal look, the square flat head, the sleepy, liquid eyes, the ill-fitting suit and black hair of the main creature of *Frankenstein* (James Whale, 1932). In other words, the monster of Honda's film is easily recognized as the American monster rather than a Japanese reinvention of the same creature. Clearly, this is not by chance, but an important choice made to appeal international audiences that were well aware of the filmic appearance of the creature and take that for granted—as if the monster could not look differently.

Like *King Kong Escapes*, this film begins in "international mode" as well, with a laboratory filled with steaming tubs and jars containing colorful liquids, a scenario easily recognizable as "mad-man laboratory" for international audiences habituated to American Universal and British Hammer horror films. Also, the scenery works as signpost to science and progress. There, a scientist—we can presume Victor Frankenstein—holds the heart of his monster. Nazi commanders come to the laboratory and request the monster's heart, which is taken away. The group of Nazis entering the castle to take

Frankenstein's heart refers to the Nazi-busting spy movies of the 30s and 40s, in which Germans are seen as an antagonistic force that irrupts from the outside to appropriate foreign work, science or art. It could be drawn a parallel between this usurpation and American occupation of Japan after Second World War when Americans took advantage of the weakened Japan.

Is the British doctor collaborating with the Axis? Is the action taking place in Britain? Since the doctor remains silent, a sense of concrete space and fixity is carefully avoided, clear geographical boundaries supplanted by a sense of transnationality, a sort of hybrid geography that highlights decontextualization, depoliticization and dehistoricization. A Nazi submariner takes aboard the beating monster heart to meet another sub, one conducting Japanese soldiers aboard, which have the mission to take the cargo from the Germans' hands. Scholar Jason Barr calls this scene "an unusually frank acknowledgment of World War II Japan's alliance with the Nazis" (108), since kaiju mostly obliterates this fact, preferring to depict Japan as neutral zone. But at the last minute, the ethical values of Japan are safeguarded. The Japanese soldiers seem to be in the dark about most of their mission ("what is it that they want us to take?") and when they learn about the nature of their cargo, they are disgusted, tensing the collaborations between Japan and Germany and deterring some issues about evilness through the conformation of a concept of Otherness. "They," Germans, are disgusting because their experimentations on humans, while Japan is presented as alien to the idea of experimenting upon people. However, if true that many nations in World War II experimented with biological weapons of war, particularly anthrax, "Japan was the only belligerent who pursued a wide variety of such weapons using human guinea pigs for research on a large scale, and then employing pathogens as weapons of war" (Gruhl 81) after subjecting abused human beings "to unethical experiments" (Cohen 159).

There are some hints, however, about Madame Piranha's nationality. In a scene, Nomura, Nelson and Susan are made prisoners and taken at the presence of Doctor Who. While the evil criminal and Nelson chat, the camera frames Nomura's face in close shot while he is looking intently at Madame Piranha, who cast down her gaze to avoid eye contact. Madame Piranha's attitude can be read as shame as the two recognize themselves as part of the same country, being Nomura Japanese. Lastly, she is troubled about the fact that Tokyo could be destroyed if Kong and Mechani-Kong engage in battle in middle of the city.

Deterritorialization is enhanced in both films. In fact, Frankenstein is referred as a "German scientific" rather than British, furthering the idea of placing inhuman traits only on Germany's side, and downplaying Japanese complicity. This way, an idea of "passive witnesses" is slowly formulated. Japanese are collaborating with Nazi Germany, but only to some extent. Human qualities such as the capacity of being horrified are still alive within Japan, while Germans are configured as truly monstrous and evil. Speaking of Frankenstein's heart, a Japanese scientific (Takashi Shimura) comments about the organ's properties, which can be useful to help people, especially soldiers who had died in the war. Thus, the film highlights the fact that Japan wants the monstrous organ only to make good things with it.

The laboratory containing the monster's heart is destroyed by nuclear bombing, in an explicit reference to the attack that Hiroshima suffered in August 5. The action cuts to fifteen years later, establishing the economic miracle which Japan has undergone, since the next shot is one of social progress. A close shot frames a plaque describing the International Institute of Radiotherapentics [sic] in two languages, Japanese and English; the English language already embedded at an institutional level. In addition, the institution's main physician is the blonde and American Dr. Bowen (Nick Adams). Famous for his performance as Johnny Yuma a former confederate soldier-turned novelist in TV series *The Rebel* (ABC, 1959–1961), Adams was one of the first to make "eastbound trip" (Ryfle 129) to star in films produced by Toho since from 1965–1969, the studio collaborated with Hollywood producers "to import second-tier American stars to Japan" (ibid.).

Dr. Bowen laments the aftermath of the bomb in Kazuko (Keiko Sawai), a hospitalized young girl, but he highlights the importance that these consequences have for research on human cell tissue: his Japanese collaborator just nods. Bowen is a metonymy of American power, the one who is in charge of voicing and action, while Japan is just a passive witness of the horror inflicted upon the country. Dr. Bowen also has the mission of exculpating America of the nuclear bombing: "Yeah. The story of Hiroshima is tragic, but it's giving us an opportunity to study the cellular tissue of the body. It's ironic, but science progresses this way. We've got to work to turn tragedy into happiness for the future." The future of who is he exactly talking about is ambiguous, since Bowen states his decision to return to America after finishing his investigations in Japan.

Many times Dr. Bowen ponders about Kazuko endurance in tragedy. She knows that death is close, but she hurries herself to give the finishing touches to embroidery that she is making for her doctor as a gift. Her calm attitude before death has a doubly meaning: first, she is making a gift for an *American* doctor, thus addressing him as a friend rather than an enemy guilty of her current situation. Second, the film depicts Japanese (and by extension, Japan) as stoic victims, enduring pain and tragedy in silence. According to Edwards, because of the "blanket censorship," Japan avoided looking at the deadly tragedy of the nuclear bombing as an atrocity, focusing instead on the "daily reality of survival and rebuilding their decimated landscapes and infrastructures" (69), because their survival instinct dictated to them "to serve their basic primal needs and not to drag up the atrocities of the not-so distant past" (ibid.). In this sense, Kazuko is exemplary in her total lack of any kind of grudge against the American invaders.

Bowen cooks wearing an apron and hat with the colors of the American flag while teaching love-interest Dr. Sueko Togami (Kumi Mizuno) how to cook the meat, thus reflecting the desire of the Japanese to "be like the Americans." The major contradiction of *Frankenstein Conquers the World* is that while it warns viewers of the weakness of the Japanese and their potential dependence on U.S., depicts Americans as both, pro-active and the film's real "good" guys, the ones in whom Japanese place their trust.

However, Bowen is a character with contradictions. He addresses himself as guilty of collaborating in the bomb's creation (as an American), but has ambitions to help humanity investigating the consequences of this tragedy. When Bowen and his assistant travel to the village where a monstrous child supposedly lives, both stop to visit some beautiful Japanese landscapes. Through a short sequence, a series of vistas display the beauty and exoticism of Japan, Bowen's gaze overlapping with that of the Western viewers among the audience. When describing Japan through travelogues, the obsession of Western visual culture for spectacles of Otherness is enhanced. But in the presentation at the filmgoer's gaze of the spectacle of exoticism lies a "certain disavowal of that exoticism, a desire to mark what is Other and then contain it" (Fuhrmann 193) through the exercise of soft power via visual media.

On the other hand, Madame Piranha, the only evil Asian character of the two films (being Dr. Who depicted as "an international Judas"), has contradictions of her own. As a pro-active character, she re-establishes Japan as a nation associated with pure evil, here embodied in the transnational figure of Dr. Who. As a man who does not respond either to the Soviets or Allies, Dr. Who can be read as Nazi, especially since he seems interested in world domination. Madame Piranha ruptures the framing of Japan as a mute and passive witnesses. At the last minute, however, she has a change of heart and helps Nomura, Susan, and Nelson escape from Dr. Who's hands, even if this action means her death. Like Kazuko, an Asian woman once again stoically accepts death while rewarding America. The latter can be read as the attitude that Japan takes after the nuclear bombing and its defeat after World War II. As Adam Lowenstein argues, Japan adopted an attitude of victimization, replacing responsibility for past national aggressions and colonial ventures for an image of global frailty. Through the adopting of victimization "that refuses to acknowledge connections between Hiroshima and Japanese wartime aggression" (Lowenstein 91), Japan eludes any responsibility for its own crimes, while depicting itself, as in the films here analyzed, as neutral and victimized at the eyes of the world. As we will see in the following section, the depiction of Americans as the real heroes of the film parallels the ways in which the main monsters of both films are constructed. While "American" monsters help Japan and could be read as "good guys," "real" Asian creatures are either too weak or brute, undermining any image of Japan as a potential menace to the world.

Monster Brawl: Japan 0, America 2

The first scene of *King Kong Escapes* establishes Kong as the more powerful creature and thus, implicitly, downplays Godzilla's might. It can be argued that Kong is from Skull Island rather than America; however, everything once colonized by the U.S., be it the moon or some God-forgotten island, becomes property of America once its citizens step in. If Kong is coded as an American monster, Mechani-Kong is coded as Japanese or, at least, Asian.

As mentioned earlier, there are no explicit clues about the nationalities of the film two main villains, Dr. Who and Madame Piranha. Still, both are interpreted as Asian performers. Since Mechani-Kong has been built to help those villains, he is clearly Asian in nature. In this sense, if in the first scene Kong is deemed as the strongest of all monsters, the Asian Mechani-Kong is not up to the task. After descending to the depths to extract material X, Mechani-Kong suffers from severe malfunctions caused by the substance's magnetic waves and get "stuck" and almost unusable. So, the solution is to kidnap the real King Kong, the strongest of all, to accomplish the task that this weak, emasculated and malfunctioning Japanese invention cannot properly do.

It is compelling that Kong's love interest is an American woman rather than an Asian one. Blond haired, Fay Wray–like Susan is the woman who wakes up Kong's basic instincts; thus, American women are eroticized as objects of desire, while Japanese women, both in *King Kong Escapes* and *Frankenstein Conquers the World*, follow the traditional depiction of Asian women as passive, sexless figures who exist to serve men. The latter helps built up the depiction of Japan mostly as a passive, mute witness to the events taking place before their neutral eyes.

The main monster of *Frankenstein Conquers the World* is a boy who, starved after the nuclear bombing, has eaten Frankenstein's heart (the film always refers to the doctor's name, even when it should be understood that they are speaking about the creature) and in consequence, has started to grow, until reaching towering dimensions. After 15 years, the feral boy is captured by Dr. Bowen and studied. Even when well-fed, the creature is a source of anxiety and fears, similar to the weaponry of an armed nation. The grown monster could be read as parallel to the occupation: first, the nuclear bombing has attacked those weak women (Kazuko) and children (the boy), inflicting scars, killing them with radiation or starving them. Then, like the monster itself, is (uneasily) accepted within the Japanese community and feed, fearful as they are of any potential aggression (respect to "hard" power). Finally, when the monster (Koji Furuhata) breaks free, a weakened Japan will need him to defeat ancestral Japan, which has risen in the form of the giant dinosaur Baragon, a monster which potentially will erase all cities. It should be kept in mind that the Frankenstein creature is "not Japanese, but Caucasian," as if the blood and flesh of the heart turned the Asian young boy into a Western creature. Caucasian here works as a synonym of "whiteness" in contrast with "yellow" Japanese, thus establishing a parallel between the creature and Americans. When a journalist suggests that the creature maybe has mixed blood, Dr. Bowen quickly denies this possibility: "he is definitively a Caucasian." Also, there is a possibility that the boy is not Asian at all, since there is no scene of the unmutated boy eating the heart. It is fair to conclude the menace is meant to be seen as truly foreign, as the name "Frankenstein," geographically situated outside Japan, also indicates.

The monster's captivity also exhibits American cinematic traditions as Frankenstein gets increasingly uneasy when journalists and TV reporters blind the monster with camera flashes in a scene that seems lifted from *King Kong* (Merian C. Cooper and Ernest B. Schoedsack, 1933). American popular culture is additionally displayed in another scene in which the monster watches TV. The image shows a band playing modern music and a group of young Japanese dancing boogie-woogie (with the camera doing close-ups of their butts). As John Dower argues, the Americanization of popular culture was evident in such imports as the boogie-woogie (251). Appropriating elements of American popular culture, Japanese media blended them with the values of their own country "to tie Japan's culture to that of the United States," trying to abolish cultural differences (Chun 66). The monster is shown attracted by the consumption of images and music but, prey to internal contradictions, he throws the TV out the window.

Like Shelley's monster, the creature seeks refuge within the forests (the Kizu Mountains). From there, the monster's gaze is metonymical: America looking "from above" to a diminished Japan. In the mountain Shirane, young people dance, oblivious to what is taking place to their country. Except for a girl who hears a strange noise, no one seems to notice what is happening outside, symptom of a Japan that has closed its eyes to the occupation. That noise is caused by Baragon, a monster who woke up from the bowels of earth to destroy all American paraphernalia. If "Japan's incomplete modernity is often embodied within the figure of the pre-modern monster, a revenant of traditional Japanese culture and mythology, in the horror film, which threatens apocalypse and disaster," Baragon, as a dinosaur who rises from the earth, can be read as the imperial Japan, the traditional fatherland who is shaking off modern, Americanized Japan (Balmain 8). In this scenario, Frankenstein, the foreign, Caucasian monster, must battle Japanese Baragon, which slightly resembles Godzilla since both of them are oversized reptiles. The final battle is America versus Japan; here, a Manichean approach can be observed in the origins of each character. Frankenstein is depicted as "good" since he has not caused intentional harm to anyone, while Baragon, standing for Japan, is destroying cities and humans alike.

In the epic battles closing the stories, King Kong destroys his weak, robotic counterpart. After all, Mechani-Kong, as a copy, recognizes the superior value of the American original. Within this scenario of weak, emasculated Japan, Frankenstein wins the battle, killing Baragon amidst a sea of fire, and thus reinstating the status quo of a Japan ideologically dominated by America. At the last minute, Frankenstein also succumbs and fell through the crevices that had opened in the landscape. But his honor remains intact. When Dr. Sueko mentions Frankenstein's potential death, Dr. Bowen promptly answers: "No, he's an immortal creature. He'll always survive." Japan is safe now, and the citizens are ready to spend some more time watching Japanese dance on TV, butts framed in close shots.

Conclusions

Even though Japanese filmmakers have taken kaiju and made them their own, the idea of a giant monster stomping a city is not entirely Japanese. The introduction of American monsters within the Japanese genre as kaiju makes it necessary to formulate definitions of America and national identity; thus, kaiju incorporates elements of Western film which, despite being imposed and refuted, mutates or hybridizes in cohesion of procedures and style inherited from a Japanese aesthetic that has never been abandoned entirely, not even during the occupation.

Popular culture as a form of soft power is a suitable channel to the dissemination of discourses about nationhood within the global flow. In the current era of the globalization of manga and anime, it is urgent to understand and read the many ways in which Japan has presented itself and America, the "alien" body within, to the world. Following an overpowering idea of Japan as neutral and victimized, these kaiju films with American monsters as guest stars depict Japanese characters mostly in the margins, observing rather than interacting, nodding rather than doing. Evil is placed within a vague concept of Otherness in which Nazis (*Frankenstein Conquers the World*) or transnational villains who stand for Nazism (*King Kong Escapes*) excuses Japan of any responsibility. Truly Japanese monsters stand for a traditional Japan that must be overcome by modernization (Baragon) or are merely weak copies of American creatures (Mechani-Kong). This downplaying of Japanese culture reinforces the belief that Japan stands at the margins of international affairs as neutral witnesses to American actions taking place on Japanese land.

Now, these images answer to the politics of soft power, but who is winning with these films? In fact, both the United States and Japan are positioned where they want to be. America is at the top, an image that benefits the construction of American identity, while Japan is a silent and stoic victim that legitimates and reinforces the image that Japan is trying to communicate about the global scenario in the postwar era. In brief, within the kaiju genre, the battling of monsters masks the battling of national constructions of identity; however, unlike with the creatures fighting colossal/silly battles, both countries win when the filmic depictions fit easily within their respective interests regarding nationhood. Kaiju foregrounds soft power's lasting potential for drawing two adversaries closer in vision and in practice.

Works Cited

Allison, Anne. "Cutting the Fringes: Pubic Hair at the Margins of Japanese Censorship Laws." *Hair: Its Power and Meaning in Asian Cultures*, edited by A. Hiltebeital and B. D. Miller, New York University Press, 1998, 195–218.
Anderson, Joseph L. and Donald Richie. *The Japanese Film: Art and Industry* (expanded edition). Princeton University Press, 1982.
Balmain, Colette. *Introduction to Japanese Horror Film*. Edinburgh University Press, 2008.
Barr, Jason. *The Kaiju Film: A Critical Study of Cinema's Biggest Monsters*. McFarland, 2015.
Chaong, Alan. *Foreign Policy in Global Information Space: Actualizing Soft Power*. Palgrave Macmillan, 2007.
Chun, Jayson Makoto. "Pro Wrestling and Crying Cowboys. American Influence on Early Japanese Television," *Modernization, Nation-Building, and Television History*, edited by Stewart Anderson and Melissa Chakars. Routledge, 2015, 55–73.
Cohen, Cynthia. *Renewing the Stuff of Life: Stem Cells, Ethics, and Public Policy*. Oxford University Press, 2007.
Dower, John. *Embracing Defeat: Japan in the Wake of World War II*. The New Press.
Edwards, Matthew. "Suppression and Censorship: Japanese Cinema during the Occupation." *The Atomic Bomb in Japanese Cinema: Critical Essays*, edited by Matthew Edwards. McFarland, 2015, 69–76.
Flores, Marcello. "Occupier, Occupied: The Double Reality of Japanese Identity." *Legacies of the U.S. Occupation of Japan: Appraisals after Sixty Years*, edited by Rosa Caroli and Duccio Basosi. Cambridge Scholars Publishing, 2014.
Forsberg, Aaron. *America and the Japanese Miracle: The Cold War Context of Japan's Postwar Economic Revival, 1950–1960*. The University of North Carolina Press, 2000.
Fuhrmann, Wolfgang. *Imperial Projections: Screening the German Colonies*. Berghahn, 2015.
Gruhl, Werner. *Imperial Japan's World War Two: 1931–1945*. Transaction Publishers, 2007.
Guthrie-Shimizu, Sayuri. "Lost in translation and Morphed in Transit: Godzilla in Cold War America." In *Godzilla's Footsteps: Japanese Pop Culture Icons on the Global Stage*, edited by William Tsutsui and Michiko Ito, Palgrave Macmillan, 2006, 51–62.
Kalat, David. *A Critical History and Filmography of Toho's Godzilla Series*. McFarland, 1997.
Kushner, Barak. "*Gojira* as Japan's First Postwar Media Event." In *Godzilla's Footsteps: Japanese Pop Culture Icons on the Global Stage*, edited by William Tsutsui and Michico Ito. Palgrave Macmillan, 2006.
Leheni, David. "A Narrow Place to Cross Swords: "Soft Power" and the Politics of Japanese

Popular Culture in East Asia." *Beyond Japan: The Dynamics of East Asian Regionalism*, edited by Peter J. Katzenstein and Takashi Shiraishi. Cornell University Press, 2006.

Lowenstein, Adam. *Shocking Representation: Historical Trauma, National Cinema, and the Modern Horror Film*. Columbia University Press, 2005.

Mayo, Marlene. "To Be or not to Be: Kabuki and Cultural Politics in Occupied Japan." *War, Occupation, and Creativity: Japan and East Asia, 1920–1960*, edited by Marlene Mayo and Thomas Rimer, University of Hawaii Press, 2001, 269–309.

Nye, Jr., Joseph. *Soft Power: The Means to Success in World Politics*. PublicAffairs, 2004.

Press-Barnathan, Galia. "Does Popular Culture matter to International Relations Scholars? Possible Links and Methodological Challenges." *Popular Culture and the State in East and Southeast Asia*, edited by Nissim Otmazgin and Eyal Ben-Ari, Routledge, 2012, 29–45.

Richie, Donald. *Japanese Cinema. An Introduction*. Oxford University Press, 1990.

Ryfle, Steve. *Japan's Favorite Mon-star: The Unauthorized Biography of "The Big G."* ECW Press, 1998.

Shapiro, Jerome. *Atomic Bomb Cinema: The Apocalyptic Imagination on Film*. Routledge, 2002.

Zeitlin, Jonathan. "Introduction: Americanization and its Limits: Reworking U.S. Technology and Management in Post-War Europe and Japan." *Americanization and its Limits. Reworking U.S. Technology and Management in Post-war Europe and Japan*, edited by Jonathan Zeitlin and Gary Herrigel, Oxford University Press, 2000, 1–52.

The Confused Nation
Hitoshi Matsumoto's Big Man Japan

Kenta McGrath

In Hitoshi Matsumoto's mockumentary *Big Man Japan* (*Dai Nipponjin*, 2007), Masaru Daisato (played by the director) is an unremarkable Japanese citizen who transforms into a kaiju-fighting giant of the film's title when his nipples are zapped with electricity. Employed by the Ministry of Defense, which calls upon him whenever there is a kaiju threat, Big Man Japan battles a series of grotesque foes ranging from the Stink Monster, which emits an odor as powerful as 10,000 human feces, to the Evil Stare Monster, something resembling a testicle with a massive trunk/penis, on the end of which rests a giant eyeball. Whether big or small, Daisato is low in social stature. Despite being a sixth-generation kaiju fighter of heroic lineage, he is an uncharismatic middle-aged loner living in a low-rent suburban house, separated from his wife and denied regular access to his eight-year-old daughter. And although he serves a public need, as all superheroes do in some way, the public despises him for his mediocrity. He struggles to maintain ratings for his televised bouts and is forced to rent out parts of his body as ad space by his exploitative manager (played by singer Ua). While the latter drives around in a luxury jeep and owns two Afghan dogs named Sympathy and Delicacy, Daisato rides buses, trains, and a scooter, and cares for an unnamed stray cat.

Big Man Japan is an unorthodox entry in the *kaiju eiga* ("kaiju film") genre and performs an unusual double act, from which the film derives much of its humor and meaning. It is a parody of the kaiju film that pushes the genre to ludicrous new highs—or rather, lows—but is for the most part a realist tale grounded in the everyday, observing the minutiae of a superhero's non-heroic existence within a society that fails to appreciate or acknowledge his hard work. Matsumoto's direction emphasizes both the pathos and farce of this narrative in equal measure. Most of the film comprises of a documentary crew observing Daisato's uneventful everyday life as he performs mundane tasks such as shopping, cooking and commuting. When he receives word of an imminent attack, Daisato visits a dilapidated government facility—there are three remaining in the country, down from fifty-two in the "golden years" of his (now senile) grandfather's reign—to be transformed into Big Man Japan in a low-fi backroom ceremony. In contrast to the monotony of the faux-documentary sequences, which unfold in drab suburban settings and across long, languid takes, the kaiju battles are relatively snappy and colorful affairs represented in third-rate CGI. Far from the drawn-out spectacles as seen in many kaiju films, these battles tend to be brief, usually ending with the sudden and unspectacular death of the kaiju after a few gags are offered.

What is curious about *Big Man Japan*, besides its offbeat humor, is the film's ambivalent relationship with the kaiju film. Although William Tsutsui suggests that *Big Man Japan* "combines a heartfelt nostalgia for the golden age of Toho science-fiction films with a scathing critique of Japan's cynical and troubled twenty-first century society" (210), it is only easy to agree with the latter half of this statement. It is difficult to see how exactly the film expresses a "heartfelt nostalgia" for it appears to be wholly dismissive of kaiju films, refusing to take them seriously on any level above their superficial, kitsch qualities. Matsumoto ridicules, and eventually seems to reject, this bastion of Japanese popular culture, yet the film simultaneously upholds key (albeit less obvious) tropes of the kaiju film in order to mount its critique of contemporary Japanese society. Despite Matsumoto's seeming indifference towards the genre, *Big Man Japan* remains a kaiju film all the same, and it maintains the tradition of social and political critique that began with the very first kaiju film, Ishiro Honda's *Godzilla* (*Gojira*, 1954). Like many of its predecessors, there is more than meets than the eye to Matsumoto's film. Moving beyond popular entertainment, *Big Man Japan* raises pertinent questions about Japan's troubled sense of national and cultural identity in the twenty-first century, using the kaiju film as a vehicle to mount this critique, as well as highlighting the genre as a legitimate object of critique itself.

Matsumoto/Matchan

Given that Matsumoto has a radically different public profile in Japan than outside of it, it is useful to address the filmmaker behind the film before discussing what the film does. While *Big Man Japan* served as the West's introduction to Matsumoto—the film's star, director and producer—he has long been a giant of Japanese popular culture. Like Takeshi Kitano, an elder counterpart he admires, Matsumoto started in comedy before becoming a TV superstar and turned to filmmaking with a massive reputation (and equally massive public expectations) already in place. And like Kitano, Matsumoto is a prolific multi-disciplinarian who juggles creative roles, having directed films, produced for television and radio, and written over a dozen books.

Matsumoto shot to fame as one half of the hugely popular and influential *manzai* (a traditional form of Japanese stand-up comedy) duo Downtown, of which he has been a member since 1982 with partner Masatoshi Hamada (aka Hamachan). The duo became renowned for its unconventional comedic style, centered around ad-libbed gags focusing on mundane topics, delivered in an often rambling and conversational manner (rather than the snappy and tightly choreographed banter usually seen in *manzai* acts). Matsumoto played the simple-minded fool, or the *boke* role, while Hamada played the *tsukkomi*, or the straight person, who would often reprimand Matsumoto's stupidity through slapstick violence. Kitano too shot to fame for his *boke* role in a famed *manzai* duo, Two Beat, with partner Niro Kaneko (aka Beat Kiyoshi). Both Kitano and Matsumoto have nicknames for their popular TV/comedic personas and use their full names as filmmakers: Kitano is commonly known as "Beat Takeshi," while Matsumoto is affectionately known as "Matchan."

The parallels between these two filmmakers were not lost on the Japanese media, many of whom were quick to suggest Matsumoto was Kitano's successor after *Big Man Japan* premiered at the 2007 Directors' Fortnight in Cannes. Although Matsumoto's status as a filmmaker remains far smaller than Kitano's, particularly outside Japan, *Big Man Japan* was hugely successful, debuting at the top of the Japanese box office and surpassing Kitano's *Glory to the Filmmaker!* (*Kantoku Banzai!*, 2007) in ticket sales. However, while there was a distinct split between the dark themes of Kitano's earliest yakuza films (*Violent Cop* [*Sono otoko, kyobo ni tsuki*, 1989], *Boiling Point* [*San tai Yon ekkusu Jugatsu*, 1990]) and his popular persona, *Big Man Japan* was clearly a continuation, a case of a renowned comedian extending his art into a different medium. This is so despite Matsumoto declaring in 1998, "I won't make a film. What you can do in film isn't *owarai* [a broad term for Japanese TV comedy] but comedy. Comedy and *owarai* are completely different" (quoted in "Matsumoto Hitoshi vs. Katori Shingo"; my translation). The Japanese word Matsumoto uses for "comedy" here is *kigeki*, which implies a degree of pathos, and is quite unlike *owarai*, a form of comedy associated with TV and considered to be far more lowbrow, in which gags are usually manufactured for their own sake. Matsumoto ultimately upholds both comedic traditions in *Big Man Japan*. He embraces dramatic pathos in his nuanced portrayal of a pathetic and downtrodden character, while the film simultaneously showcases a plethora of lowbrow gags that have little bearing on the film's narrative or themes. Incidentally, these two traditions are reflected in the structure of the film: the former is aligned with the documentary sequences and their focus on Daisato's quotidian reality, while the latter finds its strongest expression in the film's farcical kaiju battle sequences.

Because of Matsumoto's ubiquity within Japanese popular culture, the slow-burn, observational documentary approach in *Big Man Japan* should not be seen as an earnest attempt to create an impression of reality, but as an extension of the deadpan style that permeates his work as a comedian. Matsumoto's *boke* persona can be traced in Daisato's simpleminded character, while the drawn-out interviews and languid pacing of the documentary sequences are largely the result of improvisation; Matsumoto has revealed in an interview that there was "fundamentally" no screenplay used for the film and that over half of the interview scenes were ad-libbed, much like his stand-up work ("Matsumoto Hitoshi vs. Katori Shingo"). In recent years, Matsumoto's comedic style has relied heavily on an ill-tempered persona and his spontaneous outbursts. The former trait can be glimpsed in Matsumoto's characterization of Daisato throughout the film—he mumbles his discontent about his life and circumstances regularly in front of the camera—but the latter fails to eventuate. In a humorous series of anti-climaxes that stress his pathetic character, Daisato remains relatively subdued, submissive and mediocre even when he transforms into a giant kaiju-battling superhero; his personality fails to grow in proportion to his size and the public derides him for it.

Matsumoto's penchant for the absurd—most apparent in the film's lineup of kaiju—was already well established in Downtown's raucous variety shows such as *Downtown no Gottsu Ee Kanji* (*Downtown's "Feelin' Good!,"* 1991–1997) and *Downtown no Gaki no Tsukai ya Arahende!!* (*Downtown's "This Is No Job For Kids!!,"* 1989–present), both of which featured an array of bizarre sketches, pranks and characters. Fantastic Fest co-founder Tim League recounts his first encounter with the latter show: "[M]y mind was shattered … forever. In 30 minutes we were assaulted by a rapid-fire barrage of elaborate and gleeful torture challenges and pranks, seemingly LSD-inspired re-imaginings of Japanese monsters and costumed heroes, and sketch comedy that went from bone dry to berserk in the blink of an eye. I had never seen anything like it.…" Although *Big Man Japan* is not as excessive as the variety shows through which Matsumoto cemented his fame, the film remains a bombastic showcase of his comedic prowess—an ambitious (and at times, unwieldy) fusion of inspired and idiotic comedy, with an iconic and long-standing genre of postwar Japanese cinema. Matsumoto's eventual justification for moving into filmmaking was no less than wanting to "break cinema. To do what nobody else is doing" (Imai; my translation).

Matsumoto has also stated that *Big Man Japan* is designed specifically for Japanese, rather than foreign, audiences. At the post-screening Q&A at Cannes he expressed surprise that the audience appreciated the dried seaweed gag—one of several instances in which Daisato expresses his liking for things that expand, such as dried seaweed and fold-up umbrellas—before confirming that the film is aimed squarely at Japanese audiences (Imai). Particularly, he suggested that foreign audiences would fail to grasp the significance of the ensemble cast, which includes singer Ua as Daisato's manager; cult actor Riki Takeuchi as the Leaping Monster; the baby-faced Ryunosuke Kamiki as the Baby Monster; and fellow comedians Haruka Unabara (with comb-over intact) and Itsuji Itao (a previous cast member on one of Downtown's variety shows) as the Strangling and Stink Monsters, respectively.

Big Man Japan thus retains a heavily self-conscious quality for Japanese audiences well acquainted with Matsumoto, his career, and his comedic style, and the film plays with their expectations from the outset. In the opening shot, Daisato is sitting on a bus and looking out of the window, with his face turned away from the camera. As the interviewer asks the first of his many inane questions ("Do you prefer the hot weather?"), Daisato slowly turns around to reveal to the viewer the latest incarnation of Matsumoto's comedic persona. Far from the from-out-of-left-field cult film it may appear to Western viewers, *Big Man Japan* is in fact a high-profile work, in which many of Matsumoto's narrative and stylistic approaches resonate with those familiar with his formidable presence within Japanese popular culture.

Big Man Japan *and the Kaiju Film*

For an entertainer who had already conquered TV and a variety of other media, Matsumoto's expansion into feature filmmaking is easily understandable—but why did he tackle the kaiju film in his first attempt at it? Matsumoto had previously flirted with costumed superheroes and kaiju in sketches for Downtown's variety shows; their inherent silliness seems a perfect fit for a comedian who has built his career on innovative ways to be silly. While the kaiju and battle sequences in *Big Man Japan* allow Matsumoto to run riot with his comic inventions, these alone cannot sustain a feature-length film lest it become a series of disparate sketches with no coherent narrative. How then, besides its inclusion of the basic generic requirements—invading giant monsters, recognizable landmarks and plenty of destruction—does *Big Man Japan* sit within the genre of the kaiju film?

By virtue of being rendered in CGI, *Big Man Japan*'s battle sequences are consistent with most contemporary kaiju (and more broadly, action) films, and are at odds with early kaiju films, with their distinctive use of latex costumes and miniature models as cityscapes. However, they are similar to early kaiju films in that they both make little attempt at realism, unlike the Western tradition for special effects. The battle sequences in *Big Man Japan* have a peculiar atmosphere, set in vacant cityscapes with no presence of human beings. Obvious aesthetic differences aside, there is a strong juxtaposition established between the CGI and live-action sequences because the two modes of representation never even come close to overlapping. This runs counter to the practice of merging special effects and live-action within the same frame in both contemporary and early kaiju films (usually via CGI and trick photography, respectively), or the crosscutting between studio models and location shooting in *tokusatsu* (an umbrella term for live-action film or TV drama that relies heavily on special effects) superhero films and TV shows, in their attempt to reinforce the illusion that the action is unfolding in the same place and at the same time. The battle sequences in *Big Man Japan* are noticeably artificial, and Matsumoto gleefully exaggerates their artificiality. He refuses to integrate them with live-action images at any point, amplifying the contrast between the realist documentary sequences that make up most of the film, and the short and nonsensical CGI scenes that punctuate it. The kaiju battles in *Big Man Japan* exist in a comical aesthetic vacuum, similar to early video game cut-scenes that bear little resemblance to the actual game itself.

While its kitsch qualities clearly appeal to Matsumoto's comedic sensibilities, the broader appeal of making a kaiju film is likely to lie in the genre's dual role as popular entertainment and as a commentator for the Japanese national psyche. The original *Godzilla*, which established the template for all subsequent kaiju films, demonstrates this duality. As is well known, *Godzilla* today enjoys dual status as the pacesetter for a genre that has become an international popular culture phenomenon, and as one of cinema's most potent anti-nuclear statements. It is a major historical and cultural achievement in itself, but it is the film's latent quality—its powerful, political subtext—that has ensured the film's longevity. Through its simple narrative of a monster awakened by nuclear testing and indiscriminately wreaking havoc on Tokyo, *Godzilla* captured the shared national trauma experienced by Japanese during the war, as well as the nuclear anxiety that haunted the nation after it.

The meaning of Godzilla—the monster itself—played no small part in articulating the film's subtext. For Mark Holcomb, Godzilla serves as both "a metaphor for rapacious science" and "a manifestation of resurgent Japanese militarism" (58). According to Scarlet Cheng, for some Japanese it "embodies the souls of those who died in the atomic explosions in Hiroshima and Nagasaki" (15). For director Honda, who witnessed the devastation wrought by the atomic bomb on Hiroshima as he passed through the city on his return from China (where he served three terms as a soldier and was captured as a prisoner of war), Godzilla was not merely a "metaphor for the bomb but a physical manifestation of it" (Ryfle 52). In the many Toho offshoots following *Godzilla*, such as *Rodan* (1956) and *Mothra* (1961)—both directed by Honda—

the form of the kaiju changed but the allegorical dimensions remained largely intact.

As Susan Hayward argues, a genre's evolution "can be seen to reflect changes in the social and political environment ... so there is a cross-fertilisation between the nation's image of itself and the imaging of the nation" (101). Hence, as the *Godzilla* franchise continued, the meaning of the monster evolved. In later years, as the immediate fear of nuclear warfare subsided and the national mood became more optimistic due to accelerating economic growth, Godzilla was "transformed from a vengeful and implacable threat to Japan into a defender and champion of Japan" (Tsutsui 209). A recent version of the monster in *Godzilla, Mothra and King Ghidorah: Giant Monsters All-Out Attack* (*Gojira, Mosura, Kingu Gidora: Daikaiju Sokogeki*, 2001) sees the returning lizard "animated by the spirit of Japan's war dead, attacking a country it no longer recognizes" (Hendrix 58). In its latest incarnation in Hideaki Anno's *Shin Godzilla* (*Shin Gojira*, 2016), the monster evokes the multifaceted tragedy that befell Japan on 11 March 2011, "serving as an ambulatory tsunami, earthquake and nuclear reactor, leaving radioactive contamination in his wake" (Schilling). The original Godzilla trounced buildings and breathed fire on the city from above, evoking both the dual atomic bomb attacks and the firebombing of Tokyo and other Japanese cities. The newest Godzilla begins as an eel-like creature (it evolves throughout the course of the film) as it travels through Tokyo's river system, before spilling out onto the streets on all fours and bringing along with it a torrent of water and debris—a disturbing sight that recalls the devastating footage of the tsunami in the Tohoku region. As Jason Barr observes, the most popular kaiju icons, such as Godzilla, have "enjoyed multiple interpretations across many decades, with the themes and imagery that surround them *indicative of, and comprised of reality*" (11–12; emphasis in original).

For the most part, however, Matsumoto does not even attempt to continue this longstanding tradition of embedding kaiju with meanings grounded in reality. Even a cursory glance at the film's repertoire of kaiju will reveal that they have no relevance whatsoever to current or past social or political concerns in the country; they signify nothing and serve little purpose other than comedy. With the exception of the innocuous Baby Monster who Big Man Japan accidentally kills (it chomps down on his nipple as he cradles it in his arms, causing him to drop it), prompting his already low popularity to plummet further, and the nemesis Red Monster, who unleashes a severe beating upon Big Man Japan and forces him to flee from battle, the kaiju in the film do not have any impact on the narrative and could have been replaced with any other bizarre substitute. The glaring anomaly is the abovementioned Red Monster—a fierce and psychopathic creature that is stripped of the cute characteristics found on all of the other kaiju in the film—which clearly represents the perceived threat of North Korea, Japan's close neighbor and regional bogeyman. The Red Monster is the only kaiju in the film that is rendered entirely in CGI, and is acknowledged as a threat originating from overseas ("Apparently it's not Japanese," advises Daisato's manager after his first encounter with it). Meanwhile, all of the other kaiju are implied to be harmless domestic nuisances, as made obvious by the recognizable Japanese cast who play them, and their general lack of menace ("Don't come to the city—go out to the suburbs," Daisato scolds the Stink Monster).

Rather than exonerating the film of any social or political concerns, the meaninglessness and harmlessness of the kaiju redirect attention towards the film's true subject matter: contemporary Japanese society. For example, one of the film's understated gags is that the kaiju battles leave no actual imprint outside of the CGI sequences in which they occur. Despite the widespread destruction of bridges, buildings and other infrastructure (the standard kaiju film fare), no visual evidence of this destruction exists when the battles end. When the film reverts to live-action, life seems to continue entirely as normal and yet, the public complains incessantly! The Japanese people despise Big Man Japan for making a mess and causing inconvenience but none of this mess can actually be seen, and the public is never able to provide a persuasive reason as to how they are being inconvenienced. When people are stopped in the street throughout the film and asked to comment upon the previous night's battle in a series of vox pop interviews, some speak about it as if it were a game or sport ("That was a joke, really. I want to see a real fight"), some criticize Big Man Japan without citing any particular reason ("He winds up causing us more trouble"), some are simply cruel ("His face is huge"), and all of them do not recognize the battles as something of consequence, despite the fact that Big Man Japan is presumably saving their city from destruction. Writing about *Godzilla,* J. Hoberman notes how the film "successfully dramatized the monstrous rupture of World War II and its aftermath by integrating the fantastic and the everyday." In *Big Man Japan,* Matsumoto presents a different kind of rupture: a society no longer able to discern what exists within the realm of TV and popular entertainment, and what may have actual consequences on their lives; in other words, a failure to distinguish between what is real and meaningful, and what is not.

When Japanese people express political opinions in the film, the sentiments are frequently incoherent and hypocritical. In an extended tracking shot following Daisato's scooter ride through a valley en route to the transformation plant, he passes a series of environmentalist graffiti on the walls, condemning Big Man Japan on everything from noise pollution, wasting electricity and scaring off wild birds. In kaiju films it is typically the invading kaiju that are seen as the environmental threat, but in an ironic twist, Big Man Japan is made to adopt this burden as the superhero. After two kaiju that he attempts to repel begin having sex, newspaper headlines label him a pervert and a pimp, and Daisato's house is vandalized and plastered in leaflets that read, "Children Watch TV." The Red Monster is identified as a foreign threat and only Big Man Japan is prepared to fight against it, but after he is forced to flee from their first battle, his bravery and patriotism are called into question. In general, Big Man Japan is expected by the public to uphold an impossible commitment: repel the kaiju but do so in an orderly, noble and entertaining fashion, and assume full responsibility if something goes wrong.

There is not a single sympathetic character in sight in the film. Daisato's manager is a money-hungry narcissist who is clearly ripping him off. It is implied that his wife left him because of his lack of wealth and success. The offscreen documentary filmmaker is obtrusive, obnoxiously blunt and unethical, and at one point schemes with Daisato's manager and the government to stage a fight between Big Man Japan and the Red Monster (soldiers break into Daisato's house at night while he sleeps to transform him by force; the documentary crew pre-empt the invasion and are there to capture it all). The minor characters fare no better. The members of the public are savage in their criticism of Big Man Japan after a fight, for entirely trivial reasons; the various government workers who assist with Daisato's transformation are mindless and charmless bureaucrats; and Daisato's young daughter appears only briefly, with her face pixelated beyond recognition and her voice dropped several octaves into an ugly drawl. The closest the film has to a sympathetic character is Daisato himself, but even his sympathetic traits are offset by his frustrating submissiveness and his shortcomings as a husband and father, as revealed by his ex-wife to the documentary crew.

As these examples illustrate, the overall impression that Matsumoto paints of the Japanese is that they are petty, cynical and insular, and lacking any coherent identity or principled political stance. Steve Ryfle suggests that the original *Godzilla* affected Japanese audiences greatly because "the wounds of World War II were far from healed by 1954" (50). For the Japanese who appear in *Big Man Japan*, the traumatic events of the wartime past are a forgotten memory, and the very notions of war, violence and death seem to have become abstract concepts. As the film makes abundantly clear, the context of Japan in the twenty-first century is vastly different to that of the immediate postwar period. Matsumoto depicts a complacent Japanese society that seems to have become spoiled by peace, and whose sense of a shared national identity has all but vanished.

While *Big Man Japan* appears initially to engage with the kaiju film only on a superficial level, it in fact continues the genre's longstanding tradition of social and political critique, and its examination of the Japanese national psyche. However, Matsumoto's downplaying of the significance of the kaiju results in a kaiju film whose primary concern is the character of the Japanese people. In this respect, *Big Man Japan* is an unusual kaiju film in that its central themes are specific to its local setting and context—it lacks what Barr identifies as integral to most kaiju films, namely the "acknowledgement of worldwide anxieties" and the reflection of "greater social issues, which often supersede national boundaries" (12). The kaiju in *Big Man Japan* are mere footnotes, as reflected by their harmlessness, lack of meaning and minor position within the film's narrative. The sole exception of the Red Monster represents accentuated anxieties about the threat of North Korea, and these anxieties are particular to Japan and, of course, South Korea—two nations that are North Korea's nearest ideological enemies and which perceive its threat most directly. *Big Man Japan* may have travelled widely and garnered a cult following worldwide, yet it is a kaiju film whose key concerns are resolutely local and, as Matsumoto has asserted, aimed specifically at Japanese audiences.

Japan, America, Kaiju

Matsumoto expands his critique of contemporary Japanese society by focusing on another mainstay of the kaiju film, which relates to Japan's complex relations with the United States. Early kaiju films were often directly or indirectly critical of the United States (then still a recent enemy) through, for example, their allusions to its military actions during World War II and hydrogen bomb testing in the 1950s. Over a half-century later, *Big Man Japan* focuses instead on the impact of Japan's continuing military partnership with the United States, as well the aftermath of Japan's absorption of American culture in the postwar period as it reintegrated into the world community.

These themes are first explored indirectly through markers of Japanese culture and tradition that turn out to be quite nonsensical. Big Man Japan, like most of the kaiju that appear in the film, lacks any intelligible cultural meaning despite his historic lineage and that he supposedly embodies a nation's values (*Dai Nipponjin* translates literally as "Big Japanese"). He has a series of tattoos on his body (including the kanji character 大/*dai*, meaning "big") that hint at a vague sense of Japanese tradition, but is otherwise a ridiculous sight, adorned with characteristics that have no unifying theme (tall perm, purple underpants, flabby body, a baton as a weapon). When Daisato is transformed into Big Man Japan, the process begins with a shambolic, quasi-Shinto ceremony referred to as "The Ritual of Soul Insertion"—a ritual carried down from the past for no apparent reason and now watered down to the point of being meaningless. Even a government worker at the transformation plant concedes to the documentary crew that the ritual is unnecessary, and when the interviewer interrupts the ceremony and asks the priest to repeat a segment for the sake of the camera, he is only too happy to oblige. Like Big Man Japan's physical appearance—ostensibly Japanese but actually absent of meaning—this ludicrous ritual hints at a contemporary Japan whose sense of tradition has become diluted, and whose cultural expressions have become confused and tokenistic.

This notion of diminishing Japanese-ness is reinforced by a series of weird incongruities between Japanese and American culture throughout the film. On the way to visit his daughter (who has the Anglo name "Selina") for her birthday, Matsumoto reveals in an insert shot what Daisato bought for her as a gift: a tasteless sequin-studded bunny-hat labeled "USA CHAN" (subtitled as "Bunny Girl"); the subsequent birthday lunch is set to take place in an American-style diner called "Big Boy." After Big Man Japan accidentally kills the Child Monster, Matsumoto cuts to improbable scenes of candle-lit public vigils, with Japanese crowds holding "God Bless…" signs in English and swaying to the serenading of Gospel singers. Although these examples may only be gags highlighting the inadvertently amusing ways in which Japanese often integrate aspects of American culture, there are other instances in the film that suggest there is more at play.

In a rambling and semi-coherent interview early in the film, Daisato states that he can never take vacations because he is always on call. When quizzed about this by the interviewer, he reveals that he does not even own a passport and has never left the country:

INTERVIEWER: No trips overseas?
DAISATO: Overseas? No, never. I don't even have a passport. I just accept that's the way things are. I'm not "Anti-U.S.," but…. You see…. With protecting Japan … "Protecting Japan" is not the way I like to put it, but…. That's a factor, too.
INTERVIEWER: You don't like the United States? You said "Anti-U.S."?
DAISATO: Well, of course…. In this day and age, they're not exactly The Enemy, but…. I was brought up that way a bit. Fed some ideas…. You know.

Daisato implies that a reason he chooses not to travel overseas is because he prefers to remain in Japan and protect the nation himself, rather than allowing the United States to do so. This alludes to the United States' somewhat awkward position as the nation that devastated Japan during the war and occupied it after the war ended, but which has since become a de facto protector for a country unable to develop its own military force (due to Article 9 of the U.S.–devised, pacifist postwar constitution). Today the United States is the closest ally of Japan, where it stations some 50,000 military personnel—more than in any other foreign country and an ongoing source of contention for many Japanese.

Daisato's confused and confusing response, which hints at a restrained nationalist/anti–American sentiment without expressing it clearly, nonetheless reflects some of the ambivalent Japanese attitudes towards the United

States and its military presence in Japan. Writing about the post-war protests against American military bases in Japan, Jennifer Miller argues that the issue of bases "presented a fundamental conundrum to U.S. policymaking" in that "on the one hand, they seemingly granted security in a turbulent region, strengthening pro–American ties. On the other hand, the presence of U.S. military bases directly contradicted U.S. claims about the value of Japanese sovereignty, sparked intense local opposition to the alliance with the United States, and challenged the political foundations of the U.S.–Japanese relationship" (954). This conundrum is also reflected in the continuing ambivalence of Japanese attitudes towards the United States, its military presence, and its role in Japan's geopolitical affairs; as Carol Gluck suggests, this ambivalence amounts to Japan paradoxically "wanting [the United States] gone and wanting it there at the same time" (307). Despite this context, Daisato's point ultimately remains unclear: is it a vague expression of national pride, a desire for Japanese autonomy, a broader anti–U.S. sentiment, or simply xenophobia? His inability to articulate his views with any fluency becomes yet another example from the film in which Japanese people are unable to express a coherent political opinion.

Big Man Japan saves its most direct political commentary for its finale and it is aimed firmly at the United States. After being transformed by force, Big Man Japan is about to suffer another humiliating defeat at the hands of the Red Monster, who catches him as he flees and begins to stomp on him on the ground. There is a sudden white flash, and an offscreen voice shouts, "Freeze!" before a caption encourages the viewer to "Enjoy the rest live!" The film then cuts to a live-action studio set filled with a miniature model cityscape, and a nuclear family of superheroes, played by actors in latex suits, is introduced in turn: "American Hero" Super Justice, who resembles Ultraman; Super Justice's father; Stay With Me, the mother; Don't Touch Me, the pubescent younger sister; and Be My Baby, the infant (the captioned character names are not translated in the English subtitles). Although they resemble the iconic Japanese Ultraman family, each of these superheroes is embellished with caricatured signifiers of the United States. All of them have blonde hair, their costumes are comprised of the colors of the American flag, the mother is obese, and the father wears platforms and flared pants, and poses like a cowboy.

They proceed to unceremoniously bash the Red Monster, who is now a benign figure played by a person in a padded suit. Super Justice picks up a yellow toy bus and beats him over the head. His sister kneels on a patch of grass rolling up newspapers, passing them to her brother for him to use as a weapon. The family members take turns hitting and flipping the Red Monster onto the floor, before stripping the clothes and padding off its body. As it lies limp and unmoving, the father delivers the coup de grâce by tearing off its underpants. Throughout, Matsumoto foregrounds the artifices of *tokusatsu* filmmaking to comical extremes. The pacing of the editing is awkward because most of the action is shown continuously, as if it were filmed live (for example, Matsumoto films the entire process of the father struggling to tear off the Red Monster's underpants). Coverage is provided by multiple cameras, contrasting sharply with the rest of the film and emphasizing the studio aesthetic. And the scene unfolds to an overzealous, patriotic superhero theme song which stops and starts when blows are delivered, while the use of location sounds highlights the materiality of the fake set, costumes and props.

The Justice family then form a row and stack their hands (to the chant of "Peace!"), and oblige Big Man Japan (who has been hiding behind a building) to do likewise. A rainbow laser beam shoots out from where their hands meet and begins zapping the incapacitated Red Monster. Big Man Japan removes his hand to find that the beam works just as well without his input; "I make no difference," he mutters to himself. The Red Monster explodes. The family members link arms, with Big Man Japan in the middle, and fly off into the sky. When his shoe slips off his foot mid-flight, Big Man Japan turns to alert his American counterparts but finds that they have become creepily unresponsive—silent, eyes vacant, and flying on autopilot. In an absurd echo of the iconic image from the *Ultraman* (1966–67) series, in which the titular hero flies off into the sky after defeating his foe in every episode, the film ends with a dumbfounded Big Man Japan hanging vertically and being ferried away by his American "protectors." Ultimately, he is depicted as an ineffective superhero whose role in protecting the nation is only symbolic; when push comes to shove, it is the will and might of the United States that will get the job done.

Given the United States' ongoing involvement in Japan's geopolitical affairs, it is understandable that the greatest military power in the world should continue to resurface as a source of critique in kaiju films. It is, after all, the United States whose wartime actions against the Japanese population and postwar status as a nuclear superpower provided the impetus for the original *Godzilla* and many subsequent kaiju films. Yet, as Matsumoto's film makes plain, the kaiju film also owes its existence to the United States. *Godzilla* was inspired by, and cashed in on, the success of the American sci-fi monster film *The Beast from 20,000 Fathoms* (1953); Kim Newman goes so far as to suggest that it was "a blatant imitation" of the earlier film and that all of the earliest kaiju films "are still frank imitations of Hollywood" (11). Writing about Japan's first live-action TV superhero *Gekko Kamen* (1958– 59), Jonathan Abel proposes that the series "and its subsequent spawn, from *Kamen Rider* to *Ultraman*, are one allegorical reflection both of the growing perception in 1950s Japan that postwar justice originated from abroad and of the concomitant doubts about the possibility of a truly native Japanese justice" (188). *Big Man Japan*'s finale sequence raises this question of justice in a spectacularly unsubtle and sarcastic fashion, and exposes the kaiju/superhero film for what Mastumoto believes it to be: adults in rubber costumes, on an artificial set, playing out a phony idea of justice inherited from the United States. If *Big Man Japan* had until this point maintained a degree of ambivalence towards the kaiju film, here it ridicules it outright, framing it as the object of critique itself.

Big Man Japan presents a contemporary Japanese society unsure of its own identity, and the kaiju film becomes emblematic of this uncertainty: Is the kaiju film really Japanese, and if so, how and why? What exactly does it say about the nation? And is it effective to use the kaiju film to critique the United States when it is so heavily embedded into the fabric of the genre itself, just as the United States is so heavily embedded in Japan's geopolitical affairs in the actual world? *Big Man Japan* is a parody of the kaiju film, but the questions it raises about the genre is ultimately what differentiates it from the playful kaiju parodies of the past (for example, the numerous *tokusatsu* fan film parodies produced by Daicon Films). While all of these films satirize the genre's tropes and aesthetics, Matsumoto's film goes further, questioning the ideological roots of the kaiju film itself.

Conclusion

Kaiju and superheroes come and go, and the innovative special effects techniques that once made kaiju films so distinctly Japanese have been almost completely supplanted by CGI. As a popular genre, the kaiju film is widely understood and appreciated; as such, it has produced its fair share of weak imitations designed to do little more than cash in on what came before it. But the core premise of the genre remains robust enough to allow for the investigation of problems and fears troubling the nation at a particular point in time. It is the ongoing allegorical potential of the kaiju film which has seen filmmakers return to it, again and again.

In this light, *Big Man Japan* can be seen to uphold the kaiju film's long-standing tradition of socio-political critique, despite the film's flagrant disregard for many of its generic staples. It also expands the traditional focus of the genre: here, the nation's sense of vulnerability to disaster is a distant concern; it is instead the nation's troubled sense of *itself* that provides the primary focus of the film. Matsumoto uses the kaiju film to explore this issue, but he does so by demoting the importance of the kaiju themselves, and through the reflexive appraisal of the genre in which the film operates. While it may not be the expression of "heartfelt nostalgia" for the genre as suggested by Tsutsui, *Big Man Japan* nonetheless remains a hilarious and inventive contemporary example of it. It is a fascinating illustration of the kaiju film's flexibility and durability, and the ways in which it continues to evolve, like Godzilla, according to the state of Japan and its relationship with the world.

WORKS CITED

Abel, Jonathan. "Masked justice: allegories of the superhero in Cold War Japan." *Japan Forum*, vol. 26, no. 22, 2014, 187–208.
Anno, Hideaki, director. *Shin Godzilla*. Toho, 2016.
Barr, Jason. *The Kaiju Film: A Critical Study of Cinema's Biggest Monsters*. McFarland, 2016.
Beast from 20,000 Fathoms, The. Directed by Eugene Lourie, Warner Bros., 1953.
Cheng, Scarlet. "Zen and the Art of Monster Movies." *Asian Wall Street Journal*, 16 Oct. 1998, 15.
Downtown no Gaki no Tsukai ya Arahende!! Nippon TV, 1989–present.
Downtown no Gottsu Ee Kanji. Fuji Television, 1991–1997.
Gekko Kamen. Created by Kohan Kawauchi, KRTV, 1958–59.
Gluck, Carol. "The 'End' of the Postwar: Japan at the Turn of the Millennium." *Public Culture*, vol. 10, no. 1, 1997, 1–23.
Godzilla, Mothra and King Ghidorah: Giant Monsters All-Out Attack. Directed by Shusuke Kaneko, Toho, 2001.
Hayward, Susan. "Questions of National Cinema." *National Identity*, edited by Keith Cameron, Intellect, 1999, 92–106.
Hendrix, Grady. "They Might Be Giants: The millennial resurrection." *The Village Voice*, 25 Aug. 2004, 58.
Hoberman, J. "*Godzilla*: Poetry After the A-Bomb." *The Criterion Collection*, 24 Jan. 2012. Accessed 1 Sep. 2016.
Holcomb, Mark. "They Might Be Giants: Father of Godzilla." *The Village Voice*, 25 Aug. 2004, 58.
Honda, Ishiro, director. *Godzilla*. Toho, 1954.
____, director. *Mothra*. Toho, 1961.
____, director. *Rodan*. Toho, 1956.
Imai, Ryo. "The internationally recognised *Big Man Japan*—Matsumoto Hitoshi's directorial debut receives rave reviews at Cannes." (世界が認めた「大日本人」- 松本人志の初監督映画がカンヌで大絶賛!!) *MyNavi News*, 22 May 2007. Accessed 15 Sep. 2016.
Kitano, Takeshi, director. *Boiling Point*. Shochiku, 1990.
____, director. *Glory to the Filmmaker!* Office Kitano, 2007.
____, director. *Violent Cop*. Shochiku, 1989.
League, Tim. "Without Matsumoto There Is No *Jackass*." *Birth. Movies. Death*. 15 Jan. 2015. Accessed 15 Aug. 2016.
Matsumoto, Hitoshi, director. *Big Man Japan*. Shochiku, 2007.
"Matsumoto Hitoshi vs. Katori Shingo." (松本人志VS香取慎吾) *SmaSTATION!!*, 2 Jun. 2008. Accessed 16. Aug 2016.
Miller, Jennifer M. "Fractured Alliance: Anti-Base Protests and U.S.–Japanese Relations." *Diplomatic History*, vol. 38, no. 5, 2014, 953–986.
Newman, Kim. "Japan's Bizarre Behemoth." *Sight & Sound*. vol. 20, no. 9, 2010, 11.
Ryfle, Steve. "Godzilla's Footprint." *The Virginia Quarterly Review*, vol. 81, no. 1, 2005, 44–63.
Schilling, Mark. "'Shin Godzilla': The metaphorical monster returns." *The Japan Times*, 3 Aug. 2016.
Tsutsui, William M. "Kaiju Eiga / Monster Movies." *Japan: Directory of World Cinema*, edited by John Berra, Intellect, 2010, 206–210.
Ultraman. Created by Eiji Tsuburaya, Tsuburaya Productions, 1966–67.

Japan's Anti-Kaiju Fighting Force
Normalizing Japan's Self-Defense Forces Through Postwar Monster Films

JEFFREY J. HALL

Devastating defeat in World War II brought about a major transformation of Japanese society. Over the course of a few years, Japan transitioned from a state dominated by the military to a democracy that had legally renounced its right to wage war or maintain a military. The war-weary Japanese largely embraced the ideals of anti-militarism, including the renunciation of nuclear weapons. In place of a formal military, Japan quietly re-armed itself through the creation the Japan Self-Defense Forces (JSDF), a quasi-military that is restricted to only using its weapons for defensive purposes.

On a visit a movie theater, postwar Japanese were likely to find films that reflected the prevailing distrust of the military and abhorrence of war. Few films mentioned or focused on the Self-Defense Forces; instead, Japanese filmmakers preferred to look back at World War II, and their depictions of the Japanese Imperial Military were almost always negative. Popular anti-war films such as *Fires on the Plain* (1959), *The Human Condition* (1959–1961), and *Human Bullet* (1968) have been critically acclaimed for their depictions of an unnecessary war in which Japanese soldiers die in vain (Desjardins 95, Seaton 140). The JSDF was largely invisible in postwar cinema, perhaps partly due to the unpopularity of rearmament in the early decades after 1945, and partly due to the JSDF's own desire to keep a low profile. Unlike the United States military, which has long cooperated with Hollywood filmmakers, the JSDF did not have any formal public relations department until 1993. Until the 1990s the JSDF pursued a policy of "strategic self-preservation," believing that a lack of public attention would avoid controversy about militarization.

One JSDF officer summed up the situation by quoting an old Japanese proverb: "the pheasant would not be shot but for its cries" (*kiji mo akazuba utaremai*) (Fruhstuck 118).

In spite of these factors, it would be an exaggeration to say that the JSDF was completely absent from Japanese films in the early postwar decades. There was one particular Japanese film genre that regularly produced works featuring the JSDF: the *kaiju eiga*. After all, how could one make a film about giant monsters attacking a country without including scenes of soldiers coming to its defense? Japan's most popular kaiju film franchise, Toho's Godzilla series, with 29 films spanning the years between 1954 and 2016, is home to some of the JSDF's most epic fictional battles. Lacking official assistance from the JSDF, Toho created its own defense force, and with the use of miniatures, some military costumes on extras, and the occasional jeep, it created visually impressive scenes of Japan fighting against Godzilla and his kaiju cohorts.

Films, like any other medium of culture, serve as "storage places for meaning a particular society," and the "low data" we can gather from popular culture can often reflect general cultural themes and assumptions better than elite discourse (Neumann, Nexon 13–14). Depending on the cultural themes present, films be used to promote and assist in building consensus about the legitimacy of using military force (Davies, Philpott 50–51). Thus, when considering how Japanese society views its military, and how those views may change over time, films can serve as a useful object of analysis.

What then, can be said of the JSDF in Godzilla films? Noting the Godzilla series' "upbeat" and sometimes "gung-ho" depictions of JSDF bravery, William Tsutsui has suggested that these films may have helped erode societal taboos about celebrating military achievement (Tsutsui 95–96). On the other hand, through a more in-depth look at kaiju films, Jason Barr has argued that the JSDF has been "generally a brave, courageous, but woefully inadequate group, with even its most successful creations often leading to intentional destruction" (Barr 153). Rather than celebrating military achievement, "with only a few exceptions, the Self-Defense Forces is often the first line of defense but is eventually portrayed as another victim of the kaiju" (ibid.). Both arguments have their merits, and do not necessarily contradict each other.

Looking at the Godzilla series as a whole, the JSDF almost never succeeds in its aims. Even with the aid of sci-fi superweapons, their soldiers tend to fare quite poorly against giant monsters, and especially against Godzilla. There are, as Barr has noted, some exceptions. This essay explores a few of them, together with some of the JSDF's failures. Emphasis has been placed upon the most popular films in the franchise—the first few Showa Era films, Godzilla's 1984 reboot, and several of the later Heisei Era films. Above all of these, however, the most attention has been devoted to *Shin Godzilla* (2016), which not only gave major screen time to the JSDF, but also surpassed all other Godzilla films in Japanese box office revenue.[1] Generally speaking, the most popular films in the franchise—those that reached a wider general audience—tend to be more serious in nature and portray the JSDF in a relatively positive light. These films span Japan's postwar history, and one can observe how shifting societal and geopolitical factors have impacted the depictions of military action against Godzilla.

Historical and Social Background of Japan's Self-Defense Forces

Before delving into the world of Godzilla, it is necessary to look back at the historical circumstances that gave birth to the JSDF. As an legally odd entity in a world full of formal militaries, one cannot understand Japan's unique position without considering its history.

Japan's emergence as a modern nation state in the late 19th century occurred under the leadership of men who sought to make Japan a military powerhouse. Under the slogan "fukoku kyouhei" ("Rich nation, Strong Army"), they reformed Japan's feudal society, seeking to enrich their nation for the express purpose of militarizing it (Samuels, "Rich Nation, Strong Army"– National Security and the Technological Transformation of Japan 36–38). The Imperial Army and Navy, serving the Emperor, was a powerful institution in Japanese society. Every school in the country taught children martial values, and the military conscription system meant that millions of men had the experience of undergoing military training and education. By the 1930s, military integration into society had reached such a level that "loyalty to the army and loyalty to the hamlet and village had become synonymous" (Smethurst xvi). The military eventually became more powerful than Japan's civilian politicians, and helped drive the nation into a war that would cost millions of Japanese lives and leave the country's once great cities in ruins.

Defeat led to an American military occupation, which sought to reform Japanese government and society with the goal of making Japan into a democratic nation that would never again go down the path of militarism and aggression. Reforms included the 1947 adoption of a new Japanese Constitution, which restricted Japan's ability to wage war. Article 9 of the Constitution stated that "the Japanese people forever renounce war as a sovereign right of the nation and the threat or use of force as means of settling international disputes" and "land, sea, and air forces, as well as other war potential, will never be maintained." In other words, to avoid repeating the mistakes of the past, Japan had given up on being allowed to have a military.

The idea that Japan should never wage war or maintain military forces was an attractive one to many Japanese people. Although the majority of Japan's major cities had suffered tremendous destruction from American aerial bombardment, the populace placed a great deal of blame for the defeat and loss of life on Japan's wartime government. Few could forget that the militarist government had used schools to teach absolute loyalty and respect towards the armed forces, and that the same government has used military police to oppress civilians on the home front while carrying out acts of aggression abroad. This led to a situation in which "the balance of public opinion valued protection *from* overprotection *by* their military" (Samuels, Securing Japan 49).

Despite public support for Article 9, the geopolitical realities of the Cold War caused Japan's government to reinterpret the meaning of "war potential." With the encouragement of the United States, Japan established the National Police Reserve in 1950, a 75,000 man constabulary force armed with infantry weapons. This was then upgraded into a larger and better-armed National Safety Force in 1952, before being once again upgraded and reorganized in 1954 into the three-branch Japan Self-Defense Forces: the Ground Self-Defense Forces (GSDF), the Maritime Self-Defense Forces (MSDF), and the Aerial Self-Defense Forces (ASDF). Under the Japanese government's interpretation of Article 9 of the Constitution, it was not possible for Japan to maintain a formal Army, Navy, and Air Force; nonetheless, the 1954 organizational structure of the JSDF closely resembles that of a three branch military, and each is equipped with military weaponry.

In recent decades, Japan has spent about 1 percent of its GDP on the JSDF. Compared to percentages that most large nations spend, it is rather low. When one considers the overall size of Japan's economy, however, it makes it a significant power, with military spending close to that of France and Germany. Japan defense budget for the 2016 fiscal year was 5.05 trillion yen ($41.4 billion) and had over 225,000 personnel (Gady). The GSDF is equipped with high tech tanks, missiles, and attack helicopters; the MSDF is equipped with Aegis destroyers and attack submarines; and the ASDF is equipped with variants of F-15 and F-16 fighter jets. Its personnel are organized in a military-style command structure, wear military-style uniforms, and many live on bases that once housed the Imperial Japanese Military.

Though they have many traits of a typical military, the JSDF strives to maintain an identity of "normalcy" that downplays the fact that they are very different from other organizations. There is an unwritten rule that servicemen and servicewomen change into civilian clothes when leaving base, a rule that even extends to those serving at the Defense Ministry offices in central Tokyo. There is still a sense that wearing a military uniform in public will draw negative attention (Frühstück 62–64). In this sense, being "normal" means hiding the military face of the JSDF.

Maintaining this normalcy has been relatively easy, considering the fact that the vast majority of JSDF members have spent their entire careers stationed in Japan. Starting with a 1992 deployment to aid the UN mission in Cambodia, only very small numbers of JSDF personnel have been sent on overseas missions. These missions have been strictly non-combat in nature, focusing instead on reconstruction, humanitarian assistance, and the delivery of supplies. To overcome constitutional issues and make the deployments possible, the Japanese Diet needed to pass special laws that interpret such missions as non-military in nature. These legal restraints have pretty much guaranteed that Japan's political leaders will be extremely cautious when deciding whether or not to send the JSDF overseas. Its largest and most dangerous overseas mission was a deployment of about 600 JSDF personnel to southern Iraq from 2004 to 2006. The Japanese soldiers were placed a relatively quiet area of the country, forbidden to use their arms in any situation other than self-defense, and placed under the protection of Australian soldiers. During the two-year mission, the JSDF did not become involved in combat.

As of the writing of this essay in late 2016, the JSDF had yet to experience the death of a single soldier in combat. The JSDF and Japanese media have long anticipated the possibility of Japanese military deaths occurring during overseas deployments, but "the framing of soldiers' death is not formulated as a patriotic sacrifice." Rather, hypothetical deaths were framed within the concept of the JSDF as a force that is "doing good" in non-combat peacekeeping and other multinational humanitarian missions (Ben-Ari).

Although Japanese people have yet to see a news report about one of their soldiers engaging in or dying in combat, those that have seen Godzilla films have witnessed numerous cases of Japanese engaging in combat, and sometimes dying in defense of their country. Scenes of soldiers "doing good" in both combat and non-combat roles combine to depict the JSDF as an organization capable of more than just peacekeeping or disaster relief. On the movie screen, the JSDF is very much a combat force, putting their lives on the line to protect the Japanese people.

The Showa Era Godzilla Films

Godzilla (1954) was released the same year that the National Safety Force was transformed into the military-style Self-Defense Forces. It is only appropriate, then that a well-armed Japanese defense force appears in the film as protectors of the Japanese nation.[2]

Japan's defenders make their first appearance shortly after authorities confirm the existence of Godzilla. To respond to this threat, the government dispatches a fleet of frigates to search for the monster and destroy it with depth charges. There is no lengthy debate about the legality of sending Japanese warships into combat, nor does there seem to be much public concern about the government resorting to military force. The protagonist of the film, Dr. Yamane, opposes the naval mission, but not out of any sense of constitutional pacifism or anti-militarism. Yamane's concern is that of a scientist who wants to spare Godzilla's life so that the new creature can be researched.

Godzilla slips past the naval mission and makes his way to Tokyo Bay, where Japanese soldiers are already waiting on the shore with machine guns. Their weapons prove ineffective, even when they later bring in tanks. Japan's next step is a plan to use the JSDF and Coast Guard to construct an electrified fence along the coast and evacuate residents from the area. In the scene discussing the fence plan, one can observe that the civilians in suits are the ones in power, and the soldiers are there to follow their orders. Whether or not this was a deliberate choice, it reinforces the notion that Japan's postwar JSDF does not hold unreasonable influence over the elected government.

None of the JSDF's efforts in the film seem to achieve much, a pattern that will repeat itself in many of Toho's later kaiju films. There is, however, a noteworthy battle scene about one hour into the film, in which a squadron of Japanese fighter jets appears and fires rockets at Godzilla. It occurs at a point when Godzilla was already on his way back into Tokyo Bay, after having destroyed large areas of the city. We are shown a crowd of Tokyo residents watching the display, cheering on the ASDF's attack as upbeat music plays in the background. Their rockets lack the punch to seriously harm Godzilla, but at the very least seem to annoy him. It's a minor victory at best, but it is a patriotic scene in which the people are happy to see Japanese fighter jets inflicting some pain on the monster that hurt so many people.

The ultimate defeat of this Godzilla in this film is thanks not to the military, but to Dr. Serizawa, an anti-military scientist who developed a superweapon known as the Oxygen Destroyer. Serizawa, fearing what could happen to the world if mankind learned about his weapon, would rather die than let the secret of his technology get into the wrong hands. He acts on his convictions by carrying out a suicide attack that also kills Godzilla.

The first film in the series places a strong emphasis on the suffering faced by the civilian victims of Godzilla. Scenes of civilians being burned to death evoke the horrors of Hiroshima, Nagasaki, and World War II, but in this case, Japan's political leadership and its military cannot be blamed for the destruction being wrought upon their nation. None of the civilians were killed due to friendly fire, and Godzilla was created by American nuclear tests, not Japanese misdeeds. Scenes linking Godzilla to the nuclear bombings and air raids on Tokyo, together with Dr. Serizawa's anti-military beliefs, make this a powerful anti-war film, yet the film does not portray the use of force by the

JSDF as harmful. All of the JSDF's attacks, weak as they may be, are primarily aimed at protecting people from Godzilla.

In contrast to the minor role in the first film, its sequel, *Godzilla Raids Again* (1956), gave the JSDF a more central role in the defeat of Godzilla. The leading protagonists, Shoichi Tsukioka and Koji Kobayashi, are initially shown to the audience as civilian pilots working for a fishing company, but one later finds out that they served as pilots in the Imperial Japanese Armed forces during World War II.[3] Through their war experience, they have ties to airmen serving in the ASDF, including an airman named Tajima, who flies alongside them in the later battle against Godzilla. Throughout this film the JSDF as shown in a positive light, seeking to protect Japan while respecting civilian authority. In government meetings concerning the crisis, instead of suggesting a ham-fisted plan, they defer to the judgment of Dr. Yamane, agreeing to his plan to use flares to lure Godzilla away from populated areas. As Godzilla approaches Osaka, their jet-dropped flares almost succeed, failing only when an accident starts a fire and attracts Godzilla's attention. When facing Godzilla's inevitable attack on the city, they put their lives on the line, fighting from tanks and airplanes, with some vehicles—and presumably their pilots and drivers—being wiped out in the process.

Although the JSDF failed to stop Godzilla's attack on Osaka, it plays a central role in the final battle that defeats Godzilla. Tsukioka is given special permission to pilot one of the ASDF's F-86 fighter jets in the battle, but only after being reminded that by taking on this job of a JASDF pilot, he will be doing "work that puts your life on the line" (*inochigake no shigoto*). Together with a combined force of JSDF ground troops and fighter pilots, Tsukioka succeeds in causing an avalanche that buries Godzilla and Anguirus. In the process, Godzilla is able to destroy several aircraft, but they bravely continue the attack until victory is achieved. Unlike the 1954 film, which relied on a fantasy weapon to save Japan from Godzilla, this is a victory that was achieved through the use of the conventional weaponry possessed by the JASDF in 1955. It presents an example of the actual capabilities of the JSDF being utilized to save Japan from a menacing threat.

A notable feature of the 1955 film is the location of the final battle against Godzilla: the Kuril Islands. These islands, which lie north of Hokkaido, were occupied by the Soviet Union in late 1945, and have remained under Russian control until the present day. Japan considers several of the islands, known in Japanese as the "Northern Territories," to be unjustly occupied, and has made numerous unsuccessful attempts to negotiate for the return of these islands. Had such a battle with Godzilla occurred in the real world of 1955, it is extremely doubtful that the Soviet Union would have allowed the JSDF to enter its territorial waters and airspace. Nonetheless, the film calls the island by a Japanese, not a Russian name, and there is no discussion of the Soviet

Union. The island is treated as Japanese territory in the film, so it is only natural that the JSDF take on the role of defending it from Godzilla.

The reference to the Kuril Islands probably had no special meaning for international viewers, but Japanese in 1955 would have likely been aware of the Soviet Occupation of former Japanese territories. Viewers of the film would have included some of the thousands of Japanese citizens who had been expelled from the islands following the Soviet occupation, as well as residents of Hokkaido who felt the unease of Soviet military bases being built on nearby islands. Since its creation, a significant portion of the JSDF's strength has been based in Hokkaido, largely due to its proximity to the Soviet Union. To this day, a tense situation remains along the maritime border with Russia; the scrambling of ASDF jets in response to Russian military aircraft probing Japan's northern airspace is a common occurrence, even in 2016 [Kelly]. It is no stretch of the imagination to interpret *Godzilla Raids Again* (1955) as a film that brings to mind the JSDF's role in protecting Japan from the Soviet Union.

The third and fourth films in the franchise, *King Kong vs. Godzilla* (1962) and *Mothra vs. Godzilla* (1964), marked the beginning of a pattern that would characterize many subsequent Godzilla films. The focus of these films shifted away from humans struggling to defeat monsters, and towards stories in which the main attraction was Godzilla battling against other kaiju. The JSDF make appearances in both films, but their attempts to defeat monsters with tanks, airplanes, and electric shocks prove to be woefully inadequate. In some scenes, JSDF soldiers in *King Kong vs. Godzilla* seem more interested in guessing the outcome of the kaiju battle than in coming up with a new solution to drive the monsters away from Japan. The soldiers, like moviegoers, are there to see the kaiju showdown.

Over the next two decades, Godzilla films declined in both popularity and seriousness. As many of the movies took place in a timeline that acknowledged the events of the previous films, the JSDF within that timeline gradually equipped itself with advanced weaponry that had yet to be invented in the real world. This included Maser Cannons, satellite dish-shaped weapons that fired laser-like beams of electricity at kaiju, as well as various types of rockets and flying machines that had little resemblance to the actual weapons of the JSDF. In response to this development, Japanese fans came up with an official term for the defense forces in these films: the "Toho Defense Force." As one Japanese Godzilla fansite puts it, the existence of such a JSDF equipped with sci-fi superweapons would have been a "major international issue." Although such fantasy weaponry was rarely effective against kaiju, when considered in the context of a world inhabited by other human nations, it would have made Japan's military frighteningly powerful. Such issues, however, are not addressed.

The Godzilla films of the late 1960s and 1970s, with their campy monster battles, fantasy weapons, and space aliens, were quite far from the serious tone of the 1954 original. In several films of this era, the JSDF made no appearances. For example, *Son of Godzilla* (1967) takes place on Monster Island, far from Japan and its military. Even films with monster battles in Japan, such as *Godzilla vs. Mechagodzilla* (1974), have no scenes involving responses from a Japanese defense force.

The 1984 Reboot and Beyond

The Godzilla franchise received a fresh and well-funded reboot with a 30th anniversary reboot in 1984; *The Return of Godzilla* (1984) brought the series to the serious world of the 1954 original, ignoring all post-1954 films and setting its story in a kaiju-free world in which Godzilla was long ago defeated.

Its world is geopolitically similar to the real world of 1984, placing Godzilla and Japan as actors within the framework of the Cold War. It is a world dominated by the rivalry between the United States and the Soviet Union, one in which Japan cannot make decisions without considering the Cold War consequences of its actions. The Japanese government in the film aims to avoid public panic by keeping Godzilla's re-appearance secret, but Cold War considerations force an abandonment of this policy. Godzilla sinks a Soviet submarine and the United States is blamed for the attack, risking a nuclear war until Japan steps up and releases the data it has gathered on Godzilla.

In a reflection of the power dynamics of the time period, the two Cold War superpowers go so far as challenge Japan's freedom to respond to an attack on its own soil. The American and Soviet governments find common ground in insisting that they be allowed to use nuclear weapons against Godzilla. This solution is extremely undesirable to the Japanese in the film. Considering the historical tragedies of Hiroshima and Nagasaki, it is clear most Japanese moviegoers would find such plan to be abhorrent; nonetheless, the Japanese cabinet ministers in the film clearly feel pressured into considering the nuclear option. Interestingly, one of the strongest voices against the use of tactical nuclear weapons is the representative of the JSDF, who questions their effectiveness against Godzilla. As an expert on weaponry, the JSDF officer doubts the military effectiveness of such weapons systems, which are largely unproven, and suggests that the Americans and Soviets may be more interested in weapons testing than protecting Japan from Godzilla.

Japan responds to these demands with a strong refusal to a third nuclear weapon being dropped on its soil. The Prime Minister in the 1984 film confidently refuses to back down in the face of angry American and Soviet representatives. He justifies his decision by citing Japan's principled opposition to nuclear weapons, mirroring the public stance that Japan has long held in the real world since 1971. By asking the Americans and Soviets if they would be willing to nuke one of their own cities if Godzilla had first landed in their country, he convinces them to back down.

The Japanese Prime Minister in this film is a decisive and confident man, a reflection of the historical conditions and mood in Japan at that time. It was an era in which there seemed no end to Japan's economic growth, and many experts believed that Japan had the potential to become the world's leading economy, eclipsing the United States. Leading Japanese politicians of this era, such as Shintaro Ishihara and Ichiro Ozawa, urged their country to be more assertive on the world stage. A bestselling book, *The Japan That Can Say No*, urged Japanese to start looking out for its own interests, even if it meant angering the United States. In *The Return of Godzilla*, Japan's leadership can and does say "no" to the Americans, refusing to let foreign countries tell them how they should defend their own nation. Later events in the film show that Japan had not yet built up a level of international respect to be trusted to defend itself, and a foreign country intervenes without Japanese permission, but Japan's doubts about the effectiveness of nuclear weapons are proven to have been entirely correct.

One example of Japanese assertiveness can be found in the development and deployment of weapons technology. Although the situation has gradually changed in recent years, generally speaking, postwar Japan has not had a particularly large weapons industry. Whereas American arms manufacturers often make considerable profits through the sale of high tech military hardware to allied nations, Japanese law bans the export and sale of most weaponry. Coupled with defense spending that has usually been less than 1 percent of GDP, this creates a situation in which Japan prefers to purchase weapons systems instead of investing large sums of money into research and development. Conditions are apparently different in the Japan depicted in many Godzilla films, and *The Return of Godzilla* film is no exception. The JSDF fields superweapons—such as Maser Cannons—that would have cost a fortune to develop and manufacture.

The JSDF's most powerful superweapon in *The Return of Godzilla* film is the Super X, a heavily-armored flying ship that can withstand Godzilla's famed atomic breath. Until Godzilla's reappearance, the Super X was a tightly-held secret, and like any secret superweapon, it is formidable. Its specially-developed shells succeed in nearly killing Godzilla, and probably would have had it not been for the intervening electromagnetic pulse from a stray Soviet nuclear weapon. Japan, it would seem, had the military capability to defeat Godzilla, but meddling from other countries fouled it up. This annoying setback embodies the mood of those who believed that Japan was capable of achieving greatness, but was being held back by its reluctance to act independently.

The weaponry of the JSDF may fail to defeat their foe in *The Return of Godzilla*, but Japanese ingenuity nonetheless saves the day. After the failure of Super X, a Japanese scientist gets a chance to try out an experimental device that lures Godzilla into a volcano. The JSDF has no role in the development of this technology, but its helicopters and personnel cooperate in getting the scientist and his data delivered to where they need to be. Godzilla's ultimate demise is a product of cooperation between civilians and the military, with the military in a subordinate role.

Subsequent Godzilla films veered into the territory of focusing on monster-on-monster battles, weird fantasy technology, and an SDF that could achieve very little. For example, *Godzilla vs. King Ghidorah* (1991) has time travelling UFOs and a JSDF that willingly unleashes Godzilla on Japan in an attempt to defeat another kaiju. *Godzilla vs. Mechagodzilla* (1993) takes place in a world in which telepathy is real and the United Nations is capable of creating a mechanical kaiju to battle Godzilla. In light of such fantastic circumstances, it is hard to imagine moviegoers treating these films as serious commentaries on the state of Japan.

As the films entered the Millennium era, Toho continued to avoid reality. The 25th film in the franchise, *Godzilla vs. Megaguirus* (2000), takes place in an alternate universe in which the JSDF is equipped with one of its most fanciful weapons—a satellite that can create black holes (as one might expect, black holes turn out to be just as dangerous as giant monster attacks). *Godzilla Against Mechagodzilla* (2002) revived the idea of mechanical kaiju, this time in the form of Kiryu, a cyborg drawing power from the bones of a previous Godzilla and piloted by a special anti-kaiju squadron of the JSDF. Like many of the Millennium era Godzilla films, these two films were firmly placed within the realm of fantasy and aimed more at Godzilla fans than a general audience.

An interesting exception to this trend is *Godzilla, Mothra and King Ghidorah: Giant Monsters All-Out Attack* (2001—hereafter referred to as *GMK*), was one of the most well-received films of the Millennium era. Like the 1984 film, *GMK* takes place in a world in which Godzilla has not been seen since his defeat in 1954. From start to finish, the JSDF are shown as men and women dedicated to the defense of the Japanese people and nation. It would be fair to say that *GMK* contains one of the most positive portrayals of the JSDF ever seen in Japanese cinema. One of the main protagonists of the film, Admiral Taizo Tachibana (played by rock musician Ryudo Uzaki), embodies the patriotic ideal of self-sacrifice for one's country. After Godzilla has defeated every other kaiju in the film, Admiral Tachibana and the JSDF are the last hope for Japan's salvation. Tachibana heroically decides to carry out a suicidal submarine attack on Godzilla, miraculously killing the monster and surviving unscathed.

The Godzilla franchise went into temporary retirement following the costly flop of *Godzilla: Final Wars* (2004). In the 12-year gap between Final Wars and the next film in the series, major changes took place in Japan's domestic and international politics. In 2009, the Liberal Democratic Party (LDP), which had held a ruling majority for most of Japan's postwar history, suffered electoral defeat and was replaced by the Democratic Party of Japan (DPJ). This meant the reigns of Japan's foreign policy, defense policy, and disaster management systems were handed over to relatively inexperienced politicians. In its handling of foreign policy crises, such the disagreement over the relocation of an American military base in Okinawa and clashes between Japanese Coast Guard vessels and Chinese fishing boats near disputed islands, the DPJ appeared weak and indecisive. It also had the misfortune of preceding over the 3/11 disaster, at times facing criticism over not clearly communicating the state of the nuclear accident, as well as not doing enough to help disaster victims. Along with these issues came a sense of general dissatisfaction about the DPJ administration, which had campaigned on Obama-esque slogans of "change," but had failed to live up to most of their promises.

Japan's 2012 election resulted in a crushing defeat for the DPJ and an overwhelming majority for the LDP. Shinzo Abe, who had built his political career on promoting nationalism and talking tough about Japan's Asian neighbors, became Prime Minister. Abe succeeded in achieving one major change to the laws governing the JSDF's actions. In September 2015, the LDP majority in the Diet passed a law reinterpreting Article 9 of the Constitution to allow the JSDF to engage in acts of "collective self-defense" when serving overseas. Under the previous interpretation, Japanese soldiers were banned from using their weapons to help defend friends and allies. The new interpretation allows the JSDF to enter into combat even if an enemy was not directly attacking Japanese soldiers or citizens. Anti-war activists in Japan saw this as a move that could lure Japan into unwanted overseas conflicts, and large protest marches were held in Tokyo. Despite the protests, and despite opinion polls showing that a majority of Japanese opposed the new law, Abe pushed it through the Diet with relative ease.

The 2015 reinterpretation was a step towards something that Japanese conservative politicians have wanted for decades: the elimination of Article 9 and the conversion of the JSDF into a formal military. Abe, the LDP, and grassroots nationalist groups make no secret about their desire for an amendment to the Constitution; however, unlike changing the law, changing the Constitution would require a national referendum.

Public opinion has remained firmly against constitutional revision. One particular public opinion survey, conducted by an international polling firm in 2014, strongly underlines the lack of enthusiasm that many Japanese feel towards war. When asked, "Would you fight for your country?" only 11 percent of Japanese responded affirmatively, making Japan dead-last among the 65 countries polled (the average was 61 percent). Support of Article 9 is deeply entrenched in Japanese society, and the situation seems unlikely to change in the immediate future. Some conservatives are content to play the long game, and are seeking to promote nationalism and pro-military ideals through gradual changes to the education system and culture as a whole. The head of Nippon Kaigi (Japan Conference), the country's largest conservative/nationalist lobbying organization, has estimated it could take 10 years or more for revision to gain enough support (Yoshida).

Despite his nationalist leanings, Prime Minister Abe has enjoyed much better public approval ratings than any his predecessors. As a result, he is the first Prime Minister since 2006 to have remained in power for more than a year, and will likely maintain his position until at least 2018 (Wijaya). Under his rule, Japan faces major challenges: a weak economy, the continuing problems at the Fukushima Daiichi nuclear plant, a shrinking population, and hostile neighbors in Korea and China. It is a time of anxiety and uncertainty about Japan's future.

Shin Godzilla

The creation of a new Godzilla film offered a chance for the series to address the state of present day Japan. It was also a chance for Toho to revive a previously profitable franchise that had experienced disappointing box office earnings in the Millennium era. Toho launched an ambitious new project that brought together some of Japan's most acclaimed actors and filmmakers. Hideaki Anno and Shinji Higuchi, who had worked together to create the famed anime *Neon Genesis Evangelion*, were hired as director/writer and special effects director. The film was given an enormous budget by Godzilla standards, as well the creative freedom to reimagine Godzilla. The selection of the title *Shin Godzilla* ("New Godzilla") emphasized the intent to do something new and fresh with the franchise.

Shin Godzilla (2016) has special significance for two reasons. First of all, it was a huge hit in Japan, surpassing Toho's expectations and earning over $60 million in box office revenue (Blair). It was seen by millions of Japanese moviegoers, beating out every other live-action film released in Japan in 2016. More importantly, it surpassed the Japanese domestic box office earnings of any other Godzilla film, including the highly-successful 2014 Hollywood film. It stands far and out above any of the Toho kaiju films produced in the last two decades. This was a film for a general audience, not only fans of the kaiju genre.

Secondly, the 2016 film has a unique trait that sets it apart from Toho's other Godzilla films: it is completely divorced from the timeline of the original 1954 Godzilla. Although Toho has rebooted the Godzilla franchise several times over the years, films such as *Return of Godzilla* (1984) and *GMK* (2001) have faithfully remain tied to the original. The previous reboots were built on the premise that Godzilla had first appeared in 1954, attacked Tokyo, and disappeared after being taken out by the Oxygen Destroyer. *Shin Godzilla* is a completely clean reboot, taking place in Japan that is indistinguishable from the real Japan of 2016.

The world of *Shin Godzilla* is a realistic. Like our own world, it has no known cases of kaiju attacks or encounters with space aliens and time travelers. The international relations of the film mirror those of the real world—there is no multinational task force in place to fight against science fiction enemies. And, most important of all to the theme of this essay, the Japan Self-Defense Forces of Shin Godzilla are the same as those that exist in today's Japan. The only weapons they possess are those available to the JSDF in 2016: tanks, artillery, missiles, attack helicopters, and jet fighters. They do not have giant ray guns, mecha-kaiju, or the ability to set up gigantic electric shock weapons at a moment's notice.

Official movie posters for the film contained a slogan that unambiguously introduced the main focus of the film "Nippon vs. Godzilla." This takes the series back to its 1954 roots: a realistic Japan confronts a totally unexpected and unbelievable enemy. In order to achieve realism, the producers of Shin Godzilla regularly met with representatives of the JSDF. They wanted the lines in the script to reflect the actual way that the Japanese military spoke, and wanted to accurately portray the legal complexities of deploying Japanese troops into combat (Ushio). Combat scenes were also filmed with the assistance of the JSDF, which provided actual tanks, airplanes, and helicopters, along with soldiers and airmen to star in the film as extras. Given that cooperation extended to the level of consulting about the contents of the movie script, it is perhaps not surprising that the film depicts the JSDF in an overwhelmingly positive light. It is unlikely that official cooperation would have been given to a film that was anti-military.

One of the most striking features that sets *Shin Godzilla* is its focus on political debate and bureaucracy. The main protagonist in the film is Rando Yaguchi (played by Hiroki Hasegawa), a young politician who holds the rank of Deputy Chief Cabinet Secretary within the Japanese government, a relatively minor position that limits him to sitting at a side table during cabinet meetings. The top-level cabinet posts are occupied by much older politicians, none of whom will go on to play a major role in stopping Godzilla. These older politicians, especially the Prime Minister, seem more concerned about politics than taking decisive action.

Shortly after Godzilla first appears in Tokyo Bay, Yaguchi, who has been monitoring the situation on social media, tries to bring up the idea that the mysterious sighting could be a large animal. His superiors dismiss the suggestion as ridiculous, and Yaguchi is warned about talking out of place when his superiors are the ones who should be talking. This pattern of frustration continues through several meetings, as Yaguchi and other mid-level officials begin to realize the grave situation, but cannot act because they must defer to their superiors. Eventually, all of Yaguchi's predictions come true, much to the embarrassment of the cabinet ministers, who had foolishly decided that it would be best for the Prime Minister to hold a press conference confidently announcing unfounded conclusions about the safety of the situation.

Japan's leadership is neither decisive nor bold. Numerous people are killed by Godzilla while the Prime Minister and other leaders continue to hold meetings discussing what is happening. When it is suggested that the Prime Minister send in the JSDF to attack Godzilla, he hesitates. If the order were given, it would make the first time in Japan's postwar history that a government has invoked Article 88 of the Self-Defense Forces Law and ordered a "defensive deployment" (*boei tsushitsu*) legally authorizing the use of force "to the limit necessary for protecting the country" (Yamaguchi). Such a move could have political fallout, and the Prime Minister is afraid to take that step. It seems almost absurd, as scenes of Godzilla smashing cars and buildings appear between scenes of the Prime Minister vacillating on the issue. The Governor of Tokyo prefecture impatiently demands to know why the order hasn't been given yet, wishing he could call in the JSDF himself.

This does not, however, mean that the JSDF is sitting on the sidelines. While some soldiers await their orders to fight, many others are shown evacuating civilians. These scenes mirror the television coverage the JSDF has received for disaster relief, helping with evacuation and rescue efforts in the aftermath of events such as the 2011 Tohoku earthquake/tsunami and the 2016 Kumamoto earthquake. Such actions have received a great deal of positive press, helping improve the image of the JSDF among the Japanese people. Scenes of the JSDF using helicopters and trucks to help evacuate civilians and scenes of soldiers dishing out food at evacuation shelters no doubt reminded Japanese moviegoers of the contributions that the JSDF has made in the real world.

After much delay, the Prime Minister in the film finally decides to issue a defensive deployment order to the JSDF. Attack helicopters swiftly appear on the scene of Godzilla's rampage, spreading out in front of the monster and readying their weapons, but the soldiers hold their fire. Despite the best efforts to evacuate all civilians from Godzilla's path, some remain nearby. In this case, the JSDF spots two civilians near Godzilla's feet, causing the helicopter gunners fear the possibility of collateral damage. The Prime Minister, who holds the ultimate responsibility for making tough decisions, once again hesitates.

At that moment, Godzilla retreats into Tokyo Bay, allowing the Prime Minister to avoid issuing an order to open fire. Although they do not know it at the time, Godzilla will eventually evolve into a form that is impervious to the JSDF's weaponry, and will end up killing countless numbers of Japanese civilians. Had the Prime Minister actually ordered the helicopters to open fire, it is conceivable that Godzilla could have been defeated with minimal effort.

The hesitance of politicians to let loose the JSDF might appear strange to longtime fans of the Godzilla franchise. After all, the other Godzilla films, including those that aimed for seriousness, lack such a focus. The other films often had their own scenes of tense discussion in government situation rooms, but none approach *Shin Godzilla*'s seeming obsession over the legality and morality of having the JSDF deploy against Godzilla. This is likely because the other post–1954 films took place in a timeline in which Japan had a historical precedence for sending its troops into combat. Much like the Japan of *GMK,* in which Admiral Tachibana gives lectures about "the only time" the JSDF had seen battle, people in those films would have known about the JSDF's 1954 battle against Godzilla, and would have less qualms about sending them to battle again.

In its depiction of the political issues surrounding the JSDF, *Shin Godzilla* is arguably the most realistic film in the entire franchise. One review in the *Yomiuri Shimbun*, Japan's largest newspaper, noted that *Shin Godzilla* was remarkable for its realistic approach to depicting the politics of national defense. The scenes in which politicians hesitate and debate whether the JSDF should be sent into action against Godzilla demonstrate to audiences that the JSDF is firmly under civilian control, and that it cannot act without the approval of the Prime Minister (Fujita). Obviously, if a weak Prime Minister is in office during a national emergency that requires swift action, it could be very dangerous for Japan. Numerous articles and reviews in the Japanese press have echoed this assessment of the realistic feel of the politics in the film, and its criticism of the indecisiveness of present day politicians. It seems to show that Japan gravely requires military-minded leader and a revision of legal restrictions on JSDF deployments, a message that echoes the agenda of Prime Minister Abe and other hawks within the Japanese political establishment.

This view has been disputed by at least one influential expert. Former Defense Minister Shigeru Ishiba, a leading figure in the Liberal Democratic Party, called out the film's use of a defense deployment as unrealistic. Ishiba has argued that Godzilla is not a foreign country or a foreign military, meaning that a kaiju attack would not fulfill the legal requirements for a defense-related deployment of the JSDF. He has compared Godzilla to a rampaging bear or wild boar, which is nothing more than an animal under the law. This would make the entire debate surrounding a defense deployment a pointless endeavor. As an expert who has not only held the top position at the Ministry of Defense but has also been a life-long military geek, Ishiba believes the most likely legal means the government would take in such a scenario would be to classify a JSDF deployment as a response to a natural disaster. By classifying Godzilla as a natural disaster, the controversy surrounding defensive deployments could be avoided. Under the law, the JSDF is allowed to use "tools" when responding to natural disasters, and as long as weaponry targeted only Godzilla (and not other humans), tanks, artillery, and missile-launching aircraft could be legally interpreted as "tools" (Ishiba).

It might be fair to say that most moviegoers in Japan are not as knowledgeable as Ishiba when it comes to the nuances of bending Japan's laws to allow for combat with invading monsters. Like movie reviewers, they would have found it plausible that the Japanese government would need to order a combat deployment in order to use the JSDF's weaponry against Godzilla.

That weaponry is finally put the test when Godzilla launches his second attack, making landfall near Kamakura and heading towards Tokyo. Seeing the destruction, the Prime Minister once again orders the JSDF to attack, this time making it clear that there will be no restrictions on their use of firepower. Every weapons system at the JSDF's disposal is prepared for action and a defense line is set up along the Tama River. As Godzilla approaches the river the JSDF opens fire with its attack helicopters. Weapons are employed in order of destructive power, starting with helicopter-mounted cannons and moving on to rockets, tank cannons, artillery, long-range missiles, and aerial bombardment. As each weapon makes its appearance on the screen, subtitles announce the name of the weapon and the JSDF base from which it is being deployed. Cameras zoom in on the weapons as they are fired, and the resulting explosions are spectacular. Those who are familiar with Hideaki Anno's earlier works might notice that these scenes are very similar to the scenes of weapons being fired at monsters in *Evangelion*. Although the weapons are incapable of harming Godzilla, the audience is shown the incredible firepower at the disposal of an organization that is supposed to not be a formal military. These scenes could be described as a form of fan service for military otaku—the subset of Japanese anime and film viewers who are obsessed with weapons technology.

The JSDF's weapons fail to stop Godzilla, with tank crews dying in action as Godzilla plows through their defense line and into the densely populated center of Tokyo. The Japanese Prime Minister decides to invoke the U.S.-Japan Security Treaty and ask their American allies for assistance. The Americans, as it would turn out, doubted Japan's capabilities and had already had bombers in the air waiting for the order to attack Godzilla. Unlike the JSDF's weaponry, the American bombs have a large blast radius that would put numerous civilians at risk. Much like Japan in 1945, civilians are ordered to take shelter from American bombing, but this time, it is ironically a bombing requested by the Japanese themselves.

The American bombs succeed in visibly wounding Godzilla, but the success is short-lived. Enraged by the attack, Godzilla lashes out and shoots beams from his body, destroying the bombers and anything else nearby. Godzilla's outburst is, far more than in previous Godzilla films, truly devastating. The beams fired from his body demolish areas of Tokyo in a manner comparable to a nuclear explosion. In the process, Godzilla manages to decapitate the Japanese government by shooting down the helicopter that was evacuating the Prime Minister and 11 of his cabinet ministers. The old guard politicians are wiped out, leaving the future of Japan in the hands of the next generation.

In the aftermath of the destruction of Tokyo the Japanese government is relocated to a JSDF base in the western area of Tokyo prefecture, far from the city center. The Prime Ministership of Japan falls into the hands of a minor cabinet minister who was not on the ill-fated helicopter. The new Prime Minister, overwhelmed by the situation, relies on the work of younger men, including the aforementioned Yaguchi. Yaguchi and his comrades, who were previously not important enough to deserve a helicopter evacuation from Tokyo, are now calling the shots in the desperate struggle against Godzilla.

Unlike the Japan in *The Return of Godzilla* (1984), the Japan in *Shin Godzilla* lacks confidence and influence over other countries. The events in Tokyo convince America and other world powers that conventional weaponry is useless and nuclear weapons must be used to stop Godzilla. Japan's political leadership are horrified by this prospect, but realize there is little they can do to stop it. The Japan of 2016 is not the Japan of the 1980s—it is a country that knows it is in decline, and after losing its most economically important city, it is reduced to a condition of extreme weakness. The leaders of Japan know that when it is all over, they will be in desperate need of international assistance if they want to rebuild their country. To Japanese viewers, many of whom are keenly aware of their country's weakening position in the world order, it is an understandable conclusion.

Thanks to some personal connections from a member of the Japanese government, Japan receives help from an unlikely ally—France. The French intervene at the United Nations and persuade other countries to give Japan some extra time to attempt Yaguchi's non-nuclear solution to the Godzilla problem. Yaguchi's team includes officials from several parts of Japanese society: government bureaucrats, civilian scientists, and members of the Self-Defense Forces. His solution is not a conventional military plan, but it heavily depends on the cooperation of the JSDF, who happen to be up to the task. Gathering industrial equipment, construction vehicles, and chemicals from other across Japan, they assemble an attack force that will spray coolant into

Godzilla to shut down his nuclear innards. Civilians work out the details of the plan and gather the necessary materials, but it is the JSDF that will put their lives on the line to carry it out.

The men of the Self-Defense Forces are ready and willing to put Yaguchi's plan into action. When he thanks GSDF generals for their cooperation, they respond by telling him that there is no need to thank them for risking their lives: it's their job. Shortly before they set the plan into motion, Yaguchi delivers a speech to the Japanese soldiers who have assembled for the operation, telling them that they, the JSDF, are the last line of defense for their country, Japan's final hope. It is made very clear that, despite this being a plan that doesn't involve the JSDF firing their weapons, it is still something that cannot be done without Japanese soldiers. The necessity of a military force is evident.

The final battle against Godzilla receives an interesting assist from Japan's longtime ally. The Americans send a huge force of aerial drones to fire missiles at Godzilla, forcing the monster to shoot beams until he tires out and needs to rest. This military effort costs no human lives, underlining the fact that only Japanese soldiers will take part and die in the final assault. The Japanese do their part by packing unmanned trains full of explosives and ramming them into Godzilla. The use of trains—including the famous Shinkansen and an array of JR line trains—seems highly impractical. Sending in these trains, well-known symbols of Japanese technological achievement, is a uniquely Japanese solution. After that explosive attacks, Yaguchi sends in two successive waves of construction vehicles piloted by Japanese soldiers. Godzilla annihilates the first wave, but the second wave drives forward without hesitation, finishing the job and spraying coolant into Godzilla until he freezes.

The victory in Shin Godzilla is a victory achieved through the hard work and sacrifice of Japanese soldiers. The film's portrayal of petty and stupid Japanese political leadership serves as a scathing criticism of the current state of politics in Japan, but there is no such criticism of the JSDF. There are no bad soldiers or officers in the film—they all appear deeply committed to the protection of the Japanese nation and its people, and they achieve that mission. "Nippon vs. Godzilla" is a costly battle, but it ends in patriotic victory for Japan. It is a film that is highly agreeable to fans of the JSDF and supporters of constitutional revision and increased defense spending. Because the final plan required the aid of the United States, it underlines the necessity of Japan's alliance with America, something that right-leaning Japanese tend to recognize as a strategic necessity.

Shin Godzilla also follows an interesting pattern established in the 1954 film and respected in subsequent films. Godzilla destroys many famous landmarks in Tokyo, but there is apparently no attack on the Imperial Palace; moreover, in the midst of a major crisis that forces the government to flee from Tokyo, there is not a single mention of the Emperor or the Imperial Family.

Perhaps it is a reflection of the filmmakers' respect for political taboos (Kushner 49), or it could be a nod to the idea that Godzilla is an embodiment the souls of Japan's Pacific War dead (Inuhiko 107–108). Regardless of the reason behind it, not including the Imperial family in the film avoids a controversial issue that could have provoked intense reactions from nationalist and conservative groups. In fact, the film has been generally well-received by Japanese conservatives. Its depiction of a weak and indecisive Prime Minister who baulks at the thought of utilizing the JSDF has been interpreted by some conservatives as a criticism of politicians who do not support their reform agenda.

Conservative columnist Tsunehira Furuya, a longtime fan of the Godzilla series, has called Shin Godzilla the best Japanese film of the 21st century. He sees it as reflecting Japan's current circumstances, in which Japan has a dark future, has lost hope, but still must fight on. To achieve this, the Japanese people and Japan need to change and become, like Godzilla, "new" (the "shin" in Shin Godzilla) (Cross Cut). Tsunehara, a supporter of constitutional revision, believes that establishing a stronger and legally-sound military is part of the path towards a new and better Japan.

Film critic Yukichi Maeda, a regular contributor to the nationalist web broadcaster Nihon Bunka Channel Sakura, has praised the film as a "realistic political simulation." Maeda has suggested that Godzilla may be a metaphor for real world foreign threats to Japan, such as China. Commenting on the JSDF's appearance in the film, he notes that their weaponry had 100 percent accuracy, always hitting Godzilla, and usually in the face. He states that this accuracy reflects the professional reality of the JSDF. There is a contrast between the conduct of the Americans—who are ready to drop large bombs, including nuclear weapons, with the expectation of civilian casualties, and the JSDF—who put the lives of the Japanese people first, even if it means holding fire for the sake of just two civilians. To Maeda, this shows the folly of relying on other countries to protect Japan, because that protection will not necessarily benefit the Japanese people (Nihon Bunka Channel Sakura).

As a film that is agreeable to the political goals of Japanese conservative and nationalist groups, Shin Godzilla could be placed in the same category as the recent war film *The Eternal Zero* (2013). Both films were top earners at the Japanese box office, demonstrating that stories that appeal to a general audience, combined with well-known actors and high budgets, can produce highly successful works that transmit right-leaning political views to general audiences.

Conclusion

In one of the world's most anti-military nations, the Japan Self-Defense Forces have spent most of their history avoiding public attention. While this may have been a useful survival strategy in the early postwar years, changing geopolitical and societal conditions have led to a reverse course, with the JSDF actively cooperating with film producers.

Regardless of official support, Toho has spent the last 50 years producing monster movies that feature the JSDF, often in positive roles. Looking back on its most popular film franchise, the Godzilla series, one can observe some instances in which the JSDF was portrayed as heroic defenders of Japan, and many in which it was a mere sideshow to monster-on-monster battles. Nonetheless, these films have consistently shown the Japanese people that their country, despite constitutional restrictions, possesses a heavily armed military force that is well-prepared and eager to act in the defense of Japan and its people. Some of the most famous and serious films in the franchise, such as *Godzilla* (1954), *Godzilla Raids Again* (1955), *The Return of Godzilla* (1984), and *GMK* (2001) tend to emphasize this message.

The most recent addition to the Godzilla franchise, *Shin Godzilla* (2016), criticizes Japanese politicians' timidity towards the use of military force while depicting the JSDF in a glowingly favorable light. Its story of a new Godzilla that can only be defeated by a new Japan can be seen as an argument in favor of a newfound appreciation of Japan's quasi-military. Amid conservative and nationalist calls for constitutional revision and conversion of the JSDF into a formal military, it is a film that strongly advocates the advantages of military force. Although Japan's political and military future is clouded in uncertainty, it is evident that the Godzilla franchise has served to remind the Japanese public of the fact that their country possesses military capabilities, and through its most recent film, it has spread a pro-military message to millions of viewers.

Notes

1. As this is an essay discussing the films in the context of Japanese domestic politics, the films examined are the original Japanese language versions, not English dubs. To avoid confusion, the American names for each film are used.

2. About half of the pre–1984 films the Japanese military force is referred to as the "Defense Force" (*boeitai*) instead of the word used for the "Self-Defense Forces" (*jieitai*). There seems little consistency or meaning behind the selection. For example, in *King Kong vs. Godzilla* (1963), the Japanese have "Self-Defense Forces," but in several later films, including Terror of Mechagodzilla, there is instead a "Defense Force." As I cannot observe a special reason for this naming variation, I refer to all Japan's defense forces as the JSDF in the remaining sections of this essay.

3. Interestingly, the English language subtitles in the American DVD release of this film do not fully translate Tsukioka's conversation with his former flying comrades. American viewers are told that they were old buddies from college. Their remarks about serving in the same squadron are not translated.

Works Cited

Barr, Jason. *The Kaiju Film: A Critical Study of Cinema's Biggest Monsters.* Jefferson, NC: McFarland, 2016.

Ben-Ari, Eyal. "Death and the Japanese Self-Defense Forces." Podoler, Guy. *War and Militarism in Modern Japan*. Kent: Global Oriental, 2009. 173–185.

Blair, Gavin J. "Japan Box Office: 'Godzilla Resurgence' Becomes Biggest Live-Action Film of Year With $60M." *Hollywood Reporter* 5 September 2016. http://www.hollywoodreporter.com/news/japan-box-office-godzilla-resurgence-925708. Accessed 6 September 2016.

Cut Cross. "Furuya Tsunehara: Shin-gojira wo miru beshi! Sore demo *bokutachi ga kono kuni de ikiteiku tame ni gojira sengoshi—Anno Hideaki kuronikuru ~ gojira eiga wo gekijo de mita koto arimasu ka?*" 古谷経衡「シン ゴジラみるべし！ それでも僕たちがこの国で生きていくために 『ゴジラと戦後史』」 庵野秀明クロニクル～ゴジラ映画を劇場で観たことがありますか？ [モーニング[モーニングCROSS]" [*Furuya Tsunehira: "You should see Shin Godzilla! 'Godzilla & Postwar History' that will help us live in this country." Anno Hideaki Chronicle~Have you seen a Godzilla film in the theater?*]. Youtube, Website. 4 August 2016. https://www.youtube.com/watch?v=dNiJFKgVa_ M. Accessed 16 August 2016.

Davies, Matt, and Simon Philpott. "Militarization and Popular Culture." Gouliamos, Kostas and Christos Kassimeris. *The Marketing of War in the Age of Neo-Militarism*. London: Routledge, 2013. 43–59.

Desjardins, Chris. *Outlaw Masters of Japanese Film*. London, I. B. Tauris, 2005

Fruhstuck, Sabine. *Uneasy Warriors*. Berkeley: University of California Press, 2007.

Fujita, Ryota 藤津亮太 "Dai Hitto Eiga Shin Gojira wo mita hito ga kataritaku naru riyu" 大ヒット映画「シン・ゴジラ」を見た人が語りたくなる理由 [Why people want to talk about the hit movie Godzilla Resurgence]. *Yomiuri Shimbun* 読売新聞 3 September 2016. Online. http://www.yomiuri.co.jp/fukayomi/ichiran/20160902-OYT8T50007.html? page_no=1. Accessed 4 September 2016.

Gady, Franz-Stefan. *Japan Approves Record Defense Budget*. 28 December 2015. Website. http://thediplomat.com/2015/12/japan-approves-record-defense-budget/. Accessed 15 July 2016.

Inuhiko, Yomota. "The Menace from the South Seas: Honda Ishiro's Godzilla." Stringer, Julian and Alistair Phillips. *Japanese Cinema: Texts and Contexts*. New York: Routledge, 2007. 102–111.

Ishiba, Shigeru 石破茂 "Ohatsubon goaisatsu nado" お初盆ご挨拶など [Hatsubon greetings and other topics]. Ishiba Shigeru Blog 石破茂ブログ, Web. 19 August 2016. http://ishiba-shigeru.cocolog-nifty.com/blog/2016/08/post-55fa-1.html Accessed 25 August 2016.

Kelly, Tim. "Japan jets scramble at Cold-War levels as Chinese and Russian incursions increase." *Reuters* 14 April 2015. http://www.reuters.com/article/japan-airforce-scramble-idUSL4N0XC2ZC20150415. Accessed 15 July 2016.

Kushner, Barak. "Gojira As Japan's First Postwar Media Event." Tsuitsui, William and Michiko Ito. *In Godzilla's Footsteps*. New York: Palgrave Macmillan, 2006. 39–49.

Neumann, Iver B., and Daniel H. Nexon. *Harry Potter and International Relations*. Lanham: Rowman & Littlefield, 2006.

Nihon Bunka Channel Sakura. "Maeda Yukichi ni kiku! Shin Gojira no miryoku to natsu yasumi osusume eiga—Nacchanchi Mayuchanchi #79" 前田有一に聞く！「シン ゴジラ」の魅力と夏休みオススメ映画◇なっちゃんち まゆちゃんち #79 [*Ask Maeda Yukichi! Recommendations for Summer Vacation Films & the Appeal of Godzilla-Nacchanchi & Mayuchanchi #79*]. Youtube, Web. 16 August 2016. https://www.youtube.com/watch?v=h3d8GQiu21k Accessed 20 August 2016.

Samuels, Richard J. *"Rich Nation, Strong Army": National Security and the Technological Transformation of Japan*. Ithaca: Cornell University Press, 1996.

———. *Securing Japan*. Ithaca: Cornell University Press, 2007.

Seaton, Philip A. *Japan's Contested War Memories: The 'Memory Rifts' in Historical Consciousness of World War II*. London, Routledge, 2007.

Smethurst, Richard J. *A Social Basis for Prewar Japanese Militarism: The Army and the Rural Community*. Berkeley: University of California Press, 1974.

Tsutsui, William. *Godzilla On My Mind*. New York: Palgrave MacMillan, 2004.

Ushio, Masato. "Gojira taiji ni, jieitai ha boei shitsudo dekiru ka?" ゴジラ退治に、自衛隊は「防衛出動」できるか [Could a defensive deployment of the JSDF be used against Godzilla?]. 日経ビジネスオンライン [Nikkei Business Online], 5 September 2016. http://business.nikkeibp.co.jp/atcl/opinion/16/083000015/083100001/. Accessed 6 September 2016.

Wijaya, Trissia. "Abenomics Is Failing. So Why Is Abe Poised to Win Big in Japan's Elections?" *The Diplomat, Web.* 5 July 2016. http://thediplomat.com/2016/07/abenomics-is-failing-so-why-is-abe-poised-to-win-big-in-japans-elections/. Accessed 3 August 2016.

Yamaguchi, Noboru. *Japan's Security Legislation from an Operational Perspective.* 3 November 2015. http://www.tokyofoundation.org/en/articles/2015/security-legislation-operational-perspective. Accessed 31 August 2016.

Yoshida, Reiji. "Nationalist leader predicts constitutional revision in 10 years." *The Japan Times*, 13 July 2016. http://www.japantimes.co.jp/news/2016/07/13/national/nationalist-leader-predicts-constitutional-revision-10-years/. Accessed 31 July 2016.

The Ideology of Disaster
Godzilla, Gorillas and Geopolitics in the Global 21st Century

JAMIE MACDONALD

In 1954, Godzilla made its first appearance on cinema screens in a Japanese film which has been widely read as a powerful and somber anti-war allegory.[1] In 2014, Godzilla made his first appearance on water skis, in an American television advert for the Snickers chocolate bar ("Godzilla–New Snickers"). Godzilla's status as metaphor for the nuclear devastation visited on Japan by the United States at the conclusion of World War II in Ishiro Honda's original *Gojira* (1954) has frequently been explored; the creature is radioactive, can breathe nuclear fire, and has the burned black skin of an atomic blast victim. One might well question how the star of a film which contained such a strong expression of anti-war and potentially anti–American sentiment has become so embedded into the pop culture consciousness of the United States. In the U.S., Godzilla has advertised everything from soft drinks ("Godzilla and Dr. Pepper") to cars ("Fiat 500"), has been featured in television shows ("Thirty Minutes Over Tokyo") and movies (*Godzilla* 1998), and has even made a contribution to the English language through popularization of the suffix "-zilla" ("-zilla, comb. form"). Godzilla has been repackaged, redeployed, and repeatedly commodified since the creature's debut appearance, but the political significance of Godzilla movies has evolved over time to reflect and respond to political shifts in the monster's parent nation.[2]

Godzilla's fame in the United States is rivaled by only one other giant movie monster: King Kong. While King Kong's record of six major cinematic releases pales in the shadow of Godzilla's 30+ starring roles, the titanic gorilla has nevertheless become a cinematic icon with a similarly global reach; Cynthia Erb characterizes Kong as "one of the best-known characters ever produced by the Hollywood cinema, and a figure repeatedly activated in art and mass culture, both in the United States and abroad" (13). Much as Godzilla has come to signify Japan for many Westerners, King Kong is a national icon of the United States. Kong's origin contains elements which, like Godzilla's, seem to exist uneasily with the creature's massive pop culture appeal. For instance, as several critics note, an important part of *King Kong*'s (1933) reception history is its relationship with the ethnographic film.[3] *King Kong* directors Cooper and Schoedsack were creators of ethnographic productions in the 1920s (Rony 159), a style of cinema which sought to capture images of exotic lands and peoples for a Western audience. Though the stated aims of such studies were often scientific, Rony characterizes ethnographic spectacle as a "long-established tradition ... in which indigenous peoples are exhibited and dissected–both visually and literally" (190). Such a reading of *King Kong* links the titular creature with the natives of the film's Skull Island, with the ethnographic subject, and consequently with a racist depiction of the non-white male. As Rony elaborates: "The lineage of King Kong should be obvious: the filming, capture, exhibition, photographing, and finally murder of Kong takes its cue from the historic exploitation of native peoples as freakish 'ethnographic' specimens by science, cinema, and popular culture" (159). Erb, in a similar reading, proposes that "King Kong's status as an ape activates long-standing Western assumptions about the process of evolution. In the myth of King Kong, the ape sees the white woman and in reaching for her, reaches for the possibility of evolving, or becoming human" (16). As evidenced by these readings, the initial portrayals of both Godzilla and Kong have ideological stakes which pose questions about the transmission and reception of political thought through popular culture.

Modern viewers may not be aware of the original political relevance of their favorite creatures, but recent years have seen the proliferation in the United States of giant monster movies that renew focus on the ideologically-charged aspects of their predecessors. Even when not explicitly adapting their forebears, these new films reactivate, reevaluate, and update the significance of the giant monster in the popular imagination. While King Kong is in many ways emblematic of the American giant monster movie, the colossi which Hollywood populates cinema screens with in the 21st century look rather different to the iconic ape. Instead, there has been a discernible shift in the imagery and content of American productions towards the Japanese *kaiju eiga* tradition which began with *Gojira*. This shift appears to be mainly the result of two factors. Firstly, as the technology and techniques of computer generated effects have continued to advance, filmmakers have been able to depict larger and more believable monsters than ever before; creatures which rival the scale of the stars of kaiju eiga have become easier to realize. Secondly, the late twentieth century saw what Anne Allison terms "a new fad or fetish for Japan in the American imagination, particularly among youth" (100).

According to Allison, the rise of Japanese popular culture to new levels of "global prominence" led to "the 'Japanization' of even U.S.–made pop culture, as seen in the movies *The Matrix* and *Kill Bill* and with pop stars such as Gwen Stefani and her Harajuku Girls" (100–101). This Japanese turn in American pop culture, it seems safe to suggest, has had an influence on 21st century American monster cinema. The significance of this turn is multi-faceted and complex.

This essay will consider three American kaiju movies: Matt Reeves' *Cloverfield* (2008), Guillermo Del Toro's *Pacific Rim* (2013), and Gareth Edwards' *Godzilla* (2014), and will propose that each enters into a dialogue with its predecessors, reflects contemporary anxieties, and updates the political relevance of the kaiju film. The essay will base the analysis of how each film engages with the objects of collective anxiety on elements of Susan Sontag's 1965 essay "The Imagination of Disaster," in which she proposed that "we live under continual threat of two equally fearful, but seemingly opposed, destinies: unremitting banality and inconceivable terror. It is fantasy, served out in large rations by the popular arts, which allows most people to cope with these twin specters" (42). Sontag's conclusions can be applied productively to *Gojira* as a way to understand the film's use of its atomic metaphor as a form of coping mechanism for anxieties surrounding the use of nuclear weapons. While kaiju films frequently dwell on such anxieties without specifically working to dispel them (Barr 17), merely through inviting audience confrontation with a source of collective trauma in the safe environment of the cinema Sontag posits that such films can "normalize what is psychologically unbearable, thereby inuring us to it" (42). The collective fears which constitute the modern imagination of disaster bear little resemblance to those Sontag considered, but the response of pop culture to mass anxiety continues to be relevant to the understanding of fantasy, science fiction, and kaiju cinema.

The essay will base its political commentary on Fredric Jameson's writing on the political unconscious and the geopolitical unconscious. Jameson casts interpretation generally as "an essentially allegorical act, which consists in rewriting a given text in terms of a particular interpretive master code" (*The Political Unconscious* x) and characterizes the political interpretation of texts as "the absolute horizon of all reading and all interpretation" (*The Political Unconscious* 1). Our political unconscious operates to "map our fellows in class terms day by day and fantasize our current events in terms of larger mythic narratives" (Jameson *The Geopolitical Aesthetic* 3), and political readings of kaiju reveal elements of an "interpretive master code" which consists of rich political narratives reflected and reinforced by such films. The geopolitical unconscious is an expansion of the political unconscious which takes into account not just national-level political conditions but responds to the increased inter-connectedness of global politics by attempting "to refashion national allegory into a conceptual instrument for grasping our new being-in-the-world" (Jameson *The Geopolitical Aesthetic* 3). Kaiju films can consequently be read effectively as geopolitical "maps" of the world system, and this essay will argue that contemporary American kaiju cinema attempts to re-conceptualize the role of the United States in an increasingly volatile global community. Such an effort is not only productive for domestic viewers in that the films explore anxieties related to the United States' placement in contemporary world politics, but also fulfills an important role in shaping perceptions of the United States worldwide through the exporting of American pop culture. The essay will also explore the relevance of modern kaiju cinema to U.S.–Japan relations, the balance of power in the world system, and the way the proliferation of pop culture shapes the perception of contemporary global anxieties.

Cloverfield presents New York City under siege; a building-sized monster causes chaos as it rampages through lower Manhattan, while we watch a group of 20-something New Yorkers attempt to make their way through the broken urban landscape. In a break from both traditional American monster films and Japanese kaiju eiga, *Cloverfield*'s action unfolds from the perspective of a single diegetic camera wielded by the film's protagonist, and is delivered to the viewer supposedly unedited. An elaborate series of opening frames establishes *Cloverfield* not as cinema but as "DOCUMENT #USGX-8810-B467," the contents of an SD card which we are informed is the property of the U.S. Department of Defense. Most of the camerawork and narration is handled by the character of Hud (T. J. Miller), whom we are introduced to during the film's opening scenes, and the film relies entirely on diegetic music save for one orchestral piece used during its end credits. This music, entitled "Roar! (*Cloverfield* overture)" bears clear similarities in its heavy use of driving strings and deep horns to Akira Ifukube's score for *Gojira*. Similar acknowledgments of the film's Japanese predecessors litter the early parts of *Cloverfield*; the movie opens with a leaving party thrown for Rob (Michael Stahl-David), who is moving to Japan in order to take on a new job, and the apartment venue is populated with a number of objects which reference Japanese culture. From the reproduction of the iconic Hokusai woodblock print *The Great Wave off Kanagawa* to the miniature Japanese flag which sits next to a quintessentially American red plastic cup, these objects, as supposedly captured incidentally by Hud's camerawork, implicitly link *Cloverfield* to the kaiju eiga genre. The integration of these items into the naturalistic party scenes constructs the apartment as a hybrid American-Japanese space, and the apartment exists almost as a microcosm of the wider film; *Cloverfield* takes some situational cues from the Japanese kaiju eiga tradition, but uses its American stage to confront contemporary issues in the U.S. imaginary.

Contemporary pop culture spreads more freely beyond national borders than ever before. Ideas and icons cross continents in an age of global media distribution, and are frequently adapted, remade and rebooted far from media's country of origin. The sharing of pop culture across national borders is not a new phenomenon: to take just one example, *Gojira* was undoubtedly influenced by Eugene Lourie's *The Beast From 20,000 Fathoms* (1953). However, what has changed is the frequency and magnitude of such exchanges. The free movement of pop culture itself has strong political potential, as proposed by Joseph Nye, Jr., in his work, "Soft Power." Nye, Jr., suggests a division between a country's *hard power*, which can broadly be conceived of as power arising from a country's military strength its wealth, and *soft power*, which "is the ability to get what you want through attraction rather than coercion or payments. It arises from the attractiveness of a country's culture, political ideals, and policies" (x). Exported pop culture is part of a nation's political influence, and the prevalence of Japanese imagery in the opening of *Cloverfield* gestures towards the attractiveness of Japanese culture to American citizens; the Japanese turn in American pop culture can consequently be understood as an ideologically charged process. In depicting the apartment as a hybrid Japanese-American space, *Cloverfield* speaks back to its Japanese influences through its homage to kaiju eiga.

As the film's monster approaches, *Cloverfield*'s jubilant tone is shattered. Panic and confusion is engendered by the film's visuals and its shot style; people run in terror, jump cuts are used more frequently, and the film's camerawork is more generally frantic. The monster's demolition of a building causes a cloud of dust to engulf the road as Hud retreats into a harshly-lit shop. When our perspective returns to the street, the film's imagery strongly resembles recordings of the September 11, 2001, terrorist attacks on the World Trade Center. The omnipresent dust, the falling scraps of paper, and the images of fleeing civilians construct the visual style of *Cloverfield* in the image of 9/11 news reports.[4] The film's amateur style builds on an established sense of naturalism during these moments to evoke the multitude of public-filmed accounts of the attack. In this respect, *Cloverfield*'s allegorical structure resembles Sontag's imagination of disaster; our perspective, aligned with Hud's, allows us to experience the terror of a fictionalized attack in total safety. Like *Gojira*, *Cloverfield* heavily references a traumatic event, but distances viewers from the event itself through the use of fantastical elements. Individual traumatic experiences are those which "are not assimilated or experienced fully at the time, but only belatedly" (Caruth 4). The imagination of disaster is driven by collective trauma; cinema allows mass audiences to re-confront and assimilate aspects of a traumatic event without fully re-experiencing it.

Notably, while Sontag points to the influence of "historical reality" on science fiction and fantasy films, *Cloverfield* reveals the imagination of disaster to be a phenomenon driven by media depictions of this historical reality (45). The influence news reports had on public perception of the events of 9/11 is foregrounded by James Stone: he suggests that "Minutes after American Airlines Flight 11 collided with the North Tower of the World Trade Center, television news began to offer astounding images that 'looked like a movie' to many viewers" (168). J. Hoberman goes further, proposing that "For many, and not just those in Hollywood, the events of September 11, 2001, provided the ultimate movie experience—spectacular destruction predicated on fantastic conspiracy ... watched by an audience, more or less simultaneously, of billions" (27). Hoberman argues that the widespread diffusion of images of 9/11 challenged cinema with its dark and intense depiction of reality, leading to Hollywood adopting a raw aesthetic he terms "New Realness" (29). Indeed, through explicitly evoking visual accounts of 9/11, *Cloverfield* appropriates several aspects of the footage which made the attack such a terrifying spectacle.

Integral to the experience of the attacks for those not immediately affected by 9/11 was the massive and multi-faceted media attention the destruction received (Stone 170). W.J.T. Mitchell argues that the repeated transmission of 9/11 marked the beginning of what he calls the "war of images" which characterized "the era of the War on Terror and the Bush presidency" (2–3). Mitchell further proposes that

> Our time has witnessed, not simply *more* images, but a *war* of images.... This war has been fought on behalf of radically different images of possible futures; it has been waged against images (thus acts of iconoclasm or image destruction have been critical to it); and it has been fought by means of images deployed to shock and traumatize the enemy, images meant to appall and demoralize, images designed to replicate themselves endlessly and to infect the collective imaginary of global populations [3].

Pop culture, similarly, thrives on memetic images which spread virus-like across the world, and the persistence of both Godzilla and King Kong in the American imagination can undoubtedly be attributed in part to their iconic designs. The overwhelming number of images which circulated during the War on Terror is an aspect of the conflict which permeates *Cloverfield*; Hud's camera provides one explicitly mediated perspective, but the film's frame frequently presents other viewpoints. During the party scene, for example, our view of Rob's entrance is refracted and doubled by the screen of a guest's phone as they film the occasion. Numerous television news reports are captured by Hud as he travels through the city, and this sense of the overwhelming proliferation of images reaches its most powerful expression in an electronics shop. A raft of televisions greets Hud upon entry, fragmenting the frame into multiple smaller images. Hanging above this display is an advert which promotes the store's "AUDIO/VIDEO *BLOWOUT!*" This sign could easily describe the cacophony of noise and imagery which characterizes the frantic tone of the film itself, and acts as an analogue to Mitchell's war of images which defined the period of U.S. history immediately before *Cloverfield*'s release.

Reeves' film attempts to capture the intensity of 9/11 eyewitness accounts, but its aesthetic also bears other influences from images circulated during the War on Terror: the dusty orange tones of its frames in early parts of the film, for example, bear a striking resemblance to images captured of the United States' "Shock and Awe" campaign of Iraq nighttime bombings. The filming and transmission of these operations are characterized by Mitchell as America's "iconic counterattack" after the horrors of 9/11 (3). Sontag's imagination of disaster is thus revealed not merely as a reflection of reality, but as a collective consciousness that can be manipulated and directed through mass media depictions. *Cloverfield* does not simply replicate amateur footage of 9/11, but emulates the relentless amalgam of images and video which made up the ideological battleground of the War on Terror; the film acts as an expression of fear and confusion engendered not only by one day, but by an era of media-saturated chaos.

It follows that the creature itself has a part to play in this symbolic order, but Stone proposes a problem in that,

> Unlike terrorists, monsters are not driven by ideology.... Its violence is "senseless," a term favored by many a media pundit unwilling to confront the root causes of the attacks. Certain politicians and political commentators flourished by portraying 9 /11 as a straightforward "us-and-them" scenario, thereby allowing Americans to support the notion of "payback" in the war zones of Afghanistan and Iraq. *Cloverfield* presents us with an "us-and-it" scenario, the enemy reduced to an individual monster that is an easily definable, visible, and therefore killable threat [172–73].

This reading of *Cloverfield* fails to take into account several key aspects of the film's style. While the monster of *Cloverfield* is "individual," for the most part Hud, and by extension the audience, only catch brief glimpses of it before the film's conclusion. It seemingly appears from nowhere several times, and a large part of the film's tension is generated through the audience's lack of knowledge about the creature; we don't know where it came from, we don't know why it's destroying New York City, and we (mostly) don't know where it is. The creature is not "easily definable," or "visible," and despite the best efforts of the U.S. military, nor does it seem to be "killable" as Stone proposes. Rather, the beast, and the film itself, act as a metaphor for the nature of contemporary terror; much as terrorism's power arises from its shock value and its invisibility, the *Cloverfield* monster is similarly inscrutable. The U.S. military is depicted as disarrayed, and ill-equipped to take on a creature which seems unflinching in the face of conventional military might. The terrorist attacks of September 11, 2001, marked a shocking threat to American power that resonated around the world. If Godzilla embodied the power of nuclear annihilation, *Cloverfield*'s monster is emblematic of the insidious fear of fear itself that characterized the War on Terror and its global media coverage.

The modern imagination of disaster has myriad subjects to draw from, as Marina Levina and Diem-My T. Bui argue in their 2013 book: "In the past decade, our rapidly changing world faced terrorism, global epidemics, economic and social strife, new communication technologies, immigration, and climate change, to name a few"(1). Levina and Bui go on to argue, in the vein of Sontag's work on the topic, that "Popular films and television shows ... have allowed us to deal with the profound acceleration in changing symbolic, economic, and technological systems" (1). The imagination of disaster has expanded, and the fears faced in the 21st century function differently to those Sontag imagined. One of the factors which has contributed to this change is the process of globalization, a process which, as Jan Aart Scholte proposes, is commonly thought of as being a process affecting the "connected-ness" of the world system:

> A global (in the sense of transplanetary) social relation is one that ... can link persons situated at any inhabitable points on the earth. Globalization involves reductions of barriers to such transworld social contacts. With globalization people become more able—physically, legally, linguistically, culturally and psychologically—to engage with each other wherever on planet Earth they might be [59].

In an increasingly connected world, our problems are shared; as Peter Hough notes, in a globalized world "Events occurring in other states, such as disasters or massacres, are increasingly deemed to be of political significance for people not personally affected" (2). The contemporary imagination of disaster in the United States draws on anxieties surrounding not only what will directly impact the nation, but those which threaten change in the world system more broadly. For example, Beeson and Bisley note the fresh threats which emerge as a consequence of the world's increased connectedness: "That questionable regulation in America's banking sector can play a tangential role in the near collapse of the Greek economy is testimony to the complex political and social consequences of contemporary globalization" (4).

Anxieties surrounding potential global issues frequently defy the simple "power politics" interactions between states that typifies the "realist" approach to international politics in which states typically seek to advance their own interests[5]; as Hough notes, the realist approach faces the dilemma that "The security of one's own state is likely to be enhanced at the expense of another state" (Hough 3–4). For issues which threaten world security, this approach is clearly inappropriate. As Beeson and Bisley suggest,

> Many of the key problems of world politics fly in the face of existing structures of political authority. For example, even if we might agree in principle that climate

change is a threat which necessitates some form of collaborative action, it is far from clear what form this action should take, who should pay for it, how it should be done, or what the underlying rationale for such action should be. At the heart of such problems lies the continuing salience of national forms of politics and the robust reality of sovereignty in the minds of so many [3].

Cloverfield, Pacific Rim and Gareth Edwards' *Godzilla* can all be read as attempts to come to terms with an increasingly globalized world, and with the changing sources of anxiety in the 21st century. Acts of terrorism themselves are made more effective in an increasingly connected global community, owing to improvements in communications technology and the ability for news and images to reach more people more quickly than ever before. Contemporary global anxieties challenge the nature of sovereignty and disregard state borders, and each of these films explores the nature of threat response during such a disaster. *Cloverfield* depicts a threat to the United States which allegorizes the power of non–state actors, and exemplifies the potential ineffectiveness of traditional responses to such threats.

Guillermo Del Toro's 2013 film *Pacific Rim* depicts a more optimistic view of responses to global disaster. The film itself tells the story of the invasion of near-future Earth by a horde of giant monsters which emerge from a portal between dimensions at the bottom of the Pacific Ocean. In response, massive humanoid robots are built by humanity to fight the creatures, and the film follows the efforts of a team of robot pilots tasked with winning the war. We are told in *Pacific Rim* that "the world came together, pooling its resources, and throwing away old rivalries for the sake of the greater good." Del Toro's film discards the "us-and-them" rhetoric which dominated the War on Terror and continues to influence modern political discourse, and paints an optimistic portrait of a globalized world. The increasing export of Japanese popular culture is undoubtedly an aspect of globalization,[6] and Del Toro's film goes a step further than *Cloverfield* in its integration of concepts from Japanese media. *Pacific Rim* opens with a definition of the word *kaiju* as "giant beast," and specifically cites the word's Japanese origin. While the film's massive creatures are all original creations, *Pacific Rim*'s filmmakers pay homage to the kaiju eiga's costume-based "suitmation"[7] effects through the design language of its monsters; thought was given to how a human could theoretically portray each of the film's computer generated beasts ("Featurette: Honoring the Kaiju Tradition"), which resulted in the creation of vaguely humanoid designs that are evocative of the kaiju eiga stars. *Pacific Rim*'s giant robots, meanwhile, termed *Jaegers*, are operated from within by human pilots. These enormous machines exhibit elements inspired by the *mecha* genre, a narrative form featuring human-controlled robots originating in Japanese manga and anime.[8] Thus, Del Toro's film can read in terms of its status as an amalgam of two definitively Japanese genres: kaiju eiga and mecha.

Pacific Rim's Jaegers require two pilots to control, and Raleigh Beckett (Charlie Hunnam) opens the film as one of the pilots of the Jaeger called Gipsy Danger. His brother Yancy (Diego Klattenhoff) is his co-pilot. The system to control the machines is based on the two pilots uniting their thoughts, memories, and emotions. Both of Gipsy Danger's pilots are American, and the mechanism which delivers the Jaeger to the water is emblazoned with the stars and stripes of the United States. In addition, the design of Gipsy danger itself is reminiscent of American World War II aircraft, and its riveted chest panel is emblazoned with a pin-up image evocative of fighter plane nose art. Gipsy Danger's explicit national symbolism casts both the vehicle and its operators as representative of the United States. When Yancy is killed, however, Raleigh instead partners with the Japanese pilot Mako Mori (Rinko Kikuchi). As each pilot is partially responsible for the control of the Jaeger, Gipsy Danger, like the apartment in *Cloverfield*, becomes a hybrid space which is shared by both Japanese and American influences. *Pacific Rim* heightens this sense of hybridity through the use of contrasting color palettes for each character; Raleigh is visually coded with warm hues such as gold and light brown in his introduction, whereas Mako is coded by the cool blue tones which typify her scenes. At several points during the film the color palette and lighting of Gipsy Danger blends these hues, an aspect which is visible during the moment in which the robot's grey-blue plating is removed to reveal the warm orange-cast underlying machinery. *Pacific Rim* uses national symbolism and its color palette to optimistically depict the results of close collaboration between the film's signifiers for the United States and Japan, in a narrative which liberally blends influences from both nations' pop culture. Much as Raleigh and Mako are confined to the interior of Gipsy Danger's "head," Del Toro's film conceives of the United States and Japan as bound together in a mutually beneficial partnership.

The rest of *Pacific Rim*'s casting decisions have a similarly international focus, and *Pacific Rim* revels in the cosmopolitan aspects of a globalized multi-polar world system; the other Jaegers featured in the film are operated by Chinese, Australian, and Russian pilots. While similar Hollywood productions tend to favor American locations, *Pacific Rim* mainly takes place around and within Hong Kong, a city which has a unique role to play in global politics; after being colonized by both the British and the Japanese, Hong Kong has taken on an integral position in the dynamics of the world system as part of the sovereignty of China. The city regularly ranks very highly on A.T. Kearney's Global Cities Index ("Global Cities, Present and Future"), a list which "aims to measure how much sway a city has over what happens beyond its own borders—its influence on and integration with global markets, culture, and innovation" (Frankel "The Global Cities Index 2010"). The monsters of *Pacific Rim* threaten Hong Kong specifically, but the film makes clear that the beasts are a threat to worldwide security; the director states that "I wanted this movie to not be about a country saving the world. I wanted it to be the world saving the world" ("Featurette: Shatterdome Ranger Roll Call"). The film's international cast become representative of their respective state actors on the world stage, much as Raleigh and Yancy open the film as representative of the United States. *Pacific Rim* consequently proposes a model of globalization built from the level of Scholte's transplanetary social relationships upwards: it uses interpersonal relationships to allegorize international ones, and argues that trust and understanding form the basis of international cooperation.

Pacific Rim grounds its fantastical threat of monster invasion in contemporary threats to world security. Though we do eventually learn that the creatures are part of a structured attack, initially they are described in terms of natural disasters; the beasts are graded on a category system according to their size, a system which is clearly evocative of the hurricane-measuring Saffir-Simpson scale. Furthermore, the film opens with a montage of news broadcasts which echo disaster reports. This effect is achieved through the montage's focus on the aftermath of monster attacks rather than the monsters themselves: divorced of the rampaging beasts, the footage is near-indistinguishable from real-life after-images of earthquake or hurricane zones. It is significant that in *Pacific Rim* the monsters arise from seabed; the threat is not an external one, and instead comes from *within* the Earth itself. Climate change, tsunamis, and other threats to global security are dangers which effectively rise from the oceans, and *Pacific Rim* leverages this resonance to more effectively allegorize a global disaster. Even in entirely computer generated segments of *Pacific Rim*, the mechanics of an imagined camera are well observed in order to strengthen the film's quasi-documentary style; the film uses jump pans and rapid zooms, while mainly restricting the point of view to helicopter- or ground-level locations in order to build an illusion that the camera exists within the world of the film. Light blooms in the digital camera lens and flecks of water cover it during rain. The film's highly saturated color palette and fantasy aesthetic prevents it from aspiring to full realism, but this quasi-documentary style instead works towards its positioning of its monster invasion as an allegory for a global security threat familiar to contemporary audiences. Such threats require a re-thinking of traditional state-level responses, and *Pacific Rim* conceptualizes a multi-polar world system which is able to effectively co-ordinate global solutions.

Pacific Rim is a melting pot of pop culture influences. The direction and rapidity of pop culture's spread is influenced by geography, politics, and the development of communications technology, but is influenced perhaps most strongly by economic factors. Hollywood cinema was, in the past, consumed primarily by audiences in the United States; however, in recent years the importance of international markets has increased and has led to production decisions being directly based on potential overseas box office grosses (Brook). *Pacific Rim* made a massive 75.2 percent of its box office gross outside the United States ("Pacific Rim" *Box Office Mojo*), and over a third of its international box office gross was made in China ("Pacific Rim" *Box Office Mojo*). As Iwabuchi notes: "Malaysia, Singapore, and China have advocated for the protection of "Asian" values from decadent Western morality transmitted through the media" (4). However, Japanese pop culture has been widely promoted and distributed in East and Southeast Asia (Iwabuchi 2). American kaiju films exported to East and Southeast Asian markets effectively extend the reach of Japan's soft power apparatus by promoting elements of Japanese pop culture while simultaneously espousing American ideals and values. The aspects of *Cloverfield* and *Pacific Rim* which re-conceptualize the place of the United States in the world system function in these markets as contemporary myth-making, and as Hollywood continues its attempts to capitalize on growing Asian markets through mass culture, its ideological stance is consumed by larger numbers of people.

Gareth Edwards' *Godzilla*, like *Pacific Rim*, allegorizes contemporary disasters through its aesthetics. Edwards' film is the second Hollywood adaptation of the Godzilla series, though it is not a direct sequel to any of the previous atomic reptile films. In the 2014 *Godzilla*, a version of the iconic nuclear beast that had been dormant since 1954 emerges from the ocean to hunt two giant monsters dubbed MUTOs (Massive Unidentified Terrestrial Organisms). Like *Pacific Rim*, Edwards' film takes cues from the documentary style for its photography; cameras often scramble to keep the creatures in full view, and the beasts are often shot from ad-hoc locations such as through the windscreen of a nearby car. This allows the film to elicit emotions associated with footage captured of real disasters. For example, the opening Japanese power plant catastrophe is unmistakably suggestive of 2011's Fukushima Daiichi nuclear disaster, and the images of the tsunami which hits Hawaii are reminiscent of footage captured during the 2004 Indian Ocean earthquake. In the film's conclusion Ford Brody (Aaron Taylor Johnson) attempts to reunite with his family in a stadium, a scene which closely resembles images of the relief effort which followed the destruction caused by Hurricane Katrina in 2005.

Though Edwards' film is more specific in its referencing of real disasters, both *Pacific Rim* and *Godzilla* explore and visualize the origins of multiple anxieties: one disaster blurs into another. The films cast the modern imagination of disaster as changeable, relentless, and driven by media depictions. Levina and Diem propose that this type of anxiety is specific to the 21st century, arguing that "we have been terrorized by change" and that "monstrous narratives of the past decade have become omnipresent specifically because they represent collective social anxieties over resisting and embracing change in the twenty-first century" (2). *Pacific Rim* and *Godzilla* respond to an expanded imagination of disaster, and allow audiences to explore the sources of such anxieties in a safe environment. The sources of these anxieties in *Godzilla*, much as in *Cloverfield* and *Pacific Rim*, are revealed as impossible to overcome with military power alone. As Barr notes, in Edwards' film the American military is portrayed as completely ineffectual against the threat of the MUTOs (148).

While *Pacific Rim*'s allegorical structure proposes, perhaps idealistically, that global catastrophes can be overcome through massive international cooperation, *Godzilla*'s narrative positions itself as far more U.S.–centric than Del Toro's film. As Tsutsui noted after the release of Edwards' movie, the American influence and presence in *Godzilla* is made pervasive through the prominence of the U.S. Navy and the film's disregard for much of the rest of the globe outside the United States: he uses this aspect of the movie to argue that "the 2014 *Godzilla* reinforces political assumptions common in the United States today—that the United States is the only global power, that Europe (here in the persona of NATO) barely rates passing mention, and that the developing world, including China, would still do best to submit to U.S. military might" ("For Godzilla and Country"). Such a reading gains an increased significance when one considers the minor role which China does play in the film. Throughout *Godzilla*, the MUTOs undergo a process of Othering; their life cycle is bizarre, they are the enemies of the central U.S. military, and they are defined in opposition to the bulky titular beast through their relatively spindly design language. The MUTOs invade San Francisco to breed during the film's climax, and lay a massive number of eggs in a cavernous nest. They choose to build this nest among the red lanterns of Chinatown.

In depicting the MUTOs doing so, the film implicitly links a pit out of which are soon to crawl an uncontrollable number of insect-like monsters with the world's most populous country. Beeson and Bisley see China's rise as a "challenge to American dominance," noting that "China is the world's most enduring civilization" (2, 4). Meanwhile, Edwards' *Godzilla* seems to reflect an anxiety about the threat posed by China to its U.S.–centric worldview. Towards the film's conclusion, protagonist and EOD (Explosive Ordnance Disposal) expert Ford Brody takes it upon himself to flood the Chinatown nest with gasoline which gushes plentifully from a nearby tanker truck. As the nest fills, the film focuses on the severed head of a stone Chinese dragon while the rising level of flammable liquid engulfs it. The ideological symbolism becomes clearer when the nest explodes; the fiery explosion is framed by rows of traditional Chinese lanterns. Thus, *Godzilla* allegorically associates its hero with the U.S., its monstrous villains with China, and has the potential rise of these villains obliterated by the efforts of an American soldier. *Godzilla* consequently invites its viewers to rejoice in the success of Brody over the MUTOs, but implicitly asks them to celebrate the re-assertion of America's unquestioned dominance.

Cloverfield, *Pacific Rim* and *Godzilla* all enact differing strategies in their attempts to deal with the prospect of a globalized world system in which the United States is no longer as dominant a power as it once was. Reeves' film invites its audience to revisit an era of shock and terror, allowing viewers to come to terms with the potential for U.S. dominance to be questioned. *Pacific Rim* celebrates the possibilities of a non–U.S.-centric world system; Del Toro's film allegorically enacts idealized methods for the world, and consequently its audience, to cope with contemporary global anxieties. *Godzilla*, contrastingly, reacts to the possibility of a multi-polar world as a threat in itself and creates a representational environment in which the U.S. can retain its grip on global superpower status.

In 1954 Godzilla made its first appearance on cinema screens, in a Japanese film which can be read as an anti-war and potentially anti–American allegory. In 2014 an American adaptation of the giant monster series was presented with a Japanese governmental award for efforts made to popularize Japanese culture for a worldwide audience (Siegemund-Broka). The ideological meta-narrative of these films is one of power dynamics and cultural reach, centered primarily on the role of the United States in an increasingly globalized world system. In imagining this role, each of the films considered by this essay conceptualizes the relationship between the United States and Japan; the hybrid space constructed by *Cloverfield*, the relationship between Mako and Raleigh in *Pacific Rim*, and the collaborative elimination of the MUTO threat by Godzilla and Ford in Edwards' film all gesture towards a powerful alliance between the two nations. In addition, each film furthers the soft power goals of both the United States and Japan. The geopolitical terrain between the two nations shifts endlessly, and is mapped partially by the films considered in this essay.

Pop culture reflects and responds to the imagination of disaster much as it responds to and reflects contemporary political narratives. As Jameson notes, "all thinking today is *also*, whatever else it is, an attempt to think the world system as such" (*The Geopolitical Aesthetic* 4). Mass media distributes alternative models of the world system, and itself represents elements of contemporary thought. In July 2014, the Japanese government approved alterations to its pacifist Constitution to enable Japan to deploy its military overseas if its allies are under threat (Carney). For the United States, this was perhaps welcome news; while the Constitution which contains Japan's military prohibitions was initially written by the Unites States, Packard notes that

> The U.S. Government soon regretted this language: Japan could invoke it as an excuse to stay out the United States' future wars. Indeed, Japanese Prime Minister

Shigeru Yoshida found ways to resist Washington's urgings to build up Japan's army. Not only had the United States undertaken to come to Japan's defense in case of an attack while Japan had no reciprocal obligation, but Japan insisted that its constitution prohibited it from exercising the right of collective self-defense and thus from ever sending troops or vessels to help Americans in combat operations [93–4].

This has now changed. Japan's defense budget for 2016 ranks it 8th in the world, and 2016 marked the "fourth consecutive rise in defense spending since Shinzo Abe assumed office in December 2012" (Gady). In 2016 Godzilla made its most recent appearance on cinema screens, in Hideaki Anno and Shinji Higuchi's *Shin Godzilla*. The Japanese military of Anno and Higuchi's film is portrayed as a massive, but ultimately impotent force. The U.S. and the U.N. push for the use of nuclear weapons in *Shin Godzilla*, and the U.S.–Japan relationship is portrayed as not entirely equitable; while ultimately helpful, the U.S. of *Shin Godzilla* withholds data about the titular kaiju from their Japanese allies. *Shin Godzilla*—and the kaiju cinema discussed in this essay—reimagines, reinterprets, and ultimately participates in discourse that reshapes the relationship between the U.S. and Japan. In a globalized world, the potential for cinema to be driven by and to interact with the master code of international political narratives is increasingly relevant. Kaiju cinema is interwoven with this code, and its colossal cast allegorizes global issues.

Notes

1. See Kalat *A Critical History and Filmography of Toho's Godzilla Series* and Noriega "Godzilla and the Japanese Nightmare" for discussions of this topic.
2. See Barr for frequent discussions of the continued political relevance of Godzilla movies to Japanese politics.
3. See Berenstein, 160–97, and Rony, 157–91 for two perspectives on this issue which also highlight several previous texts critical of this element of *King Kong* (1993).
4. Stone, 167–74 concurs, and reads the film along similar lines.
5. For an account of "realism" in International Relations, see Hough, 2–4.
6. See Iwabuchi *Recentering Globalization* for a discussion of this topic.
7. For a description of the mechanics of this technique, see Rickitt, 300.
8. For an analysis of some of the thematic elements of the mecha genre, see Lunning, 268–82.

Works Cited

A.T. Kearney. "Global Cities, Present and Future: 2014 Global Cities Index and Emerging Cities Outlook." *Ideas and Insights A.T. Kearney*, April. 2014. Web. 15 Nov. 2016 www.atkearney.com/research-studies/global-cities-index/full-report.

Allison, Anne. "The Attractions of the J-Wave for American Youth." *Soft Power Superpowers: Cultural and National Assets of Japan and the United States*. Eds. Watanabe Yasushi and David L. McConnell. Armonk, NY: M.E. Sharpe, 2008. 99–187. Print.

Barr, Jason. *The Kaiju Film: A Critical Study of Cinema's Biggest Monsters*. Jefferson, NC: McFarland, 2016. Print.

Beeson, Mark, and Nick Bisley. "Issues in 21st Century World Politics: an Introduction." *Issues in 21st Century World Politics*, 2nd edition. Eds. Mark Beeson and Nick Bisley. Basingstoke: Palgrave Macmillan, 2013. 1–12. Print.

Berenstein, Rhona J. *Attack of the Leading Ladies: Gender, Sexuality, and Spectatorship in Classic Horror Cinema*. New York City: Columbia University Press, 1996. Print.

Brook, Tom. "How the Global Box Office is Changing Hollywood." *BBC Culture*. 21 Oct. 2014. Web. 15 Sep. 2016. www.bbc.co.uk/culture/story/20130620-is-china-hollywoods- future.
Carney, Matthew. "Return of the samurai: Japan steps away from pacifist constitution as military eyes threat from China." *ABC News*. 19 Aug. 2014. Web. 15 Nov. 2016. www.abc.net. au/news/2014-08-19/japan-expands-their-military-amid-growing-tensions-with-china/ 5672932.
Caruth, Cathy. "Trauma and Experience: Introduction." *Trauma: Explorations in Memory*. Ed. Cathy Caruth. Baltimore, MD: Johns Hopkins University Press, 1995. 3–12.
Erb, Cynthia. *Tracking King Kong: A Hollywood Icon in World Culture*. Detroit, MI: Wayne State University Press, 1998. Print.
"Featurette: Honoring the Kaiju Tradition," *Pacific Rim*. Dir: Guillermo Del Toro. London: Warner Home Video, 2013. Blu-ray Disc.
"Featurette: Shatterdome Ranger Roll Call." *Pacific Rim*. Dir: Guillermo Del Toro. London: Warner Home Video, 2013. Blu-ray Disc.
Fiat. "Fiat 500—Comercial Godzilla." Youtube video, 0:45. Posted by "FIAT PERU." 16 Jan. 2015. Web. 15 Nov. 2016. https://www.youtube.com/watch?v=aHR0IvpTBps.
Gady, Franz-Stefan. "Japan Approves Record Defense Budget." *The Diplomat*. 28 Dec. 2015. Web. 15 Sep. 2016. www.thediplomat.com/2015/12/japan-approves-record-defense- budget/.
Gojira. Dir. Ishiro Honda. London: British Film Institute, 2012. DVD.
Hoberman, J. *Film After Film, Or, What Became of 21st Century Cinema?* London: Verso, 2013. Print.
Hough, Peter. *Understanding Global Security*. London: Routledge, 2004. Print.
Iwabuchi, Koichi. *Recentering Globalization: Popular Culture and Japanese Transnationalism*. Durham, NC: Duke University Press, 2002. Print.
Jameson, Fredric. *The Geopolitical Aesthetic: Cinema and Space in the World System*. Bloomington: Indiana University Press, 1992. Print.
Jameson, Fredric. *The Political Unconscious: Narrative as a Socially Symbolic Act*. Oxon: Routledge, 2002. Print.
Kalat, David. *A Critical History and Filmography of Toho's Godzilla Series*. Jefferson, NC: McFarland, 2007. Print.
Levina, Marina, and Diem-T. Bui. "Introduction: Toward a comprehensive monster theory in the 21st century." *Monster Culture in the 21st Century: A Reader*. Eds. Marina Levina and Diem-T. Bui. London: Bloomsbury Academic, 2013. 1–14. Print.
Lunning, Frenchy. "Between the Child and the Mecha." *Mechademia* 2 (2007): 268–282. Print.
Mitchell, William John Thomas. *Cloning Terror: The War of Images, 9/11 to the Present*. Chicago, IL: Chicago University Press, 2011. Print.
Noriega, Chon. "Godzilla and the Japanese Nightmare: When *Them!* Is U.S." *Asian Cinemas: a Reader and Guide*. Eds. Dimitris Eleftheriotis and Gary Needham. Edinburgh: Edinburgh University Press, 2006. 41–55. Print.
"Pacific Rim." *Box Office Mojo*, n.d. Web. 15 Nov. 2016. www.boxofficemojo.com/movies/? page=intl&id=pacificrim.htm&sort=percoftotal&order=DESC&p=.htm.
Packard, George R. "The United States–Japan Security Treaty at 50: Still a Grand Bargain?" *Foreign Affairs* 89, 2 (2010): 92–103. Print.
Rebecca Frankel. "The Global Cities Index 2010." *Foreign Policy*. 16 Aug. 2010. Web. 15 Nov. 2016. www.foreignpolicy.com/articles/2010/08/11/the_global_cities_index_2010.
Rickitt, Richard. *Special Effects: The History and Technique*. London: Aurum Press, 2006. Print.
Rony, Fatimah Tobing. *The Third Eye: Race, Cinema, and Ethnographic Spectacle*. Durham, NC: Duke University Press, 1996. Print.
Scholte, Jan Aarte. *Globalization: A Critical Introduction (Second Edition)*. Basingstoke: Palgrave Macmillan, 2005. Print.
Siegemund-Broka, Austin. "Legendary's 'Godzilla' to Receive Japanese Governmental Award." *The Hollywood Reporter*. 14 Aug. 2014. Web. 15 Nov. 2016. www.hollywoodreporter. com/ heat-vision/legendarys-godzilla-receive-japanese-governmental-725714.
Snickers. "Godzilla—New Snickers TV Commercial 2014." YouTube video, 0:46. Posted by "Fun Guru." 3 Mar. 2014. Web. 15 Nov. 2016. https://www.youtube.com/watch?v=mcQ-gvOM9UE.

Sontag, Susan. "The Imagination of Disaster." *Commentary*. October (1965): 42–48. Print.
Stone, James. "Enjoying 9/11: The Pleasures of *Cloverfield*." *Radical History Review* 2011, 111 (2011): 167–174. Print.
The Verge. "Godzilla's 60 years of destruction and Dr. Pepper: 90 Seconds on The Verge." Youtube video, 1:30. Posted by "The Verge." 16 May. 2014. Web. 15 Nov. 2014. www.youtube.com/watch?v=NiRt4R6tLAQ.
"Thirty Minutes Over Tokyo." *The Simpsons*. Fox network, 16 May. 1999. Television.
Tsutsui, William. "For Godzilla and Country: How a Japanese Monster Became an American Icon." *Foreign Affairs*. 27 May. 2014. Web. 15 Nov. 2014. www.foreignaffairs.com/ articles/ 141472/william-m-tsutsui/for-godzilla-and-country.
"-zilla, comb. form." *Oxford English Dictionary, 3rd ed.* Oxford University Press, 2009. Print.

FILMOGRAPHY

King Kong (RKO Radio Pictures: dir. Merian C. Cooper and Ernest B. Schoedsack, 1933).
The Beast from 20,000 Fathoms (Warner Bros.: dir. Eugene Lourie, 1953).
Gojira (Toho: dir. Ishiro Honda, 1954).
Godzilla (TriStar Pictures: dir. Roland Emmerich, 1998).
Cloverfield. (Paramount Pictures: dir. Matt Reeves, 2008).
Pacific Rim. (Warner Bros. Pictures: dir. Guillermo Del Toro, 2013).
Godzilla. (Warner Bros. Pictures: dir. Gareth Edwards, 2014).
Shin Godzilla (Toho: dir. Hideaki Anno and Shinji Higuchi, 2016).

"We are eating Gamera"
Mystery Science Theater 3000 *Consumes the Kaiju*

Karen Joan Kohoutek

The 1960s Japanese *kaiju* films featuring Gamera, the giant, flying, flame-throwing turtle and friend to children, were a mainstay of the cult television series, *Mystery Science Theater 3000 (MST3K)* (1988–1999). In MST3K's most absurd premise, mad scientists send bad movies to a space station, where they're watched, while they play to the TV audience, by the show's marooned host: soft-spoken, easy-going Joel Robinson (Joel Hodgson). Along with Tom Servo and Crow, a pair of sarcastic robots, or 'bots, Joel created out of everyday objects on board his satellite, he makes running comedic commentaries. Humorously riffing on the English-dubbed versions of Gamera films, the show's characters act out the part of American consumers, with all the darker connotations that word conveys, using products of another culture for amusement value. The episodes work as a vehicle to introduce its Middle American viewers, well-known for its racial homogeny and used to the conventions of their own popular culture, to entertainments that originated in a very different environment, using humor to mediate the encounter of unsuspecting audiences with these international popular culture artifacts; this mediation may have even reached beyond the passive-aggressive culture dubbed "Minnesota Nice," which has often been considered a way of keeping perceived outsiders, including people of color, at a distance while maintaining a superficial friendliness. As we gaze over the silhouetted shoulders of Joel and the 'bots watching the film, viewers become part of this sideways, fictionalized documentary. Before analyzing the connection between Gamera films and MST3K, it is crucial to explore Japanese kaiju film production in greater depth.

After the worldwide success of the quintessential Japanese monster movie, Toho studio's original *Godzilla* (1954), many imitators followed, as they would more than a decade later in the United States when *Jaws* became a phenomenon. Perhaps the "most successful" of these Japanese competitors, however, was the rival studio Daiei, which created Gamera: "huge, green, and generally bipedal, with flame-thrower breath and massive, superfluous tusks … [and] the peculiar ability to fly through the air, almost Frisbee-like, using fiery jets from under its shell" (Tsutsui 180).

Merely the fact of Gamera being a giant turtle would probably have been unusual enough, but since his hallmarks are qualities that turtles don't possess, including the ability to fly and shoot flames, he becomes an even stranger kind of monster. This strangeness is both familiar to and different from already-established kaiju, especially since the flames spout from his mouth similar to Godzilla, and from the part of his shell into which his head and limbs retract. This certainly makes one wonder about the mechanics of his anatomy, and where he goes inside his shell to allow this to happen. Even his flying is relatively unique; unlike other kaiju like Mothra, Rodan, or Gaos (alternately spelled "Gyaos," a vaguely bird-like monster fought by Gamera in 1967, and again in films from the 1990s and the 2000s), Gamera has no wings or any elements of his physiology that should allow him to fly. The "Frisbee-like" flight might be an attempt to explain this ability—showing the turtle propelling through the air—but Gamera is also seen cruising through the sky with head and legs extended (as in an extended sequence in 1969's *Gamera vs. Guiron*), like Superman, if he were a giant turtle.

With this level of imaginative oddity intrinsic to the very conception and design of the creature, the films seem to revel in their freedom from the narrative constraints of logic, at least when the monsters are onscreen in scenes of destruction or battle. As William Tsutsui says, "if the Gamera series … could boast anything, it was monstrous adversaries, movie plots, and special effects yet sillier, more outlandish, and more hilariously cheesy" than those of other kaiju filmmakers (184).

In 1995, Gamera would be revived in a trilogy of films, beginning with *Gamera: Guardian of the Universe*. These films boasted obviously higher budgets than their predecessors and contemporary special effects, consequently treating the monster and his stories in a more serious fashion; however, he retains the essential characteristics from the earlier films, even, for example, his position as a "friend of all children." In the 1960s, Gamera's friendship was presented without explanation; of the five films from the 1960s that were shown on *MST3K* only one (*Gamera vs. Barugon*) doesn't include a special bond between Gamera and a Japanese child or children. Sometimes these children, as in *Gamera vs. Gaos* and *Gamera vs. Guiron*, seem unconcerned about dangerous situations, since they can call on their turtle friend at any time for rescue. In the more serious cycle of 1990s films, Gamera is also shown to have a connection to a young character, the teenage Asagi, in this case positing a psychic and spiritual link.

While the Gamera series of the 1960s was originally made for a Japanese audience, as with *Godzilla*, the filmmakers included American actors "for the benefit of overseas audiences," and sold rights to American distributors, who dubbed and re-edited the films for viewers in the United States (Tsutsui 182). Producer Sandy Frank, also responsible for repackaging a Japanese television series as a movie called *Fugitive Alien*, which was also popular on *Mystery Science Theater 3000*, released the edited versions in the United States, and it is these versions that appeared in the screening room of MST3K's spaceship set known as the Satellite of Love.

A combination of creativity and budgetary constraints brought Gamera with accompanying commentary to American audiences, as MST3K began in "a scrappy little independent UHF TV station, KTMA," located "in the bustling industrial park regions of east central Minneapolis" (Beaulieu xxx). Comedian Joel Hodgson and producer Jim Mallon enlisted a crew for a locally-aired program in which Hodgson's character, also named Joel, was stranded in space and forced to watch bad movies. To "keep his sanity," as the show's theme song put it, he created a group of wise-cracking robots, who joined him in commentaries on one film per episode and in various comedic skits. Kaiju films, including the five Gamera films, were among the original batch of local shows, since KTMA already had them in their film library. Their low budgets and general absurdity, especially in the available versions, which had been badly dubbed into English by the Sandy Frank team, made them a natural fit with *MST3K's* comedic style. Tsutsui describes this as a "trademark brand of spoofs, encyclopedic popular culture references, and irreverent commentary," which provided "some of the most entertaining, intelligent and biting material" on kaiju films (Tsutsui 136–137).

Before long, *MST3K* graduated to an early version of the well-known cable channel Comedy Central, and later to the Sci-Fi Channel. This movement from local access to basic cable allowed the show creators to upgrade the sets and spend more time on writing scripts, thereby upping the pace of the riffs that the characters could deliver. The show ran for eleven years and became a beloved popular cultural touchstone in its own right, even after Hodgson left the show he had created, to be replaced by head writer Michael J. Nelson. Many MST3K episodes were later released as DVD box sets, and all five Gamera films were released as a special edition DVD collection in 2011.

All of the Gamera episodes in the box set came from the revamped show's third season, airing in 1991, while Hodgson was still the host. In *The Mystery Science Theater 3000 Amazing Colossal Episode Guide*, written by members of the show's cast and crew, Mary Jo Pehl says that "when we were informed that we could acquire the rights to the Gamera series," the original members "jumped at the chance, as they had done them with great success at KTMA" (Beaulieu 54). Hodgson further reflected on the importance of the Gamera films to the show's development: "I have to say, when we were at KTMA, I felt like our whole thing solidified around the Gamera movies. Once those happened we found our place in the universe, we knew that this was going to work ... they were so perfect for what we did" (Begy and Fierro 189). While other episodes are perhaps more iconic (for example, *Manos, the Hands of Fate* and *Santa Claus Conquers the Martians* have been collected as *MST3K* "Essentials"), it is interesting to note that the peculiar qualities of Gamera as a monster and as a film series could have helped to inspire the success of something that has, from its humble beginnings, had such a strong influence on the pop culture landscape.

The Minnesota in which *MST3K* took root was a place with a strong racial divide between its white majority and everyone else. In a 1990 census, two years into MST3K's 11-year run, and the year they would move up to the Comedy Channel, bringing them to a national audience (Beaulieu 2), 78.4 percent of the Minneapolis population was white. In contrast, African-Americans made up 13 percent, and the category of Asians and Pacific Islanders was only 4.3 percent (City of Minneapolis). Looking at the state as a whole, the percentage is even smaller. Information from the United States Census shows Minnesota's total population in 1994 was 4,375,099, and the Asian population was 77,886 people: only 1.78 percent.

It's no wonder, then, that Asian-American Minnesota writer David Mura says "We're invisible," and that he knows "I will never really ever be considered a true Minnesotan (Mura 48, 54). With such a dominatingly homogenous population, "the white people here are very white," he says, despite their paradoxical desire "to think of themselves as nice people" (Mura 53, 54). In a study that measured "the current integration level of whites and blacks," Minnesota ranked last overall, at 51, out of 50 states plus the District of Columbia included), Minnesota ranked last, at 51. Minnesota also rank at 50 for "Highest Gap in Median Income Level," 50 for "Highest Gap in Homeownership Rate," and 49 for "Highest Gap in Poverty Level" (Bernardo). While this study was primarily concerned with the gap between white and African-American residents of the state, it still provides a snapshot of the racial climate, and the racial divides, found in Minnesota both in the 1980s and '90s, and in the present day, which has not improved significantly despite increases in the non-white population.

Many connections have been drawn between the state's inequities and the well-known phenomenon of "Minnesota Nice," described as a "polite friendliness," combined with "aversion to conflict and confrontation," "emotional restraint," and "a massive dose of passive-aggressive behavior" (Veldof and Bonnema). For example, an article called "'Minnesota Nice' and Minnesota's Racism" baldly states that this common behavior "exacerbates the state's racism" (Plaid). With an ingrained tendency to indirect expressions of emotion and conflict avoidance, prejudices are easily unexamined, and racist attitudes cloaked in a veneer of politeness are more difficult to latch onto and confront.

In this context, the image of a white man ridiculing a cultural project from Japan could be considered problematic in these times, which are more conscious of cultural appropriation issues and the power imbalances to be found between different demographic groups, especially in a region that is so predominantly skewed to the white majority, and when that man's persona contains so many traces of that "Minnesota Nice." Of course, while the *MST3K* cast watched other films from many countries, the majority of the films shown on the program were American ones made with American audiences in mind. In context, the treatment of the Gamera films doesn't stand out as racist, despite some jokes which foreground Japanese cultural references, which draws attention to their difference from the American mainstream.

Writers analyzing *MST3K* often discuss the show's subversive elements—for example, in their mocking critique of racist and sexist tropes found in the products of earlier time periods—which can steer us to a reading of similar elements in the Gamera films as ultimately having an equally "progressive" stance.

Many examples in the run of *MST3K* can be used as evidence that this talking back to the film was in the service of progressive ideals, in addition to existing for pure comedic effect. Much "riffing" does make a commentary on stereotypes and social attitudes that seem obviously racist or sexist. This tendency can be found in many of the "social hygiene" shorts, which mock the assumption of white, middle class superiority, and in their version of a *Santa Claus* movie, filmed in Mexico, in which a pageant of ethnic stereotyping is skewered by exaggeration of it. There's no doubt that the reaction of over-the-top racial slurs is in the service of pointing out the stereotypes on the screen.

In riffing on the Gamera films in particular, Joel and "his robot friends," Tom Servo and Crow, do make fun of a foreign film, with a suggestion of schoolyard racial mockery: for example, using nonsense words to mimic an Asian language, and jokes about the pronunciation of foreign names. It's difficult to make a real case, though, that Hodgson's character represents the white male American power structure, because he so clearly does not.

Joel was created as an anonymous member of the working class, doing a thankless job as a cog in a giant corporate machine, whose "bosses didn't like him so they shot him into space," as the theme song goes, a detail with real sociopolitical relevance for its time. He was also an everyman, albeit one with an inventive streak and a brain full of pop cultural minutia, able to turn the experience of being marooned alone in space into a playground for the imagination, literally creating his own community along the way. While these would seem to be unique characteristics, he is always polite, soft-spoken and self-effacing, representing the more positive side of the Minnesota Nice stereotype.

Where most of us are subject to the pressures and influences of the mass media, we still have at least an illusion of control over our lives. Joel, though, is literally powerless over the conditions of existence, and as part of that, is literally forced into the role of media consumer. In a very Minnesota form of indirect rebellion, however, Joel reshapes his environment, proving he is always free to take what he wants from his media viewing experiences to create joy and meaning. So while in some respects he represents, and often enacts, the ways a typical—or stereotypical—white, middle-class, middle-American audience might ordinarily react to things, the overall impression is irreverent and satirical.

All of this complicates a simplistic reading of the show's relationship to the products of mass media, or what philosopher Theodor Adorno called the "culture industry" (231), and what it represents about its viewers' relationships with the same. *MST3K* is a production from the United States, with a slant of regional humor specific to Minnesota, and Joel is a white American man, as are the two other human characters who appear in this season, the "Mads" who have imprisoned him, played by Trace Beaulieu and Frank Conniff. It would be possible to read the broadcast television program as being in a position of "power over" the Japanese films, with white Americans taking a superior stance to the products originating in a different country, featuring characters with a different ethnic makeup. With that in mind, their joking responses can be seen as reframing the films and subordinating them to an American cultural framework, in a classic example of "consumption."

Much commentary exists that addresses the assumed passivity of mass media audiences; Adorno, for example, says that "they force their eyes shut and voice approval, in a kind of self-loathing, for what is meted out to them" (235). Within this kind of paradigm, it becomes hard to know where the power and influence lie: with the show that's getting the last laugh, so to speak, by putting its stamp on the original movies? Is it the original films? They were created with a goal of getting the most viewers possible, so maybe the Gamera creators are actually getting the last laugh, and perhaps influencing the viewers in ways they are largely unconscious of. If so, is the *MST3K* crew part of that viewership? Or is more influence in the hands of the ultimate mass media consumers, the audience, than is often recognized?

In the end, however brainwashed the audience might appear to be by the products of the cultural industry, and as difficult as they find it to avoid them, individuals do in the end have the power to determine their reaction to those products. This experience, playing out in a field of limited choices, with persuasive forces arrayed against the ordinary viewers, is enacted in every episode of *Mystery Science Theater 3000*.

The five Gamera films shown on *MST3K* were first produced as KTMA episodes in 1988. In 1991, they re-did them, this time airing them in chronological order, which allows us to view the films' progression. The films are:

- *Gamera* (a.k.a. *Gamera the Invincible*) (1965). Japanese title: *Daikaiju Gamera*. Originally aired 12/11/88. The second version aired 6/8/91, as episode 302.
- *Gamera vs. Barugon* (1966). Japanese title: *Daikaiju Ketto: Gamera tai Barugon*. Originally aired 12/4/88. The second version aired 6/22/91, as episode 304.
- *Gamera vs. Gaos* (1967). The word "Gaos" is frequently transliterated as "Gyaos," but "Gaos" appears on the title card of the version produced by Sandy Frank. Japanese title: *Daikaiju Kuchusen: Gamera tai Gyaosu*. Originally aired 12/18/88. The second version aired 6/27/91, as episode 308.
- *Gamera vs. Guiron* (1969). Japanese title: *Gamera tai daikaiju Giron*. Originally aired 1/8/89. The second version aired 9/7/91, as episode 312.
- *Gamera vs. Zigra* (1971). Japanese title: *Gamea tai Shinkai kaiu Jigura*. Originally aired 12/31/88. The second version aired 10/19/91, episode 316.

The first movie in the series is both the most straight-faced, and the one that most resembles the original *Godzilla*, its obvious inspiration. William Tsutsui claims that "Gamera was conceived as a bald-faced copy of the king of monsters " (Tsutsui 181), with the similarities stretching across their respective film series. For example, both monsters start off as destructive forces, in "a somber, reflective film," but each becomes "a friendly, obliging defender of Japanese society," and fighting opponents with similar names: Barugon (Gamera) vs. Baragon (Godzilla) (ibid.).

With one exception, each of the movies begins with the same credit sequence, an addition to the Sandy Frank versions shown on *MST3K*: a close-up of black and white waves, with only the movie titles and the names of cast and crew members changing from film to film. After the first movie, the riffing during the credits follows a ritualized format, including some traditional white mockery of Japanese names (much of which is quite clever, and which will eventually be overtly, if briefly, critiqued), and a series of jokes about the recurring credit for "Planning." The credit sequence in the first *Gamera* movie contains the most jokes about Asian names. For example, when the studio's name, Daiei, appears, Joel yells "Dai-EEE!" and he waves his hands as if in distress. When the producer's name comes up, Crow says "Hidemasa Nagata. That's Japanese for In-a-Gadda-Da-Vida. Or I got into the Gouda." As more Japanese names scroll, he adds, "They could tell us anything and we'd believe it," to which Joel responds, "We have to. We're at their mercy, basically." Of course, this is true of anything in English-language film credits as well, but the presence of a foreign language draws attention to the audience's position, only able to react to what it's shown.

Gamera opens in the Arctic, where a Japanese research expedition is interrupted by the crash of a jet carrying a nuclear explosion—a clear reference to the reach of Cold War politics even to remote parts of the planet. This explosion wakes up the monster which, like Godzilla, almost immediately goes off to destroy a power plant. As far as his motivations are concerned, however, he seems psychologically linked to a little boy named Kenny, whose family is forcing him to get rid of his beloved pet turtle just moments before Gamera appears, like a giant figure of turtle-related vengeance. This connection is underlined by Crow's speaking for him, in a stentorian voice, "What's all this about Kenny not being allowed to keep his turtle?"

In addition to the kinds of jokes they might make about any low-budget motion picture, the commentary of Joel and the 'bots address the foreign elements, such as "Ground Control to Major Wong," a "Turning Japanese" joke, and a self-consciously bad-taste reference when Crow jokes "This is Pearl Harbor," over news footage of fiery destruction, immediately backpedaling with "Just kidding" and "not even."

Equally, though, the riffs reference the negative elements of the United States' corporate culture and imperialistic history. For example, for a different shot of flames and destruction, Tom Servo responds in his most pompous voice, as if narrating, "Here at Exxon, we take the greatest precautions for the preservations of our fragile ecology" (1:06). Then, when the military is luring Gamera to potential destruction, he comments, "Hey, this is just like a Klan meeting!" at which Joel mutters "Without the charm." A subtly pointed comment is made early on, which is simply: "Americans. What are they doing in the film?"

There are multiple layers to the moments of cultural-historical critique. These demonstrate that the viewers of the film are not inevitably buying in to the official versions of American values, but their subversive qualities work in different directions, complicating a simple interpretation. As Gamera falls to his apparent death, they all moan. "I don't like to see this," but Crow punctures any element serious commentary by announcing "Soup for everybody!" Gamera as an entity is already ready for consumption by these peculiarly representative middle-American viewers. At the end of the episode, Joel does something relatively unusual in the show's run, and tells the Mads with sincerity, "Thanks for not sending such a bad movie this time."

With *Gamera vs. Barugon*, they continue to riff on the Daiei name ("Dai-ee-I-ee-I-o") in the credits, this time rhyming "Nagata" with "ya gotta": a very regional pronunciation. That element will become a factor in one of the skits in which the 'bots, wearing skull masks and tusks, speak in exaggerated Minnesota accents of the kind that would become famous five years later with the movie *Fargo*, play ladies lunching at a "TGI Tokyo's." This begins a pattern in which the skits fuse elements from the Gamera films with other, more familiar popular culture, which will be seen during the later episodes. This example is particularly interesting because it translates a specific kind of regional humor, about white, largely Scandinavian culture, to a Japanese environment.

Again, there are jokes based on Asian references in American pop culture: the Joy Luck Club, Bruce Lee, the Reverend Moon, and "Mr. Eddie's Father," a phrase used by the Japanese character on the situation comedy *The Courtship of Eddie's Father* (1969–1972). They also continue to make more pointed barbs at American culture. In the film plot, a group of mercenaries go to an isolated Pacific island to retrieve a jewel that was hidden by a Japanese soldier during World War II; the jewel turns out to be an egg that hatches Barugon, a lizard-like kaiju that will wreak destruction, shooting lethal rainbows out of its back. When their helicopter lands, Crow says "Hi, we're from America. We've come to decimate your jungle, convert your youth, and make you feel inferior." Tom Servo adds "It's Robert Duvall," referencing the actor's role in *Apocalypse Now*, with his famous quote about loving the smell of napalm in the morning.

In *Gamera vs. Gaos*, the now openly heroic turtle fights the birdlike reptile, Gaos. During this credit sequence, Joel and the 'bots sing the word "Gaos" to the tune of "Day-O," Tom Servo refers to Hidemasa Nagata as "Hideous Negativity," and a name is met with "Gesundheit!" After that, Joel quietly muses, "Do you think Japanese people make fun of American names?" and Tom replies, "Oh, I suppose so." While this is, like all the riffs, presented as a throw-away comment, it does raise a legitimate question, and suggests an underlying judgment on the reflective white American perspective.

This film's antagonist, Gaos, is awakened by the conflict between industrialists building a road and the farmers whose land it's going through, who are agitating for a higher price. Eventually, their ringleader comes to believe that the monster's arrival is a punishment from the gods for their greed. Almost immediately, a random shot of a tree being sawed down kicks Tom Servo into the mode of narrating an educational film: "The logging industry. Over three billion down. We work for you while we work against you. Feeding you big-time double-talk. Stealing your dreams and selling them back to you."

Through the skits that take place during certain commercial breaks, the cast begin to incorporate Gamera into their lives and their pop culture vocabulary. In this episode, they begin to act out a fusion of the kaiju films with Wagnerian opera, the "Gameradamerung," complete with Valkyrie and Viking ship; later, Joel, wearing a Gaos head and attempting to spin turtle-shaped plates, appears on a faux *Ed Sullivan Show*. Both of these skits mash up the Gamera films with more familiar pieces of Western or American culture.

Gamera vs. Guiron takes its child protagonists to outer space, where Gamera will eventually fight an exhausted-looking knife-headed monster, and rescue them from an attractive pair of cannibal space girls. In the episode's opening introduction, both Joel and the Mads are making food-related jokes, so when it comes time to send the movie, Frank describes it as "indigestible," and Dr. Forrester says "Open wide, Joel. Eat it, baby, eat it!" All of which is going to dovetail very shortly into the idea of consumption, which will carry on through the remainder of the series.

This is the film that does not have the standard credit sequence of black and white waves, instead featuring a background of orange shapes resembling lava. Where they would normally make puns on the cast and crew names, here they focus on the major American character: "Christopher Murphy? The Japanese have some funny names." References are made in the film to "Madam Butterfly" and "Yoko Ono," but when they mock the accents of the outer space women, it's because they have broadly regional American accents: "it sounds like she's from Indiana."

The major contribution of *Gamera vs. Guiron* to the *MST3K* world is the introduction of the "Gamera Song" to the show's stock of inside jokes. In the film (which is badly dubbed even by the standard of the other Gamera films), the song is untranslated, freeing them to make it whatever they want, in the way that kaiju films in general could have "a tabula rasa effect for American audiences ... allowing American audiences to place their own meanings on the film" (Barr 121, 122).

At first, the jokes involve trying to make sense of what they're hearing: "Senorita Gamera?" This will later be reprised as "Hirohito Gamera?" Almost immediately, they link the song to widely varied cultural references, likening it to the Vienna Boys Choir and "the cast of *Oliver*." Then, they make it completely their own by filling it in with the lyrics "Gamera is really neat/Gamera is filled with meat/We've been eating Gamera!" When they sing it again later, near the end of the film, they will use the line "We are eating Gamera," so the lyrics put the act of eating the giant turtle, and consuming his film series, into both the present and past tenses.

The first version of the song contains lines that directly refer to their imprisonment on the Satellite of Love, and how they usually don't complain about it, another callback to the concept of "Minnesota Nice." This version also ends with the line "Now we have commercial sign," the in-show flag that was time for the crew to cut to a commercial: an example of the way that the Gamera movies and the "everyday life" of the show were beginning to connect.

At the end of the episode, the song will appear in two other versions. First, Joel and the 'bots energetically sing nonsense lyrics to the tune, in fake schoolyard Japanese. Then, at the very end, the Mads hang on the words of an unctuous piano player (played by Mike Nelson), who sings a lounge version with "a Rodgers and Hart feel," until they abruptly decide to kill him.

The "Gamera Song," though, which will feature even more prominently in the next installment, isn't even this episode's most noticeable example of the way the characters recontextualize the kaiju. Early on, they decide the American boy in the film bears a faint resemblance to Richard Burton, and in a mid-movie skit, they perform a tribute to the actor, interspersing tidbits (both real and fictional) about his life with reenactments of some of his famous roles, through the lens of Gamera.

These include "Who's Afraid of Gamera Turtle?" and "King Arthur in the smash musical *Gamera*," but the peculiar highlight is Crow, as Richard Burton, reciting Dylan Thomas: "Gamera, Gamera, what dark despised dreams dwell in the sullen weighty bones 'neath your impenetrable shell?" This moment captures the heights to which the show could aspire, being completely absurd, the product of an individualist humor that takes whatever is at hand and connects it to anything in the known universe of history and art, whether highbrow or low. At the same time, it is, as a surprised and stricken Joel responds, "really good … very moving."

The *MST3K* crew celebrates *Gamera vs. Zigra*, their last Gamera film, with a Gamera piñata, and several other creative elements which will appear during the episode's skits, such as dioramas of scenes from the various Gamera movies. In the now fully ritualized riffing during the credits sequence, there will be a joke turning Noriaki Yuasa's name into the "Y-USA Network," followed by the self-referential "Hey look, they've got funny Japanese names." The vein of humor in the "funny Japanese names" has been so fully explored that they are able to move on from something that is no longer a novelty after "watching the same movie like six times," as they will say later.

At the end of *Gamera vs. Zigra*, as they celebrate finishing the series, Joel and the 'bots sing different versions of the Gamera song, connecting to multiple musical genres from various time periods and geographic locations. Joel does a reggae version in the style of Eek-a-Mouse, Tom does a beatnik poetry version, Crow does a rap number, and Gypsy dresses as a Valkyrie for a mock opera, echoing the previous episode's crossover with Wagner. They finish in barbershop quartet style, and, not to be outdone, the Mads do a credible punk version. These skits illustrate the way the show generally relates to the films shown on it, focusing on idiosyncratic qualities that can be connected to anything else they choose. Joel and the 'bots actively react to the media texts—turning a one-way communication into a situation that focuses on their talking back—and in doing so, they create new products out of the interaction. As Hodgson describes it, "you're collaborating with the original work and kind of working with it. Then when you add in the audience there's this element, and I think that's what makes it different" (Begy and Fierro 195).

Three seasons after the airing of the Gamera series, a random *MST3K* riff illustrates that the Gamera films themselves have become thoroughly integrated into the show's pop cultural sources. Watching a 1948 western, *Last of the Wild Horses*, Crow comments on a fistfight: "This is like *Gamera vs. Zigra*—only with cowboys." He is now using something that was once culturally foreign in order to describe a stereotypically American genre, with an implicit expectation that viewers will understand the reference.

Television viewing, and other media products which are traditionally broadcast in one direction, from active creators to an audience of passive consumers, with no opportunity for response or dialogue, is often seen as a force of "hegemonic oppression" that works to support a "status quo" (Burnham and Ewalt 34). The *raison d'etre* of *MST3K*, however, is to react to and critique those products. Their work can be viewed as part of the monolithic culture industry, but also provides an example of ways that consumers can become more conscious of how mass media works, a reminder that all people are free to re-shape the works and create their own cultural contexts. In this context, the riffing on *MST3K* "presents the tactics of resistance performed by the weak and the oppressed" (Burnham and Ewalt 35), described by various other scholars as "subversive" (McWilliams 110), and working "against hegemonic culture" (Dean 120). By providing a light-hearted corrective to the passive consumption of media, "a model of irreverence against authority," the show "exemplifies the ideal popular culture audience resisting hegemonic culture and empowering viewers to participate in that resistance" (Rees 3).

Since the original texts dealt with by the *MST3K* crew are primarily forgotten B movies, made on shoestring budgets, it may be overstating the case that they represent tools of the powerful. It's certainly difficult to imagine the Gamera films oppressing anyone; certainly not in the United States. Despite the English dubbing and some re-edits, the Gamera series is still comprised of foreign films, made in Japan with predominantly Japanese casts, for a Japanese audience. While they were willing to make them available for an American audience, as represented by Joel and the 'bots, Daiei studios clearly didn't have them in mind as potential viewers, and any intended messages were not primarily aimed at them. The films were produced according to the status quo of a very different society. Even if the films were created as hegemonic products, intended to promote the interests of the status quo, which is not the same status quo as an American viewer of *MST3K*; they were not made within the hegemony of the culture in which they are being viewed.

Complicating matters, the show *Mystery Science Theater 3000* could be seen more as the vehicle of hegemonic control. While the behavior of the crew towards the films in general can be seen as fitting as the pattern of resistance to traditional media spectatorship, their targets in this case, the Gamera films, are more outside the hegemony than they are, especially taking into account the divide between the white Midwestern creators and the Asian origin of the films, broadcast to a demographic with such a small Asian population.

An element of cultural appropriation can be seen in this, but part of the cumulative effect is that we also see an Asian hegemonic culture beginning to have an influence on one of the most white-bread regions of the United States, bringing works from the Japanese culture industry, rather than the American one, to one of the most racially homogenous parts of the country. There is always a tension in humor between mockery and celebration. The sharp focus on the source material takes the original seriously as a subject, even if the exploration itself is comedic.

Does the airing of these films on *MST3K* represent a form of media consumption that, instead of diminishing the impact of the original, serves to bring it more it more firmly into the consciousness of its demographic audience? The situation can be likened to other ways in which *MST3K* has performed a revivalist or, surprisingly, preservationist function in relation to the films on which it riffs.

This idea has been addressed by many scholars. For example, scholar David Ray Carter discusses the show's contribution to the wider popularization of "bad" movies, and says "*Laserblast, Mitchell,* and *Racket Girls* had previously only been known to a select group of initiates, but *MST3K* had exposed them to society en masse, reintroducing them into the pop culture lexicon of the time" (106). Similarly, Cheryl Hicks wrote an essay, "Revival of Forgotten Films Through Appropriation," on this tendency. She uses examples of a few mostly forgotten films, like *Manos: The Hands of Fate*, which are demonstrably more well-known today because of *MST3K*: "the use of these movies by the show brought new attention to these films, many of which had been widely unseen for many years and for the most part had been long forgotten by the public. Because of *MST3K*, these films have experienced a second life and a broader audience than they received upon their initial release" (55, 56).

The Gamera movies weren't "forgotten," as such, but they were little known in the United States. In the era before VHS/DVD and streaming video, films could only be seen as they played in physical movie theaters, and then as they were broadcast on the few existing television channels. None of the kaiju films would have aired on any of the major networks, but only on independent stations like *MST3K*'s KTMA. At the time these episodes aired, it would have been difficult to see the films any other way.

Unlike some more traditional or serious creative works that are often debated in terms of cultural appropriation, the Gamera movies are not easy to discuss in terms of art or "cinema." They are unabashed entertainments, created for profit, to be consumed, and they certainly contain an element of camp, especially by the era of *Gamera vs. Guiron*, in which Gamera swings from a bar like an Olympic gymnast, even flinging his arms wide when he swings off and lands upright on his feet, causing the 'bots to declare "Nice dismount."

Translation adds a layer of abstraction; stripped of their original language, and original context, the Gamera films have to stand on their own merits in the field of American hegemonic productions. In fact, to the extent they do not represent the mainstream of an ethnically white, middle class America, they stand somewhat in the position of the cultural outsider, themselves, in opposition to the hegemony, or as a wedge that pries open that door to let in appreciation for a wider, more multicultural range of cultural products, forged in hegemonies all over the world.

Within whatever cultural environment they find themselves in, in the very act of media consumption, individuals are free to reframe the experience, both in how they interpret new material they're exposed to from other nations and cultures, incorporating it into their worldview, and in how they interpret the hegemony itself. As the Gamera movies are viewed, mocked, and eventually made a part of the comedic, even absurdist world of *MST3K*, it creates a microcosmic of the way the larger genre of kaiju films are consumed by new audiences and integrated into their general pop cultural knowledge and interest.

Despite the superficial level of low-budget monster silliness, these films bring a different culture and a different style of cultural product to the white Midwestern audience, broadening their horizons without their even noticing. In documenting an American audience's exposure to kaiju films, the *MST3K* episodes show that this encounter can sometimes contain elements of exploitation, and moments that expose insensitivities to racial difference on the part of the white viewer, but they are still a stepping stone to accepting the cultural products of different countries into the American experience.

Works Cited

Adorno, Theodor W, and Brian O'Connor. "Culture Industry Reconsidered." *The Adorno Reader*. Oxford, UK: Blackwell, 2000. 230–238. Print.

Barr, Jason. *The Kaiju Film: A Critical Study of Cinema's Biggest Monsters*. Jefferson, NC: McFarland, 2016. Print.

Beaulieu, Trace. *The Mystery Science Theater 3000 Amazing Colossal Episode Guide*. New York: Bantam Books, 1996. Print.

Begy, Jason, and Generoso Fierro. "The Design and Speculative Technology of MST3K: Joel Hodgson and Trace Beaulieu at MIT." Weiner and Barba, 184–196. Print.

Bernardo, Richie. "2016's States That Have Achieved the Most Racial Progress." WalletHub,

12 Jan. 2016. wallethub.com/edu/states-with-the-most-and-least-racial-progress/18428/#rankings-progress.

Burnham, Jef, and Joshua Paul Ewalt. "Mystery Science Theater 3000 and the Restricted Universe of Popular Culture Production." *Reading Mystery Science Theater 3000: Critical Approaches*. Edited by Shelley S. Rees. Lanham MD: Scarecrow Press, 2013. 31–44. Print.

Carter, David Ray. "Cinemasochism: Bad Movies and the People Who Love Them Weiner and Barba, 101–119. Print.

City of Minneapolis. "1990 to 2000: Population by Race and Ethnicity for Minneapolis." Minneapolis Census, 17 Nov. 2011. www.minneapolismn.gov/census/2000/ census_1990-to-2000-population-change-by-race-and-ethnicity-for-minneapolis.

Dean, Michael. "Frame Work, Resistance and Co-optation: How Mystery Science Theater 3000 Positions Us Both In and Against Hegemonic Culture. Weiner and Barba, 120–126. Print.

Gamera. *Mystery Science Theater 3000 XXI: MST3K vs. Gamera*, written by Michael J. Nelson, Trace Beaulieu, Frank Conniff, Joel Hodgson, Jim Mallon, Kevin Murphy, Bridget Jones, Lisa Sheretz, and Colleen Henjum, Shout! Factory, 2011.

Gamera vs. Barugon. *Mystery Science Theater 3000 XXI: MST3K vs. Gamera*, written by Michael J. Nelson, Trace Beaulieu, Frank Conniff, Joel Hodgson, Jim Mallon, Kevin Murphy, Colleen Henjum, Bridget Jones, Lisa Sheretz, and Jef Maynard, directed by Jim Mallon, Shout! Factory, 2011.

Gamera vs. Gaos. *Mystery Science Theater 3000 XXI: MST3K vs. Gamera*, written by Michael J. Nelson, Trace Beaulieu, Frank Conniff, Joel Hodgson, Kevin Murphy, Colleen Henjum, Bridget Jones, Jim Mallon, and Paul Chaplin, directed by Jim Mallon, Shout! Factory, 2011.

Gamera vs. Guiron. *Mystery Science Theater 3000 XXI: MST3K vs. Gamera*, written by Michael J. Nelson, Trace Beaulieu, Frank Conniff, Joel Hodgson, Kevin Murphy, Bridget Jones, Jim Mallon, Paul Chaplin, and Colleen Henjum, directed by Jim Mallon, Shout! Factory, 2011.

Gamera vs. Zigra. *Mystery Science Theater 3000 XXI: MST3K vs. Gamera*, written by Michael J. Nelson, Trace Beaulieu, Frank Conniff, Joel Hodgson, Kevin Murphy, Peter Chaplin, Bridget Jones, Jim Mallon, and Colleen Henjum, directed by Jim Mallon, Shout! Factory, 2011.

Hicks, Cheryl. "Resurrecting the Dead: Revival of Forgotten Films Through Appropriation." Weiner and Barba, 55–64. Print.

Last of the Wild Horses. *Mystery Science Theater 3000: XXIII*, written by Michael J. Nelson, Trace Beaulieu, Paul Chaplin, Frank Conniff, Mike Dodge, Bridget Jones, Kevin Murphy, and Mary Jo Pehl, directed by Kevin Murphy, Shout! Factory, 2012.

McWilliams, Ora, and Joshua Richardson. "Double Poaching and Subversive Operations of Riffing: 'You Kids with your hoola hoops and your Rosenbergs and your Communist agendas.'" Weiner and Barba, 110–119. Print.

Mura, David. "A Surrealist History of One Asian American in Minnesota." *A Good Time for the Truth: Race in Minnesota*. St. Paul: Minnesota Historical Society Press, 2016. 43–58. Print.

Plaid, Andrea. "'Minnesota Nice' and Minnesota's Racism." *Twin Cities Daily Planet*, 5 Nov., 2015. www.tcdailyplanet.net/minnesota-nice-and-racism/.

Rees, Shelley S. "Introduction." *Reading Mystery Science Theater 3000: Critical Approaches*. Edited by Shelley S. Rees. 1–9. Print.

Tsutsui, William. *Godzilla on My Mind: Fifty Years of the King of Monsters*. New York: Palgrave MacMillan, 2004. Print.

United States Census Bureau. "1990 Census of Population and Housing Public Law 94-171 Data (Official) Age by Race and Hispanic Origin." http://censtats.census.gov/cgibin/pl94/ pl94data.pl. Accessed 6 Sept. 2016.

Veldof, Jerilyn, and Corey Bonnema. "Minnesota Nice? It's like ice." *Star Tribune*, 11 July, 2014. www.startribune.com/minnesota-nice-it-s-like-ice/266823811/.

Weiner, Robert G., and Shelley E. Barba. *In the Peanut Gallery with Mystery Science Theater 3000: Essays on Film, Fandom, Technology, and the Culture of Riffing*. Jefferson, N.C: McFarland, 2011. Print.

Collecting Kaiju
How Nostalgia Influences Adult Toy Collecting

JASON BARR

Many children go through a period when kaiju or kaiju-like creations dominate, if not their imagination, then certainly their environment. Dinosaurs, Bible stories, tall tales, film, and video games all propagate the fascination with larger-than-life beasts that can destroy modern infrastructure with but a single stomp or flick of the wrist. For many of these children, the fascination may evolve into a near-obsession, but at some point in time, the child typically "outgrows" the interest in the concept. Of course, some would argue that one never quite "outgrows" a childhood interest; it simply morphs and evolves into a new state, deadened only by the often mundane demands of adult life: bills, jobs, children of their own.

For an increasingly large number of people, however, marketing and toy companies have managed to rekindle the nostalgia of childhood through the deft introduction of retro-styled toys. These toys take numerous forms: from the homages to the cheap plastic toys of the 1970s and 1980s (complete with uninspiring cardboard packaging), to "premium" toys, which can only be described as the toys that someone would have liked to have had when they were a child, but couldn't. This phenomenon started in the late 1990s, when franchises such as Hello Kitty! and Barbie sold special, more expensive, "limited edition" products to adults. In 1998, 15 percent of Barbie sales stemmed from adult buyers (Hamilton), a percentage that has surely grown in the intervening decades.

What causes adults to collect toys? Perhaps it is simply the shift in how buyers define "toys." Many adults from the Baby Boom generation (born between 1946 and 1964), for example, collected and built scale model kits. Grandmothers across the nation still purchase puzzles. Yet, in the past thirty years, there has been a sizable shift, first in the perspective of the customers, and then, in an effort to pursue their disposable income, a shift in the perspective of manufacturers. Simply put, the idea of buying a "toy" that could not necessarily be explained away in the tropes of adulthood—action figures, for example—became more acceptable in society, and, as such, toy manufacturers and retailers were more than happy to oblige. But over these past few years, in particular, retro and adult toys have become more and more mainstream, as has collecting them. Completely forgoing the aspect of the internet for a few moments, one can walk into major retailers such as Barnes and Noble, Hot Topic, Sam Goody, Books-A-Million, and so on, and find these toys.

Interestingly, there has been little research on what makes someone collect anything, be it coins, old maps, dolls, or action figures. What research that does exist often borders on hysterical, often drawing an incredibly thin line between "collecting" and "hoarding," as if the relationship between the two was simply a part of a dangerous evolutionary process in the mind of the buyer: one day a simple collector, the next day the owner of a home whose walls are bulging from the weight of their uncontrollable impulses. For many of these works, a collector seems simply to be a hoarder with slightly less in their collection and a greater sense of aesthetics in how they display their material. Philipp Blom writes of when he suddenly understood the "more powerful, darker connotations" of collecting (7). On entering a room, Blom saw

> the books spreading everywhere like moss on wet stones. Piles of books lined the entire hallway and more were sitting on every step of the staircase leading up to the first floor. Books were creeping up the walls and occupying every inch of free space on the floor, on tables, chairs and other furniture. The rooms were accessible on through narrow canals winding through a mountainous landscape of reading matter ... [7].

Another, more recent example is a *Den of Geek* article called "Collections: How to Avoid a Hobby Becoming a Problem." The subtitle is "Spotting the Signs of a Problem." No reasoning about why people collect, or any attempt to find the source of pleasure and joy that seems to stem from collecting. Instead, the article—ostensibly geared toward adult toy collectors—focuses on the negatives of collecting and offers advice on when to sell or clean out one's collection. The article even offers a handy, although somewhat absurd, rubric: "if the collection fills a box room and you can still at least sleep in the room (or put someone else up) then it's not likely to be an issue. If it is encroaching every available space in the house, however, things might be getting desperate" (Westthorp).

The primary issue with this, however, is that a collection is often not necessarily measured by collectors in terms of physical size so much as it is by breadth and esoterica. Take, for example, coin collectors, who, one can assume, rarely have an issue with their collection filling an entire room or "encroaching every available space in the house." For these collectors, they can spend extraordinary amounts of money and descend into an almost manic expertise on the topic; yet, they are often rarely considered to have a "problem" with their collection. By their very definition, coins are often small and easy to put away. Yet, for the adult toy collector, the issue is much more obvious; many of the toys are large and often unwieldy, and the debate as to whether or not to open a package for enjoyment or to keep it sealed for pleasure is a timeless one. Still, the idea that a collection is just a few shades from a mental disorder unfairly colors much of the conversation and the research surrounding adult toy collectors, even those who occasionally pick up and display the random nostalgic piece from their local Barnes and Noble.

But kaiju toys are different. Yes, one can get some of the cheap Bandai figures at Target, for example, especially around the time of the latest Godzilla film release. Yet, to collect almost anything else requires a consistently high level of commitment and income. Many kaiju toys, as mentioned earlier, have to be imported, and the greater the rarity of the piece, the more appreciated it is by the collector, looks and functionality be damned. Spending hundreds— and perhaps thousands—of dollars on Yahoo! Japan auctions or eBay auctions to hunt down a particular piece is not unheard of; such a phenomenon, and such effort, sets apart the kaiju collector from the average "adult toy buyer." For the "adult toy buyer," many of the purchases are on a whim, and these purchases are often picked up with a sense of self-deprecation. The toys are often easily found, and they also require relatively minimal expenditure.

For the kaiju toy collector, life is considerably more difficult. It should be noted, too, that the kaiju toy collector is even more unique; although there are many kaiju cinema fans and scholars, fewer still become kaiju toy collectors. The industry leaders produce numerous toys, but these toys are often imported, either by the companies themselves or by independent resellers. As a result, these toys can be terribly expensive, especially when compared to the entry-level Bandai toys found on toy store shelves. These premium toys, often manufactured by companies such as the National Entertainment Collectibles Association (NECA), X-Plus, and Bandai, among many others, can feature numerous points of articulation, be rather large (NECA has a line of figures from *Pacific Rim* that stand over 18 inches tall), and are often incredibly expensive (those same *Pacific Rim* toys often retail for well over a hundred dollars). S.H. MonsterArts, for example, a subsidiary of Bandai (through the Tamashii Nations division—further evidence of the encyclopedic expertise required of the devout kaiju toy collector), and X-Plus routinely release limited runs of figures that are often hundreds of dollars for one figure. These figures are often "cinema quality" and look almost exactly like the creations that appear in the film. Yet, spending nearly two hundred dollars on a 12-inch replica of Titanosaurus, a B-list kaiju from *Terror of Mechagodzilla* (1975), can defy explanation for those not a part of this particular collecting community. Admittedly, Bandai releases far cheaper (and less inspiringly made) kaiju on a semi-regular schedule, so if collectors want to purchase Mechagodzilla without having to budget for it, they can purchase one with a few clicks of a mouse and around twenty dollars at most.

The kaiju toy collector, however, like the coin collector or the firearms collector, has a bible. In this case, it is Sean Linkenback's *An Unauthorized Guide to Godzilla Collectibles*, published in 1998. Linkenback, who also owns and operates the kaiju toy internet store Showcase Daikaiju, is one of the de facto experts on kaiju toys, especially vintage Godzilla-related collectibles. His guide—which, now that it is out of print, has become somewhat of a collector's item itself—includes a reflection of his own awakening into the world of kaiju toy collecting: "How did it all start? The beginning goes back to the summer of 1963 when *King Kong vs. Godzilla* was released in this country. As an impressionable 9-year-old dinosaur lover, when I saw the trailer for this film, I immediately felt something special—this was the greatest dinosaur ever!" (5) Linkenback's kaiju memorabilia collecting, from which he only plans "to get rid of something … when I die" (5), takes him into a vast and new network of people, from a convention in Chicago to "other fans in the US and Canada" (6) to the moment when he "finally decided to visit Japan in 1979" (6). At each of these waypoints in life, Linkenback, like many other kaiju toy collectors, formed a strong network of friends, acquaintances and suppliers to assist with their hobby.

There are, of course, underlying cultural reasons why people buy collectibles, and certainly, the kaiju toy industry benefits from various aspects that extend well beyond those Funko Pop! figures that one can buy at a Barnes and Noble or Gamestop. These aspects have made collecting kaiju toys a sort of subtrend, a collector's niche market buried within another niche market. And it is there, in the world of X-Plus and Y-MSF and Bandai and Marmit, where people benefit not only from nostalgia (which we will discuss later), but also from a variety of other aspects which sets these collectors (and their toys) apart from the random person with disposable income who buys the occasional retro-styled package at a Wal-Mart. In their book *Stuff: Compulsive Hoarding and the Meaning of Things*, Randy Frost and Gail Steketee write about the process of collecting:

> Once [the decision to collect] has been made, planning for the acquisition begins. A byproduct of the planning process is fantasizing about the object. The fantasies increase the object's subjective value and give it a magical quality, and soon the value of the object outstrips and becomes disconnected from any functional utility it may have. Next comes the hunt, frequently the most pleasurable part of collecting … [w]hen the acquisition occurs, it is accompanied by a wave of euphoria and appreciation of the object's features, which become a part of the "story" of the acquisition [54].

In actuality, however, Steketee and Frost's description of the *process* of collecting seems to combine or overlook the perceived *benefits* of collecting. The "byproducts," in other words, are actually the main reason for the collection itself. It is entirely possible, perhaps even probable, that starting a collection such as one featuring kaiju toys is not based on a particularly rational decision. Underneath a kaiju toy collection lies the motivations of the kaiju toy collector, and they manifest themselves not as a part of the process, but as the sole reason for the collection to begin with. It is possible to take the ideas that Steketee and Frost outline and use it as the basis for why such niche collections exist at all:

The Lure of the Exotic: The kaiju toy industry, which is centered primarily in Japan (or are American companies who carry licenses originating from Japanese production companies such as Toho), routinely creates toys that are exceptionally difficult to find within the United States. As such, a collector or buyer who manages to purchase a semi-expensive toy that represents a kaiju has done their due diligence. Purchasing a random Bandai Godzilla off the shelf at the local Target is not necessarily something to brag about or post on Facebook; however, purchasing and owning an X-Plus Gaira (from *War of the Gargantuas*) earns one a bit more cachet among fans and collectors. Although, like most collections, rarity and overall quality plays a part in the pricing, so, too, does the exoticism of the toy itself. The amount of money dedicated to a particular purchase (often well into the hundreds of dollars) is matched only by the purchaser's work ethic in tracking down the item, purchasing it, and then displaying it online and at home for all to see. The "fantasizing" of the object is based on the "hunt" for the toy itself, a movement from apparition to the real.

The Birth of Expertise: The exoticism of the toys themselves has led to a bumper crop of experts and toy sellers who have adopted the unique language of collecting toy kaiju. This, of course, creates experts where there were no experts before, and, considering the exotic nature of many of the toys, such experts are often routinely cherished by the toy collecting community. As a result, many of these collectors have created their own small industry of blogs, podcasts, YouTube videos, and so on, in order to share their expertise. These writings—often in the form of reviews of particular products—often go into extreme depth and detail regarding the toy. YouTubers such as Fresh Vinyl Reviews, DeanKnight333, and RealRetro87, among many others, often post elaborate and well-made "unboxing" videos of new toys. These videos often last fifteen to twenty minutes and take viewers through the process of first opening the toy's packaging. During the process, the YouTuber frequently holds court on articulation points, lights, cost, paint quality, and so on, going into incredibly deep detail. Herein lies the "items that have value only in certain circles, among a group of initiates whose rules and knowledge are deeply arcane and shared by only a few" (Blom 166). Although anyone can ostensibly watch these videos, they are geared in tone and technique toward fans of the genre and fans of the toys.

Like-Minded Individuals: Although it is possible, few collect items with an eye toward *not* sharing their finds. Through the process of collecting items, and through the process of publicly displaying items, one can find similar individuals with similar passions. Much like the sports fan who wears his or her favorite team's t-shirts and knowingly nods to strangers wearing that same team's apparel, the collector seeks out others with the same interests, either actively or passively. Additionally, demographics may play a part in the idea of collecting and seeking out others. A litmus test for this assertion is quite simple: imagine the typical Barbie collector. Often, we can picture middle-aged white women. Imagine the typical stamp collector: middle-aged white men. And so on. The outliers in each collecting group, such as female or African American kaiju toy collectors, may have a more difficult time not only pursuing the hobby, but finding any interest in it at all. Like kaiju cinema and fandom itself, kaiju toy collecting is demographically dominated in North American by white men.

These reasons extend well beyond the rather simple rubric put forward by psychoanalyst Werner Muensterberger, who, when referring to massive collections (once again, as an unhealthy obsession), stated that "The objects [collectors] cherish are inanimate substitutes for reassurance and care. Perhaps even more telling, these objects prove, both to the collector and to the world, that he or she is special and worthy of them" (256). Muensterberger's idea, then, is that a kaiju toy collector collects kaiju toys because it makes the collector feel wanted, and more so, provides an intrinsic importance to the collector themselves. However, the relative obscurity of collecting kaiju toys—coupled with the potential social stigma of being in such a niche field—defeats such an idea. The audience of kaiju toy collectors, at least the more "serious" ones, is so incredibly small that a sense of importance can only be derived from other collectors and fans, of whom few can be found on a casual basis. To expound, it is hard to imagine a fifty-year-old male showing visitors unfamiliar with kaiju and kaiju toys to his kaiju toy collection room and expecting them to be impressed by much more than the setup and the cost expenditure the collection represents. To take another example from fandom, it would be far easier for one to find people near them with interests in other pursuits, such as sports teams or video gaming.

But perhaps the most powerful force in collecting—and this holds particularly true for kaiju toys—is nostalgia. If collecting is truly an "individual desire across the intertext of environment and history," "an unrepeatable conjuncture of subject, found object, place and moment," then that particular intertext is nostalgia itself (Cardinal 68). It is entirely possible that a collector can purchase a toy, which invokes some form of nostalgia, and then the emotion wears off, thrusting the person into a sort of default mode of collecting. Here, to refer back to Muensterberger, who writes of a patient that "The final "conquest," as he liked to put it, had a magical, but unfortunately only momentary, healing effect on his deeply disturbed self-image, for his sense of victory was always short-lived. Once he had succeeded in his seduction maneuvers, he was in pursuit of another conquest" (11). Although in this instance, Muensterberger reflects on a patient with particular sexual peccadillos, the basics (setting aside the "deeply disturbed self-image") can be transferred to the role nostalgia plays in purchasing these toys, in particular for the kaiju toy collector, again, for whom there is precious little audience.

The "conquest" is for a particular toy (often referred to as a "grail" by many collectors), which, when obtained, creates a sense of "victory" which quickly washes away. Thus, in an effort to reclaim that "victory," the process begins anew. Although every collector has a "favorite" or more in their collection, the initial enjoyment of a piece almost certainly vanishes or diminishes as one keeps and displays the item. Nostalgia is exceptionally powerful and may, in the end, be the entire genesis for collecting. People who collect things as a hobby tend to not only exhibit the above traits, but they also discover their passion for those objects in childhood. It is hard, for example, to come to a logical conclusion about what to collect, and how. For example, I could admire 19th and early 20th century German steins, but without a motivating force, without a personal history that ties me to the objects, I have little impetus to begin to invest money in them and set aside space to display them. This lack of fascination, and this lack of nostalgia, prevents me from becoming a collector of German steins, or at least a passionate and authentic one. To turn the discussion back toward kaiju toys, I argue that, unless I am a completionist with significant cash flow, the toys I seek out will be those from which I will earn the most personal enjoyment. These particular toys will be tied to what I *personally* enjoy, and no one else can share the special relationship intrinsically built around that particular item. Thus, on a personal level, I am far more likely to purchase kaiju toys tied to the Godzilla franchise than I am the Ultraman or the Gamera franchises, as I rarely saw the latter two franchises during my own childhood.

A part of this process is, intrinsically, the desire to replicate one's own initial emotions upon seeing a particular creation for the first time. A part of this is the simple newness of a particular feeling. As Susan Neiman writes, the idea of newness really only happens once per object or idea:

> The newness of our surroundings [create] more vivid awareness and attention. Under very particular conditions this may be true in moments, but it cannot last for long. More than once I've had the good fortune to live in jaw-droppingly beautiful surroundings. My jaw did drop, the first few mornings … till the surprise of it ceased and turned into pleasure, but the wonder was gone [83].

Thus, the attempt to recapture the newness of a situation is intrinsically wrapped up in the very emotion of nostalgia. After the newness of a collector's purchase wears off, that particular item may be met with pleasure, apathy, or worse yet, dismay (based on, for example, the amount of money spent on the item). It follows, then, that children who enjoyed the newness of *Godzilla vs. The Smog Monster* (1971), for example, may find themselves more likely to pick up a Hedorah toy to add to their collection (again, forgoing completionists). Herein lies the nostalgia: an attempt to revive or relive the newness of a situation. On that first moment of purchasing and opening the toy, some semblance of the first emotions involved in that particular creature are revived. Linkenback, for example, notes that the market for kaiju model kits is not as intense as other toys because the purchases are not made "by adults seeking to regain what they once had in childhood" (42). Linkenback's observation extends beyond the simple differentiation of toys versus model kits, but also includes the very *idea* of childhood itself, which includes, at least partially, the toys. The memories—perhaps the television set, the room, or the shuffling of your parent's footsteps down the hallway—briefly gain, once more, their vivid color in the presence of this small figure that brings to life, at least partially, a small portion of childhood.

But what happens next? I argue that nostalgia, itself a nearly indecipherable and certainly ephemeral emotion, fades away. The process has thus moved the kaiju toy from desire to memory to, well, collectible. Only those collectibles with particular emotions attached to them that extend beyond the nostalgic equivalent remain in the forefront of the collector's mind. The toy signed by a Godzilla suit actor, for example, or a toy one played with as a child, or perhaps a toy purchased overseas.[1] As Svetlana Boym notes, the continued American fascination with dinosaurs, in particular, is not surprising: "Dinosaurs are ideal animals for the nostalgia industry because nobody remembers them. Their extinction is a guarantee of commercial success; it allows for total restoration and global exportability. Nobody will be offended by improper portrayal of the dinosaur.... The dinosaur is America's unicorn" (18). Kaiju, one could argue, are not strictly dinosaurs, but the resemblance, on the surface, is clear enough: overly large reptilian creatures that can provide massive amounts of destruction. Within the dinosaur, as Peter Semonin argued in *American Monster*, lies many of the dreams of American superiority. But, to make the circle from American dinosaur to Asian kaiju complete, we need only turn back to Boym, who writes "Asians and Europeans had their folklore and their dragons; Americans have their scientific fairy tales that often involve love and death of some prehistoric monster (18–19). The kaiju film industry, then, manages to successfully bridge this cultural difference. Godzilla, for example, though wholly Japanese in the minds of many fans, drew inspiration from the American film industry. In the original *Godzilla*

(1954), the love story (or, at least tension) between Serizawa, Ogata, and the woman they both love, Emiko Yamane, ties the film further to American expectations. The same with the "death of some prehistoric monster," Godzilla itself. Yet, there are few that would argue that Godzilla itself (and the continued success of the franchise, is also due to the uniquely Japanese perspective built on the cultural folklore.

Back to kaiju toy collectors, then. The process repeats itself because the very process of kaiju toy collecting is a rendition of the process of nostalgia. The kaiju toy buyer searches for a particular toy, and prior to ownership, may simply exist in the ether, an object seen online, but never touched. Then, when the purchase of that toy is made, and the toy has a "story," then the collector is temporarily sated. In this way, nostalgia is the mimicked engine of kaiju toy collecting itself. The toy, itself representative of a sort of un-reality, is itself temporarily un-real, something that does not exist until it is purchased. Upon purchase, a goal has been accomplished, and the un-real has become, at least temporarily, incredibly real, a toy replica of something that never existed to the collector, either in reality or in toy form. The collection urge for these particular toys not only combines the typical aspects of any collector, but they are also fired by the continual attempts to recreate worlds that never existed, except, perhaps, only in the childhood memories of that individual collector. To build upwards, the kaiju toy collectors happens to buy replicas of the "unicorn," the mythical never-was that yet someone exists in the mind and perhaps the idealization of childhood. From there, the kaiju toy represents not only the unattainable, an appreciation of a uniquely American mythology, but also simultaneously embodies the exoticism of a completely different culture. Objects create, or attempt to create, a state of permanence. The kaiju toy can be seen, in some ways, as an attempt to keep the genie of nostalgia firmly entrenched in the bottle.

The joy of collecting kaiju toys stems from the replication of something that is irreproducible. The most fascinating discussions on kaiju toys is how "film ready" these toys are. Many X-Plus statues, for example, are often based on the exact kaiju suits worn in the film. This increases the toy's credibility, and, as a result, the cost and workmanship put into making the toy is reflected in the cost. For those who spend the few hundred dollars, they receive something that is as close to the film as they may ever get. Yes, the kaiju toy collector may go to conferences such as G-Fest and meet the suit actors and other members of the cast and crew (and these cast and crew members may even autograph items), but, in order to "keep" the memory and maintain the authenticity, the toy must be purchased and it must be displayed. In this way, the kaiju toy collector retains some minor control over their nostalgic feelings; not only does the toy remind them of a particular film or a particular character within the film, but the toy itself becomes a story, a sort of waypost in one's life. Therein lies the strengthening of a personal relationship with kaiju that began at the very moment a creature first dared to walk onto the movie or television screen in the presence of the future collector.

Within the world of the kaiju toy collector resides heavy doses of effective nostalgia, and, as such, the kaiju toy phenomenon, even in its esoteric and rarely visited corner of collecting, remains undeniably strong. In "serious" kaiju toy collections, then, one can find an amalgamation of everything that collectors, whether they collect guns, books, or German steins, can appreciate. Ultimately, however, kaiju toy collectors, who reside in a market buried within a few other esoteric markets, are symbolic of a healthy style of collecting, which symbolizes and displays their own unique expertise. The kaiju toy collector thus represents everything about collecting, but most of all, some of the most intense sentiments of nostalgia and memory.

Notes

1. I would argue as well that the process is broken somewhat by mass market adult toys. If one purchases, for example, a ten-dollar Bandai or Jakks Godzilla from Toys"R"Us, it becomes difficult to attach any sort of lingering sentimentality to it. There is, after all, the lingering knowledge that thousands, if not tens of thousands, of people (quite possibly mostly children) have purchased that same item. As Philipp Blom notes, "[t]he charm of the endlessly produced consumer article" is offset by "a loss of authenticity" (167). Thus, the whiff of nostalgia one may feel by picking up a not-quite-collectible Godzilla toy on the shelves of a major retail store evaporates quickly, replaced by an object that may not even be displayed, except for in self-referential deprecation or an attempt to earn some "geek" cachet.

Works Cited

Blom, Philipp. *To Have and to Hold: An Intimate History of Collecting.* New York: The Overlook Press, 2003.
Boym, Svetlana. *The Future of Nostalgia.* New York: Basic Books, 2001.
Cardinal, Roger. "Collecting and Collage-Making: The Case of Curt Schwitters." *The Culture of Collecting,* edited by John Elsner and Roger Cardinal, Reaktion Books, 1997, 68–96.
Frost, Randy, and Gail Steketee. *Stuff: Compulsive Hoarding and the Meaning of Things.* Boston: Houghton Mifflin, 2010.
Hamilton, William. "Can Mommy and Daddy Come Out to Play?" *The New York Times.* December 24, 1998. Retrieved from: http://www.nytimes.com/1998/12/24/garden/can-mommy-and-daddy-come-out-to-play.html?pagewanted=all.
Linkenback, Sean. *An Unauthorized Guide to Godzilla Collectibles.* Atglen, PA: Schiffer Publishing, Ltd., 1998.
Muensterberger, Werner. *Collecting: An Unruly Passion.* San Diego, CA: Harvest Books, 1994.
Neiman, Susan. *Why Grow Up?: Subversive Thoughts for an Infantile Age.* New York: Farrar, Strouss, and Giroux, 2014.
Westthorp, Alex. "Collections: How to Avoid a Hobby Becoming a Problem." *Den of Geek.* July 29, 2016. Retrieved from: http://www.denofgeek.com/uk/other/collecting/42613/collections-how-to-avoid-a-hobby-becoming-a-problem.

About the Contributors

Emiliano **Aguilar** has a master's degree in the arts from the Universidad de Buenos Aires, Argentina. He has published articles in journals such as *Lindes* and *Letraceluloide* and in the essay collection *Orphan Black and Philosophy* (Open Court).

Jason **Barr** is an assistant professor at Blue Ridge Community College and the author of *The Kaiju Film* (McFarland). He coedited *The Language of Doctor Who* (Rowman & Littlefield) and his work has appeared in *African American Review*, *Explicator*, and *The Journal of Caribbean Literatures*, among others.

Nicholas **Bollinger** received his master's degree in film studies from Columbia University in 2017. His research interests include studies of seriality and franchising, focusing especially on transmedia narrativity across film, television, and comic books.

Jeffrey J. **Hall** is a research associate with Waseda University's Institute of Asia-Pacific Studies (WIAPS). His research interests include sociology, media studies, and Japanese history.

Se Young **Kim** is Mellon Assistant Professor in the Program of Cinema and Media Arts at Vanderbilt University. He is working on a manuscript on the violent contemporary cinema of Korea and Japan and its relationship to neoliberal crises.

Karen Joan **Kohoutek** is an independent scholar who works in the library at Minnesota State University Moorhead. She has published in various journals and literary websites and has written extensively on a wide range of popular culture topics, including cult horror and Bollywood films.

Jamie **Macdonald** is an interactive media student at the University of York. He completed an MA in film and literature in 2014. His research interests include science fiction, digital culture, comics, and the interplay between politics and cinema.

Kenta **McGrath** is a Japanese/Australian filmmaker and a lecturer in screen arts at Curtin University. He has lectured for the Japan Film Festival and the Japanese Animaton Film Festival.

Justin **Mullis** has an MA in religious studies from the University of North Carolina–Charlotte, where he lectures on topics related to religion and popular culture.

His work includes essays in edited collections and articles on Japanese science fiction for *G-Fan* magazine, *LovecrafteZine* and the blog *Maser Patrol*.

Camille D.G. **Mustachio** is an assistant professor of English at Germanna Community College. She has written on feminine empowerment and graffiti and coedited *The Language of Doctor Who* (Rowman & Littlefield). Her research focuses on the ways in which literature, culture, and higher education pedagogy intersect.

Fernando Gabriel **Pagnoni Berns** is a professor at the University of Buenos Aires in Argentina, where he teaches seminars on horror cinema. He has published essays in *Horrors of War* (Rowman & Littlefield), *To See the Saw Movies* (McFarland), *Reading Richard Matheson* (Rowman & Littlefield), and *Deconstructing Dads* (Lextigton Books), among others.

Sigmund C. **Shen** is an associate professor of English at LaGuardia Community College/CUNY. His research interests include horror and monster movies, and the politics of public higher education. He is working on a book about ideology in kaiju cinema.

Jase **Short** is a writer and blogger for several publications, including *Red Wedge Magazine* and *Against the Current*. As a student of philosophy, he has written extensively on the intersection of popular culture and social problems.

Index

Attack on Titan 7, 10

The Beast from 20,000 Fathoms 6, 8, 13, 59, 135, 165
Big Man Japan 3, 123–137
Blom, Philipp 194, 198, 202n1
Brothers, Peter 1

Cloverfield 74, 75, 163–170, 172–174

Destroy All Monsters 93, 99–102

Eco, Umberto 78, 89
Erb, Cynthia 7, 161, 162

Frankenstein 94, 107
Frankenstein Conquers the World 3, 5, 10, 109–121

Gamera: franchise 69; 1965 184
Gamera: Super Monster 4
Gamera III: Revenge of Iris 93, 103–107
Gamera vs. Barugon 179, 184, 186
Gamera vs. Gaos 179, 184, 186
Gamera vs. Guiron 179, 184, 187, 191
Gamera vs. Zigra 184, 188, 189
Godzilla: franchise 3
Godzilla (1954) 2, 60, 63, 64, 65–66, 68–69, 70, 71, 93, 95–98, 109, 112, 124, 129, 161, 162, 163, 164, 165, 184
Godzilla (2014) 15, 63, 75, 80, 106, 150, 163, 172, 173, 174
Godzilla: Final Wars 69, 149
Godzilla, Mothra, and King Ghidorah: Giant Monsters All-Out Attack 129, 148
Godzilla vs. Biollante 42, 70
Godzilla vs. Destroyah 6, 98
Godzilla vs. Gigan 7
Godzilla vs. Hedorah 70, 72
Godzilla vs. King Ghidorah 148
Godzilla vs. Mechagodzilla 84, 146, 148

Godzilla vs. Megaguirus 148
Godzilla vs. SpaceGodzilla 69
Godzilla vs. The Smog Monster see *Godzilla vs. Hedorah*
Godzilla's Revenge 6
Gojira see *Godzilla*, franchise; *Godzilla* (1954)
Gorgo 6, 8, 9

Hiroshima, atomic bombing 6, 18, 21, 29, 32, 43, 96, 110, 116, 117, 128, 143, 146
Honda, Ishiro 6, 10, 13, 37, 47, 60, 65, 80, 95, 109, 110, 112, 114, 124, 128
The Host 7, 9

Jaws 5, 179
Jurassic Park 42
Jurassic World 4

Kamen Rider 3, 17–33, 136
King Kong (character) 1, 6, 12, 83, 87, 109–121, 161–162, 166
King Kong (1933) 2, 3, 5, 6, 19, 92–107, 162
King Kong Escapes 109–121
King Kong vs. Godzilla 6, 109, 112, 145, 196

Linkenback, Sean 196, 200

Matango 4, 10
Monster Zero 93, 99–100, 106
Mothra (character) 5, 12, 26, 37, 64, 83, 179
Mothra (1961) 47, 66, 68, 128
Mothra vs. Godzilla 64, 145
Muensterberger, Werner 198–199
Mystery Science Theater 3000 3, 177–192

Nagasaki, atomic bombing 18, 21, 29, 32, 43, 65, 128, 143, 146
nationalism 98, 106, 109, 138–158, 161–175
Neo Ultra Q (television series) 39

206 Index

Pacific Rim 3, 4, 6, 9, 15, 36, 75, 77–91, 163, 169–174, 195

Q; The Winged Serpent 6
Reptilicus 6, 8, 9
Return of Godzilla 79, 139, 146–151, 158
Rich, Adrienne 92, 93, 99

Sharknado 4, 9
Shin Godzilla 3, 7, 75, 129, 139, 150–158, 175
The Simpsons 72
Son of Godzilla 4, 68, 146
Super Sentai 22

Tsutsui, William 1, 21, 40, 124, 129, 136, 139, 173, 179, 180, 184

Ultra Q (television series) 38, 39, 42, 63, 68
Ultra Q: Dark Fantasy (television series) 39, 46
Ultra Q The Movie: Legend of the Stars 39
Ultraman (franchise) 2, 9, 39, 199
Ultraman (television series) 2, 3, 19, 22, 32n3, 39–52
Uncle Grandpa 1, 2
Unit 731 28, 96–97

War of the Gargantuas 5, 10, 197

www.ingramcontent.com/pod-product-compliance
Ingram Content Group UK Ltd.
Pitfield, Milton Keynes, MK11 3LW, UK
UKHW042004140426
5217IPUK00015B/968